PANAMA
Latin America's Best-kept Secret

PANAMA

Latin America's Best-kept Secret

William Chislett

Rose Tremain and Richard Holmes,
In case you ever find
yourselves in Panama (most
unlikely!).
Best wishes,
William
August 97.

Published by
Euromoney Publications
in association with
The Private Asset Management Group
Aseguradora Mundial
Banco Disa
Banco del Istmo
Colón Free Zone
The Panama Stock Exchange

GRISELDA LOPEZ

Published by
Euromoney Publications PLC
Nestor House, Playhouse Yard
London EC4V 5EX

ISBN 1 85564 351 0

Typeset by PW Reprosharp, London
Printed in England by Clifford Press Ltd, Coventry

Acknowledgements

William Chislett was born in Oxford in 1951. He reported Spain's 1975–78 transition to democracy for *The Times*. Between 1978 and 1984 he was based in Mexico City for *The Financial Times*, covering Mexico and Central America, before returning to Madrid in 1986 as freelance writer and translator. He co-authored *Spain – The Internationalisation of the Economy* and wrote *Portugal – A New Era*; *Spain*; *Chile – Stability and Progress* and *Ecuador – The Economic Modernisation* for Euromoney Publications. He also wrote *Spain: at a Turning Point* (Banco Central Hispano, 1994), *The Spanish Media since Franco* (Index on Censorship, 1978) and contributed to *Politics in Mexico* (Croom Helm, 1985). He is married and has two adopted Mexican sons.

William Chislett would like to thank the following people for their help in researching the book: Raul Elizalde, an analyst at ING Securities; Charlotte Elton, director of CEASPA; Marco Gandásegui, executive secretary of CELA; Orville Goodin, a former minister of finance and of planning and economic policy; Juan Jované, director of the research department of the economics' faculty of the University of Panama; Nelly Lambert, adviser to the presidency; the journalist Griselda López; Fernando Manfredo, a former administrator of the Panama Canal Commission; Gustavo Pérez, Deputy Comptroller General; José María Fernández-Pirla, Chairman, and Kristian Kwiecinski, financial analyst, of The Private Asset Management; and Joseph Salterio, chief executive of Midland Bank, Panama.

Chapter 12 was provided by Ernst & Young and chapter 13 was provided by The Private Asset Management Group.

The photographs in the text were supplied by Capstone Design. The co-publishers provided their own photographs. The photograph on page 4 is reproduced courtesy of Griselda López.

Contents

Chapter One

Historical introduction

Strategically situated on the narrow isthmus joining North and South America and midway between Europe and Asia, Panama has long been an important crossroads for world trade. Panamanians proudly call their country "the centre of the world and the heart of the universe". As early as 8000 BC the Isthmus of Panama was used as a transit route by prehistoric man mirgrating through Central America to settle in South America. The Spanish *conquistador* Hernán Cortés pinpointed the country's unique advantage – and foresaw the building of the Panama Canal almost 400 years later – when he told Charles V in 1524 that the union of the Atlantic and the Southern Sea (as the Pacific Ocean was then called) "would be worth more than the conquest of Mexico".

When Christopher Columbus first reached the shores of Panama in 1502, he was so impressed by the great number of gold ornaments worn by the natives that he wrote in his journal: "In this land of Veraguas I saw more signs of gold in the first two days than I saw in Española during four years." Panama quickly became, after colonisation, the main route for shipping precious metals from Latin America, particularly the gold of the Incas in Peru, to Europe and for European goods to the region. Between 1531 and 1660 around 60 per cent of gold and silver shipped from from Latin America to Spain passed through Panama. The conquest of Peru and Chile by Francisco Pizarro and Diego de Almagro was organised in Panama.

Goods from Europe were transported across the Isthmus via the River Chagres and the *Camino de Cruces* to Panama City, and silver and gold was carried by mules from Panama City to Nombre de Dios along the *Camino Real* (Royal Road) until it was re-routed to Portobelo on the Caribbean coast, which was one of the major trading centres of the New World until the middle of the 18th century. Its fairs sold agricultural products, handicrafts, animals and precious metals from Ecuador, Bolivia, Chile, Peru and Argentina. Today, not very far away from Portobleo, a tourist site designated a World Heritage Site by UNESCO, whose only reminder of its glorious past are its fort and cannons, is the Colón Free Zone, the largest free trade zone in the Americas and the second biggest in the world after Hong Kong. The *Camino Real* has been replaced by the canal, opened in 1914.

The Spanish colonisation and independence (1501–1821)

When the Spaniards arrived Panama had around 350,000 inhabitants in several tribes in eastern, central and western regions. As in other Latin American countries, the *conquistadores* took advantage of tribal rivalry to dominate the Isthmus: but it was not an easy task. Indians in the eastern and western regions frequently raided Spanish villages and in the Veraguas province Urracá and his successor, Estiber, held off the Spaniards from their mining region until 1560. Several ethnic groups remain today, including the Emberá-Waunaan, the Kuna and the Ngobe-Buglé, the largest.

The first vestiges of human presence in the Isthmus date back 11,000 years. Agriculture began as early as 3,500 years ago. The discovery in the sacred underground reservoir at Chichen Itza in Mexico of a gold piece from Panama shows that there were contacts between the Isthmus and Mexico. Dwellers arrived in the western region from Costa Rica between the 5th and 4th century BC and established communities based on cultivating corn and beans. The American archaeologist Matthew Stirling discovered a ceremonial site at Barriles in the 1950s on the fertile slopes of the Barú volcano, which today is in the province of Chiriquí.

Vasco Nuñez de Balboa determined Panama's destiny on 25 September 1513 when he first glimpsed the Pacific Ocean from a hill in Darién. News of the seminal discovery – the distance between the world's two largest oceans is only 80 kms – soon got back to Philip V and he sent Pedro Arias Dávila to govern the Isthmus. Pedrarias, as he was known, arrived in Darién in 1514 but his efforts to settle in this inhospitable tropical region came to nothing. Pedrarias soon quarrelled with Nuñez de Balboa (after whom Panama's currency is named, though the *de facto* legal tender is the US dollar) and had him executed. More than 700 Spanish soldiers died in a month from fever and other diseases and Pedrarias moved the seat of government from Santa Maria La Antigua, on the Caribbean coast, to Old Panama on the Pacific Ocean, establishing the town in 1519.

Panama was part of the Viceroyalty of Perú from its establishment in 1542 until 1739 when Philip V created New Granada (modern Colombia and Ecuador) which included Panama. The head of Panama's colonial government lived in Lima and he was represented in Panama by a man who held the Crown's confidence. Creoles filled the political, military and ecclesiastical positions. Few Spanish noblemen lived in Panama because land and not trade – the Isthmus's *raison d'être* – was considered the only suitably dignified way to make money and Panamanian land did not provide wealth. During this period an urban merchant class linked to international trade was created, which today is still the dominant force in Panama, and not a landed oligarchy as in most of the rest of Latin America. The countryside was sparsely populated.

English pirates were attracted by the riches passing along the Royal Road. Sir Francis Drake attacked Nombre de Dios and in 1573 his men penetrated inland to Cruces, captured its treasure and burnt the town. To protect the route

Spain built forts at the entrances to Portobelo and San Lorenzo at the mouth of the Chagres, and their galleons, loaded with treasure, were escorted against attack. In 1596 Drake died of dysentery in his ship off Panama and was buried at sea in a lead coffin. Perhaps the most famous attack was by Henry Morgan in 1671. He captured the fort of San Lorenzo and then pushed inland, burning and looting Panama City which was rebuilt on a new site. Morgan loaded 195 mules with booty and returned to the Caribbean. Spain abandoned the route in 1746 and began trading round Cape Horn. The Panamanian economy then went into decline. Panama City and Portobelo (near today's Colón) remained the only poles of development and most of the rest of the country was effectively abandoned. This is still largely the case today.

Separatism swept through South America in the early part of the 19th century and Colombia and Venezuela won independence in 1811. Panama declared its independence on 28 November 1821 and joined Gran Colombia, the liberator Simon Bolívar's visionary idea of Latin American unity, with Venezuela and Ecuador.

Post-colonial Panama and birth of a nation (1821–1903)

Gran Colombia broke up in 1830, but Panama was unable to create its own nation state. Panama was a Royal Audience during the colonial era, as were Ecuador and Venezuela, and should have become independent like other nations. Instead it became a province of Colombia, separated, as it still is today, by mountains and jungle with no road between them. Although politically linked to Colombia, Panama kept its economic freedom and free trade principles. This liberalism caused repeated conflicts with the more conservative and protectionist Colombian governments and spawned many attempts at separation. Significantly, two of the newspapers founded in Panama were both called *Comercio Libre (Free Trade)* in 1832 and 1849.

General José Domingo Espinar led the first breakaway movement in 1830 but it only lasted three months before Panama, was reincorporated into Columbia. Further shortlived attempts were made in 1840 and in 1861, when Colombia was plunged into civil war. The Panamanian authorities signed an agreement with the insurgents in Colombia which granted virtual independence but it was not respected when they triumphed in the civil war.

By the mid-19th century Panama was attracting increasing attention from the United States. The discovery of gold in California lured thousands of prospectors to Panama as it was easier to travel from the east to the west coast of the United States by passing through the Isthmus than going across US territory. The Mallarino-Bidlack Treaty in 1846 between the United States and Colombia protected Colombia against English colonial aspirations and guaranteed its sovereignty over Panama in return for giving the United States the exclusive right of transit across the Isthmus "upon any modes of communication that now exist, or that may be, hereafter, constructed". US domination of transport in Panama – and US intervention – began with this treaty.

The fortunes of Panamanian merchants were revived by the opening of the transisthmian railroad in 1855. The 47-mile track required 170 bridges and culverts of 15 feet or more and 134 bridges and culverts of less than 15 feet: it was "the world's first transcontinental railroad and the most expensive line on a dollar-per-mile basis, expensive to build and expensive to travel".[1] A one-way ticket cost US$25 in gold. The gain in time and distance was enormous. From New York to San Francisco around the Horn was a month-long voyage of 13,000 miles. From New York to San Francisco by way of Panama was 5,000 miles. The cost paid in human life from cholera, dysentery, fever and smallpox was equally large. "The common story, the one repeated up and down the California gold fields, the one carried home on the New York steamer, the claim that turns up time and again in the dim pages of the old letter, is that there was a dead man for every railroad tie between Colón and Panama City. The story was nonsense – there were some seventy-five thousand ties along the Panama line – but that had not kept it from spreading, and from what many thousands of people had seen with their own eyes, it seemed believable enough."[2] A reasonable and conservative estimate of the deaths is more than 6,000. The Panama Railroad Company kept no records, except for its white workers, who represented only a fraction of the total labour force employed during the five years of construction.

Labourers were brought in from China, Europe and the Caribbean islands and – later with the construction of the canal – radically changed Panama's population mix. Today, for example, there are more than 100,000 Chinese in Panama out of a total population of 2.5 million and Colón's population is predominantly black and English-speaking. The railroad was one of the most profitable investments of that time, but that prosperity ended with the inauguration of a transcontinental railway in the United States in 1869. Between 1856 and 1866 around 400,000 people used the Panama line.

The first US military intervention in Panama took place in 1856, shortly after the railway was opened. The flash-point, worthy of a comic opera, was a slice of watermelon stolen by a US soldier. More than a dozen US citizens died in riots and marines landed "to protect the railroad".

Matthew Fontaine Maury, the pioneer US oceanographer, told a Senate committee as early as 1849 that a Panama railroad would lead directly to a Panama canal. In 1880 the Frenchman Ferdinand de Lesseps, builder of the Suez Canal, launched an attempt to construct a sea-level waterway through Panama. The French had obtained from Colombia the 99-year Wyse concession to build and operate a canal. The Compagnie Universelle du Canal Interocéanique bought out the Panama Railroad Company and the Mallarino-Bidlack Treaty guaranteeing US access to the Isthmus remained in force. Lesseps laboured for nine years but had to admit defeat because of a lack of capital and the technological impossibility of building a sea-level, rather than a locks-based canal.

The United States was never happy with the idea of a European controlled canal; as early as 1832 the Monroe Doctrine had stated that the United States would actively oppose any further European attempts to colonise the Americas, and this became a central feature of US foreign policy. President

Theodore Roosevelt saw the canal much more in empire building terms than as a commercial venture. It was "The vital – the indispensable – path to a global destiny for the United States of America. He had a vision of his country as the commanding power on two oceans, and these joined by a canal, built, owned, operated, policed and fortified by his country. The canal was to be the first step to American supremacy at sea."[3] Roosevelt was deeply influenced by Alfred Thayer Mahan's book, *Influence of sea power upon history*, published in 1890, which reached the hardly surprising conclusion that national greatness and commercial supremacy were directly related to supremacy at sea. The Spanish-American war of 1898 convinced the US military of the need for a canal between the Atlantic and the Pacific so that US naval vessels could pass easily between the oceans.

In 1903 the United States and Colombia negotiated a new agreement, the Hay-Herrán Treaty, which granted the US the "exclusive and absolute option" to build and operate a canal for a 100-year period, while Colombia would retain sovereignty and the obligation to defend the canal militarily. But, to the anger of Roosevelt, the Colombian senate refused to ratify the treaty. Panamanian secessionist movements – there were 33 attempts to declare independence between 1830 and 1903 – suddenly began to interest Washington. Philippe Bunau-Varilla, the Frenchman in charge of the canal excavation under Lesseps who, as a shareholder of the Compagnie Nouvelle, stood to gain handsomely from a US buy-out of the French rights and assets, moved to New York and, operating out of Room 1162 at the Waldorf Astoria (which he later described as "the cradle of the Panama Republic") acted as the intermediary between Washington and the secessionists. "I do not think that the Bogotá lot of jack rabbits should be allowed permanently to bar one of the future highways of civilisation", Roosevelt wrote at the time. US ships were lying offshore at Colón and Panama City when the secessionists moved. Colombia, weakened by its (civil) War of a Thousand Days (1899–1902), much of which was fought in Panamanian territory, was in no position to put up a fight and its troops left Panama peacefully. Roosevelt wielded the "big stick" and it worked. Panama's independence was recognised by Washington on 6 November 1903.

Building of the canal and US protectorate (1903–36)

Bunau-Varilla was named "envoy extraordinary and ambassador plenipotentiary" in Washington and he negotiated and signed a US–Panamanian canal treaty with Secretary of State John Hay. It was thought unnecessary to ask for any Panamanian signature. The treaty granted the United States within an expanded canal zone (10 miles wide instead of six under the Hay-Herrán Treaty) "all the rights, power and authority . . . which the United States would possess and exercise if it were the sovereign of the territory . . . to the entire exclusion of the exercise by the Republic of Panama of any such sovereign rights, power or authority". It even granted Washington these rights "in perpetuity" and not a 100-year lease as in the Hay-Herrán pact. Panamanians living

NO
ESTACIONE
ENTRADA

or working in the Zone were subject to American law and to trial in the United States right up to the 1977 treaty. Hay called the treaty "vastly advantageous to the United States, and we must confess not so advantageous to Panama".

Colón and Panama City were not part of the Zone, but the sanitation, sewerage, water supply and maintenance of public order in these terminal cities at the Atlantic and Pacific ends of the proposed canal were placed under US control. In return, the United States guaranteed the independence of Panama. When Bunau-Varilla greeted Manuel Amador, Tomás Arias and Federico Boyd, the rebel leaders, in Washington his first words were: "The Republic of Panama is henceforth under the protection of the United States. I have just signed the Canal Treaty."[1] Amador and Arias could not believe what Bunau-Varilla had done and were furious. Boyd is said to have hit Bunau-Varilla in the face.

Bunau-Varilla warned them that if they opposed the treaty and it was not ratified by Panama's Legislative Assembly the United States would withdraw its protection. The tactic worked. Washington then drove home its domination in 1904 by forcing Panama to abolish its army (Taft Agreement) and the US dollar was established as the country's legal tender. US troops intervened to put down protests.

Panama's new constitution granted the United States the right to intervene "in any part of Panama to reestablish public peace and constitutional order". Panama's love-hate relationship with the United States dates from this period when the country was sliced in two by a strip of alien territory and became a client state. Construction of the canal began and it was opened 10 years later in 1914. The canal had an enormous impact on US empire-building and on Panama. In the words of Panama's best known historian, Ricaurte Soler,[4] "The Caribbean became effectively the US's *mare nostrum*, pushing out English capital on the Pacific side of South America in favour of yankee capital and making Panama the hub not only of its economic domination but also its military and geostrategic support. For the Panamanian nation it meant the beginning of a colonial enclave which denied its sovereignty and reduced its personality in the international concert of nations." The colonial nature of the Canal Zone was such that Panamanians who wanted to drive their cars there had to request driving licences and number plates from the Zone's governor. Racial segregation in the Zone long outlasted the abolition of racist laws in the southern United States. It was possible at many points to enter the Zone by crossing from one side of the street to the other. But Panamanians had to be careful: if they were involved in a traffic offence on the wrong side of the street, they could be judged in a US court by American law.

At the peak of the canal's construction in 1913 there were 56,654 workers. By the time the "eighth wonder of the world" was completed a year later an estimated 25,000 people had died during its building, including those from the French era (500 for every mile of the canal).

Panama, after the years of economic stagnation since the collapse of the Compagnie Universelle, appeared poised to regain its position as the crossroads of world trade. The only significant development in the local economy had been in banana production which started in the 1860s in the province of

Chiriquí in plantations and came to be controlled by the United Fruit Company, the US multinational.

Between 1903 and 1936, when Panama's protectorate status was abolished by the General Treaty of Friendship and Cooperation which ended Washington's right of unilateral intervention except where necessary to defend the canal, US troops intervened nine times to quell unrest, be it in banana plantations, during elections or to put down a rent strike in 1925. During this period and for most of the time between 1936 and 1968 a couple of dozen closely linked families (often through marriage) known as *rabiblancos*, or white tails – "an incestuous set whose obsession with race, class and family lineage turns virtually all society gossip into a discussion of genetics"[5] – held office through the Liberal Party and its factions. During the three governments of President Belisario Porras (1912–24) the foundations of Panama's modern state were laid.

Arnulfo Arias and the National Guard coup (1940–68)

The populist Arnulfo Arias (1901–88), the dominant personality in 20th century Panama until General Omar Torrijos took power in 1968, broke the mould of Panamanian politics by challenging US control of the canal and the supremacy of the National Guard (created in 1953). Arias was elected president three times, but served only a year in 1940, 17 months in 1951 and just 11 days in 1968. Each time he was ousted by the National Guard, in collusion with US and Panamanian oligarchical interests, after trying to change the high command.

Arias' ideology was a strange mixture of nationalism (what he termed *panameñismo*), tinged with racism, anti-communism, fascism and social reformism (he gave women the vote, for example). Unlike the conservative parties run by the upper class, Arias had a working-class power base and it was his potential to galvanise it which worried Washington. He drew support from all those who felt excluded by the merchant élite but he did not bring workers and peasants into the circles of political power. As a demagogue Arias was a wild card for US governments and he was never trusted until he spent 10 years in exile in the United States, after the 1968 coup, and became friends with Ronald Reagan, then governor of California. Arias' lack of a coherent policy was underscored when he joined ultra-right Republicans and opposed the Torrijos Carter canal treaty negotiations in the 1970s on the grounds that the canal was being handed over to "communists".

On 9 January 1964, when the government was headed by Roberto Chiari, clashes took place between students, who were attempting to fly the Panamanian flag next to the US flag at Balboa High School in the Canal Zone, and Zonians. President John Kennedy had earlier decreed that a Panamanian flag could fly wherever the Stars and Stripes were displayed. US troops were called in and 21 people were killed and more than 300 wounded. Panama severed diplomatic relations with the United States for three months. The riots

– 9 January is commemorated as a "national day of mourning" – brought to a head simmering nationalistic sentiment.

Arias won the 1968 elections but his stay in the presidential palace was shortlived. The National Guard not only saw Arias as a threat to the power and privileges it had accumulated, but it was also unhappy at the country's drift under the bickering oligarchy, divided between reformist elements, who supported President John Kennedy's Alliance for Progress, and reactionaries who opposed reform at all costs. Although the 1960s saw rapid economic expansion, with GDP growth averaging 8 per cent a year, Panama's income distribution was one of the most skewed in Latin America.

The Torrijos era and the canal treaties (1968–81)

The arrival of the National Guard broke the dominance of the oligarchy. The Guard grew out of the police force in 1953 but by the mid-1940s was a power in its own right. In 1952 José Antonio Ramón Cantera stepped down as police chief and ran successfully for the presidency at the head of a new conservative coalition called the National Patriotic Committee. By the time of the coup the National Guard was well along the road to becoming a full-scale army, with 5,000 men, 465 officers and US$3 million a year of assistance from the United States, despite Panama's tiny size and the umbrella of US protection. Officers generally trained in military academies in the region (Torrijos went to El Salvador) and then undertook courses at the United States School of the Americas in the Canal Zone, a training centre for Latin American armies which was the centre of a hemispheric military strategy to fight communism.

Initially, it looked as if the National Guard would return power to civilians: their first communiqué said they had "decided to act with high patriotism to install in the republic a provisional government that will pave the way for a return to the democratic order upset by ambitious and misguided politicians". But the Guard remained the *de facto* political power until the US invasion at the end of 1989. During its first year in power it had to contend with pockets of guerrilla resistance in the countryside and in Panama City.

While General Omar Torrijos, the son of teachers and the first head of the National Guard not linked familially to the oligarchy, was in Mexico City on 15 December 1969 he was telephoned at his hotel by a senior officer and told he should not return to Panama. In a press communiqué released in Panama a group of colonels, with the support of the National Council of Private Business, accused Torrijos of being a "communist". Torrijos and the group of officers with him hired a plane to take them to El Salvador where a veteran pilot friend of Torrijos, known as Red Grey, took them on to Panama. The plane, in a risky flight, landed at night at David, the capital of Chiriquí, where Torrijos had been in charge of the military region and which was then controlled by Lt.-Colonel Manuel Antonio Noriega (whose later rise to power dates from this allegiance).

Torrijos, in the words of Graham Greene,[6] was a "lone wolf" in a region dominated by right-wing military dictators. He told the novelist Gabriel

The entrance to the Panama Canal

García Márquez, another close friend, that "we don't follow a set of ideological rules, for we would run the risk of being narrowly patriotic without being truly nationalistic". Above all else, Torrijos was a nationalist and he believed in consensus politics, though he outlawed political parties until 1978 and imprisoned or exiled some of his opponents. Close to 100 politically related deaths were attributed to the National Guard by human rights organisations.

Leftists and some communists were brought into the Ministries of Education, Labour, Health, Agriculture and Foreign Policy and businessmen into planning, finance, commerce and industry; he also co-opted the Moscow-line People's Party. According to Marco Gandásegui,[7] one of Panama's leading sociologists, *torrijismo* was an "Alliance between the productive bourgeoisie (industry and agriculture) and financial capital. This alliance was politically co-ordinated by the military which, in turn, acted as the intermediary with popularly organised sectors (workers, employees, farmers, peasants and smallholders). The military co-opted popular organisations and divided them." It was the military which now carried the banner of national sovereignty, the recovery of the Canal Zone, agrarian reform, and educational reform.

Torrijos, "maximum leader of the Panamanian revolution" under the 1972 constitution, nationalised electricity and telecommunications, created state companies in the banana, sugar and cement sectors and substantially increased spending on education, housing and health. Public sector employment accounted for two-thirds of the new jobs created between 1970 and 1979. A public investment programme provided services to wide sections of the population which had not previously enjoyed them. A new labour code was established that was much more favourable to workers (collective bargaining and the right to strike were allowed and job security was guaranteed after two years). The reforms had a profound effect on Panamanian society, opening the doors of society and politics to the middle class and the poor, particularly the black population. Illiteracy and infant mortality rates came down significantly.

At the same time Torrijos was careful not to alienate the private sector; he gave into pressure from business sectors in 1976 and reformed parts of the labour code, making it easier to hire and fire workers. He safeguarded the élite's interests by creating a haven of peace in a turbulent region. The business élite was won over by his creation of an international financial centre (more than 100 banks) and by the Colón Free Zone (established in 1948) which quickly expanded to become the world's second largest after Hong Kong. Torrijos and his planners realised that Panama's future lay in maximising its strategic location as a service-oriented economy.

The Guard benefited from the transformation of the economy and a military business complex took root which enriched senior officers, particularly in the Colón Free Zone. Favours and bribes became a commonplace of business practice particularly during the 1983–89 Noriega regime. Officers were involved in contraband and trafficking drugs from neighbouring Colombia, the world's largest cocaine producer. The size of the Guard grew to 15,000 by 1978 and its budget increased tenfold. Senior officers were the country's Mafia chiefs. Panama embarked on a process of militarisation which was to have disastrous consequences after Torrijos' death in a mysterious plane crash in 1981.

After the 1964 riots the Johnson administration agreed to draft a new set of treaties which would be more favourable to Panama. The 1967 draft would have perpetrated US control until 2067, affirmed the legality of the US military bases and given the United States the exclusive right to build a sea-level canal in Panama. Torrijos refused to accept the treaties and raised the international stakes of the canal issue. "I don't want to enter into history books," he said, "I want to enter the Canal Zone." Working in concert with other regional and non-aligned countries, he persuaded the UN Security Council to hold a special session in Panama City in March 1973 and told participants that Panama "will never be an associated state, colony or protectorate and nor do we want to add another star to the US flag". The Council passed a resolution favourable to Panama which was vetoed by the United States.

The canal issue was seized on by right-wing Republicans in the run-up to the 1976 US elections, particularly Ronald Reagan, a contender for the Republican presidential nomination. "We bought it, we paid for it, it's ours and we should tell Torrijos and company that we are going to keep it", Reagan said.

The Democrat Jimmy Carter won the election and proceeded to conclude new treaties which were signed in September 1977, 13 years after the process was begun. Although far from satisfying Panamanian and Pan-Latin American aspirations, the treaties were a substantial improvement. The main points were:

- The Canal Zone ceased to exist and Panama assumed territorial jurisdiction.

Two-thirds of its land area reverted almost immediately to Panama, including the railway and the ports at the Atlantic and Pacific ends.

- The United States retained the right to operate the canal until the year 2000, but under a new nine-member commission (five US and four Panamanian citizens).
- Panama would gradually assume greater control over the canal, and in 1990 a Panamanian would become the head of the commission.
- An increased percentage of tolls would go to Panama.
- No sea-level canal would be built in Panama without US consent; there would be no US negotiations on a sea-level canal with any other Western hemisphere nation.
- US military bases and training areas would remain under US control until the year 2000.
- The canal would be "permanently neutral"; the primary responsibility for defence would rest with US military until that year; the United States would retain authority to defend the canal's neutrality.

The treaties were very narrowly approved by the US Senate (68–32 on an issue requiring a two-thirds majority) and one-third of voters in Panama's referendum rejected them. This gives an idea of the extent to which the issue had become polarised.

The Legislative Assembly, made up of 505 representatives from Panama's *corregimientos* (the name given to municipalities divided into subdistricts), appointed Aristides Royo president in 1978 and Torrijos formed the Democratic Revolutionary Party (PRD). Both moves were part of a planned gradual return to democracy. The PRD, whose emblem was the number 11 on the national flag (11 October was the date of the coup), was modelled on Mexico's Institutional Revolutionary Party (PRI), the world's longest ruling party, which provides a corporatist vehicle for trade unions, peasants and the private sector. The PRD was created to compete in local elections in 1980 and general elections in 1984. Torrijos intended to retire from the helm of state, though he would probably have remained the power behind the throne.

Reagan's arrival at the White House in 1981 changed US policy towards Central America and a much tougher stand was taken against left-wing revolutionaries in the US's "backyard". Torrijos aided the guerrillas in Nicaragua and, to a lesser extent, in El Salvador, to the anger of Washington. Torrijos first established contact with the Sandinistas in 1975 and Panama sent a brigade to fight along their side in Nicaragua. The Somoza dictatorship was toppled in July 1979. According to Greene,[6] Torrijos wanted "a social democratic Central America, independent of the United States, but representing no menace to justify intervention". The United States favoured military solutions.

The new and tougher US policy towards Latin America, and Panama in particular, was set out in a document known as Santa Fe I which criticised the Carter administration's accommodation with Panama and said the country was "under the control of the left wing of the military regime which, according to the CIA, was the intermediary in the shipment of arms from Cuba and the United States to the Sandinistas in the Marxist conquest of Nicaragua". When

Torrijos received a curt message from Secretary of State Alexander Haig in February 1981 he returned it with the words, "I cannot acknowledge receipt as it has been sent to the wrong address. It should be sent to Puerto Rico." In July Torrijos died in a plane crash and Panama began to disintegrate.

The Noriega regime and the US invasion (1983–89)

Torrijos' death laid bare the infighting in the government and the National Guard which was kept at bay while he was the final arbiter. Colonel Florencio Flórez became the new head of the Guard and in 1982 the "leftist" President Royo was forced to resign. He was replaced by Vice-President Ricardo de la Espriella. Flórez was then ousted in a palace coup by Colonel Rubén Dario Paredes who quickly promoted himself to General. Paredes resigned in 1983 to run as the PRD candidate in the 1984 elections. General Manuel Antonio Noriega, head of G-2 (military intelligence) and a long-serving CIA asset, became commander in chief. He reorganised the National Guard and renamed it the Panama Defence Forces (PDF), incorporating the tiny navy and air force, the police, the Canal Defence Force, the traffic department and the immigration service. Noriega was advised by Mike Harari, a former member of Mossad, the Israeli Intelligence Agency. The president could not dismiss the PDF commander. The Pentagon saw the strengthened forces as a key element in the process of handing over the canal to Panama (the Batallon 2000 was specially created to defend it) and as part of its policy of containing revolution in Central America.

As early as 1971 the US Drug Enforcement Agency had sufficient evidence to indict Noriega after a shipment of marijuana was seized from Panama, but the US Attorney's office in Miami decided not to proceed. Noriega's CIA contacts probably saved him.[7] Noriega's activities also came out during the closed-door hearings in the US Senate in 1978 as part of the canal treaty ratification process. When Noriega became head of the Guard, the US ambassador in Panama wanted an investigation into his activities, but he was overruled by the CIA station chief, who valued Noriega's intelligence gathering services. Noriega was recruited by the CIA when he attended the Peruvian military academy in 1960.[8] President Carter's CIA chief, Admiral Stansfield Turner, revealed that the CIA was paying Noriega US$100,000 a year before he took him off the payroll in 1977. After Reagan became president in 1981, vice-president George Bush, a former CIA chief who first met Noriega in 1976 when he was head of Panamanian military intelligence, insisted that Noriega be re-hired.

By 1984 the Panamanian economy was in recession. GDP shrank 0.4 per cent in 1984 after expanding 0.6 per cent in 1983 and 5.5 per cent in 1982. A lot of the investment had been financed with foreign debt and debt servicing amounted to US$566 million in 1984, more than the value of merchandise exports. However, as the US dollar is Panama's legal, tender the foreign debt is a fiscal and not a balance of payments problem, an important difference which foreign bankers tend to overlook. Nevertheless the economy felt the shock waves from Mexico's 1982 foreign debt crisis. Growth in the banking sector was less than half that of preceding years, while value added in tourism and in the Colón Free Trade Zone declined sharply. Private investment fell in real terms after completion of a transisthmian oil pipeline. The government loosened the reins on expenditure and the consolidated public sector deficit reached 11 per cent of GDP, almost double the amount stipulated in Panama's IMF standby agreement.

Under pressure from the Reagan administration Noriega appointed Nicolás Ardito Barletta, a former planning minister and a vice-president of the World Bank, as the PRD candidate in order to revive the sagging economy. Paredes was ditched. A few months before the elections President Ricardo de la Espriella refused to appoint a list of cabinet replacements handed to him by Noriega as part of his plans to ensure that Barletta won the elections, and resigned. Many more military men ran state entities under Noriega than under Torrijos.

Barletta, a pupil of US Secretary of State George Shultz, faced Arnulfo Arias who had returned from 10 years in exile at the end of the 1970s. Arias, aged 83, was the rallying point for the growing anti-Noriega forces. Polls predicted an Arias victory and by all accounts it was an overwhelming one, but Barletta was declared the winner by the slender margin of 1,713 votes. The US Embassy in Panama City was well aware of the fraud but Barletta's "victory" was not challenged. Noriega, despite his drug dealings, business with Cuba (to get around the US trade embargo) and violent past, was proving to be extremely useful to the CIA, particularly in shipping arms to the US-backed Contra rebels fighting to overthrow the Sandinistas. In February 1985 Noriega was invited to speak at the John F. Kennedy School of Government at Harvard University.

Noriega's long and drawn-out downfall began on 13 September 1985 when Hugo Spadafora, a former deputy health minister under Torrijos and leader of the Panamanian brigade that fought with the Sandinistas in Nicaragua, was murdered by Noriega's henchmen near the border with Costa Rica. Spadafora was returning from exile in Costa Rica to Panama and intended to reveal details of Noriega's involvement in drug trafficking. There was nothing new about Spadafora's claims. Noriega and his activities had been the subject of several White House-level reports. What was new, and disturbing for Noriega, was that Spadafora was going to document his charges in articles and radio talks. Noriega was in Paris when he received a call[11] on his satellite line (which was monitored by the US National Security Agency). The conversation was brief. "We have the rabid dog", Noriega was told. "You know what to do with a dog that has rabies", Noriega replied. Spadafora was beheaded.

Spadafora's brutal death stunned Panama and brought thousands of protestors into the streets. The tide began to turn against Noriega. Barletta announced that a commission would be established to investigate the murder. Noriega was furious and forced Barletta to resign, allegedly at gun point. He was replaced by the vice-president, Arturo Delvalle. Washington's support of Noriega now began to wane. Noriega's double dealings – shipping arms to left-wing guerrillas in El Salvador as well as to the Contras, providing intelligence to both the CIA and the Cubans, and his close links with the Medellín drug cartel, formed in 1981 – began to make him a liability for the Reagan administration. The 12 June 1986 issue of *The New York Times* carried a story that detailed Noriega's involvement in the Spadafora murder, election-fixing and drug trafficking. Again there was nothing new in the details. What was important was that sectors of the US administration were leaking information in order to undermine Noriega who by then was a key element in Colonel Oliver North's illegal activities in support of the Contras (money raised by the sale of arms to Iran was being diverted in secret to the Nicaraguan "freedom fighters"). It was the first shot fired in public in the politically expedient campaign to demonise the "monster" created, to some extent, by Washington. It is easy to portray the struggle against Noriega, as the US government did, in the simplistic terms of the "good guys against the bad guys" but the issue was much more complex than this. The wily Noriega responded to the article by publishing the many letters he had received from the US Drugs Enforcement Agency praising him for his co-operation.

A little under a year later Colonel Roberto Díaz Herrera, the chief of staff and second in command of the Panamanian Defence Forces, who had been led to believe by Noriega that he would move up to the top slot, was relieved of his post. Noriega promised Díaz Herrera a lucrative post abroad, but he reneged on the deal. Díaz Herrera then wielded his only weapon – he spilled the beans about Noriega's activities in a press conference on 7 June 1987, particularly regarding the rigging of the election. Díaz Herrera also admitted that he had enriched himself, selling Panamanian visas to Cubans who wanted to get into the United States. His accusations were of seminal importance because it was the first time that a senior officer had broken ranks and washed dirty linen in public. Middle class opposition groups, who by then had formed a Civic Crusade for Justice and Democracy, took to the streets. They turned up, as P. J. O'Rourke wrote in *Rolling Stone* magazine "in nice ties and linen dirndl skirts . . . in BMWs and Jeep Wagoneers . . .". Foreign journalists joked that the numbers turning out to protest depended on the available parking space.

Noriega, in the words of Roger Fontaine, a member of the US National Security Council, had become an "irritant". On 26 June the US Senate voted in favour of a resolution calling for Noriega to step down, an independent investigation of corruption charges against senior officers, and elections. In August, Washington suspended aid to Panama. There was a run on deposits in Panama City's banks and by the end of 1987 the deposits had dropped to US$23 billion from US$32 billion a year earlier.

Not even the indictment on drug-trafficking charges by US attorneys in February 1988 had any effect on Noriega, who cleverly exploited the growing opposition at home by portraying the *rabiblancos* as tools of the United States. Noriega, of humble origin and swarthy complexion, played on Panama's underlying racial tensions to his own benefit, winning support from the poor. Encouraged by the CIA, President Arturo Delvalle tried to fire Noriega, but he himself was ousted by the Legislative Assembly and replaced by the Education Minister, Manuel Solís Palma. Delvalle, the fourth president in six years to be ousted by the military, sought refuge on a US military base and then went into exile in the United States where Washington recognised him as Panama's legitimate head of state. Over the next year there was a failed US-inspired coup attempt in October 1989, widespread strikes, further sanctions (the US government froze Panama's assets abroad and ordered US companies not to pay taxes or social security to the Panamanian government) and attempts to strike a deal with Noriega. The suspended payments from the Panama Canal Commission deprived the government of around US$80 million, a sizeable sum for an economy whose GDP was US$4.5 billion. Not surprisingly, in December 1987 the government suspended capital and interest payments on the public foreign debt which had grown to US$6 billion from US$190 million in 1970 and the country's banks were closed in March 1988 for nine weeks to stop the run on deposits. Debt service payments plummeted from US$461 million in 1987 (8 per cent of GDP) to US$28.1 million in 1988. US sanctions decimated the economy and GDP shrank 16.7 per cent in 1988 and 1989, the steepest decline of any Latin American country for several decades according to the United Nations. Open unemployment climbed to 20 per cent in 1989 from 12 per cent in 1987.

In return for Noriega stepping down, the Reagan administration was prepared to drop the drug-trafficking charges against him, but the general refused to go. He took comfort from George Bush's victory in the presidential election, believing that his former paymaster would not run him out of office.

In May 1989 businessman Guillermo Endara, the head of the Democratic Alliance of Civic Opposition, won Panama's presidential election which was held in the presence of several hundred foreign observers, including former President Jimmy Carter who had signed the canal treaties in 1977. But Noriega refused to accept the massive defeat of his candidate, Carlos Duque of the Democratic Revolutionary Party, who headed a coalition of forces loyal to the regime called COLINA, and nullified the election on the grounds of irregularities. Washington had given US$10 million to ADOC to fund its campaign. Noriega sent his paramilitary Dignity Battalions into the streets: the photo of vice-presidential candidate Guillermo Ford, covered with the blood of his murdered bodyguard and under attack from Noriega's thugs, shocked the world and probably did more than anything else to convince Bush, under fire at home for being a "wimp", to press ahead with plans for an invasion.

It came in the early morning of 20 December, but only after another failed coup attempt in October. By then Noriega's *ad hoc* parliament had appointed him head of state with unlimited powers. The invasion, involving 30,000 troops and christened Operation Just Cause, was the most extensive US military operation since the Vietnam war, and involved the largest combat paratroop drop since the Allied attempt to seize the Rhine bridges in 1944. The CIA station chief in Panama City at the time believed the invasion was excessive and that other means could have been used to force Noriega to step down. The eminent historian Eric Hobsbawm[12] called the invasion "pointless" and said it was undertaken to demonstrate the "unchallengable supremacy and invulnerability of the USA".

Residents of the exclusive Punta Paitilla district took to the balconies of their high-rise apartments, some with champagne glasses in their hands, and applauded as the headquarters of the Defence Forces, in the middle of the El Chorrillo slum area, was pounded to the ground. The wooden tenements in El Chorrillo caught fire and the district was erased. Officially, 314 members of the Defence Forces and 202 civilians died. An independent commission of enquiry whose members included former US attorney general Ramsey Clark concluded that "as many as 4,000 to 7,000 people may have been killed". Many people killed were hastily buried in secret mass graves.

Noriega gave himself up after taking asylum in the Papal Nunciature, the Vatican's embassy in Panama City. He was flown to Miami and imprisoned, after a trial, for 40 years.

The Endara government (1990–94)

Guillermo Endara, the winner of the May 1989 election by a two-to-one margin, was sworn in as president at Fort Clayton, a US military base, in the early hours of the invasion. Endara, a founding member of the Authentic Panameñista Party, a conservative populist party headed by Arnulfo Arias until his death in 1988, and his vice-presidents, Ricardo Arias Calderón, a Christian Democrat, and Guillermo Ford of the National Liberal Republican Movement (Molirena) headed the ADOC coalition. Although none of the three parties had a popular base, ADOC galvanised anti-Noriega votes and won more because people were fed up and wanted a change than for its own particular merits. Its victory represented a return to the political *status quo* that existed when the National Guard overthrew Arias in 1968. Endara was the equivalent of the Planning and Economic Policy Minister in the Arias government.

The invasion caused an estimated US$1 billion of damage, and including the impact of US sanctions and three days of looting, losses were much higher. Despite a promise by President Bush that the United States would grant aid of this amount, Congress only approved US$420 million in March 1990. For several months after the invasion, Panama reverted to being a US protectorate; military personnel were stationed in all ministries which had been ransacked by Noriega's supporters and by looters. Banco Nacional de Panamá, the largest Panamanian bank and the government's fiscal agent (Panama does not have a central bank that issues currency as the US dollar is the legal tender), had negative reserves of US$1.2 billion at the end of 1989 and the foreign debt had reached US$6.3 billion, making the country (population 2.3 million) one of the most heavily indebted in the world in per capita terms. The task facing the new administration was daunting: it had simultaneously to re-establish democratic institutions and respect for the rule of law, revive an economy which had suffered a 16 per cent drop in real terms in two years, and restructure the economy to correct extreme distortions inherited from the past. Real output had fallen to below the 1980 level, and real per capita production was below that of 1978. More than 40 per cent of the labour force lacked steady employment. The aid was so slow in coming through that the overweight Endara staged a two-week fast "in solidarity with the people of Panama".

One of the first measures was to sign a drugs accord with the United

States and to abolish the Panamanian Defence Forces which were replaced by a police force (largely recruited from the former military as only senior officers were purged). By 1990 military spending represented 2.5 per cent of GDP compared with 0.1 per cent in 1960. Expenditure was the equivalent of 34 per cent of the spending on health and education (2 per cent in 1960). Washington tied a chunk of the aid to Panama's approving anti-narcotics legislation, in particular a Mutual Legal Assistance Treaty, which committed the government to supplying documentary and other evidence required in drugs cases. The Panamanian parliament quickly ratified the treaty but the US Senate did not ratify it until May 1995. Republicans (who gained control of the US Congress after the Pérez Balladares government took office in September 1994) such as Jesse Helms, chairman of the powerful Senate Foreign Relations Committee and a key player in the downfall of Noriega, imposed conditions, reserving the right to deny information on drugs investigations to Panamanian officials suspected of being involved with drug barons.

New controls were also put on the banking system to try to curb laundering of drug money (Panama City was known as the "washing machine" under Noriega). Banks have to report all deposits and withdrawals of more than US$10,000, as done in the United States.

The Endara government began to negotiate a Brady-style foreign debt rescheduling agreement with its commercial bank creditors, but no accord was agreed. It also started to clear up US$685 million of arrears to the International Monetary Fund (IMF), the World Bank and the Inter-American Development Bank (IDB). As a result, the IMF approved a support programme and this was followed by a structural adjustment loan from the World Bank and a credit granted by the IDB for the reform of public enterprises. However, more than US$200 million in scheduled disbursements was withheld during 1992, mostly because of delays in fulfilling conditions agreed upon.

The tax code was also reformed. The law approved in December 1991 simplified personal and business taxes, reduced the differences in rates between small and large companies, decreased the levels and the range of personal tax rates, and lowered the number of personal tax brackets from 209 to 11. The new code made the system more equitable by increasing the deductions for dependants, the minimum taxable income and the personal exemptions. To compensate for the lower rates, the government increased from 5 per cent to 10 per cent the value-added tax on beverages and cigarettes and from 2.5 per cent to 5 per cent the import duty on tourist goods.

The economy began to expand again, growing 4.6 per cent in 1990, 9.6 per cent in 1991 and 8.6 per cent in 1992. A boom in construction, mainly luxury apartments and not homes for the poor, was the main motor of the economy.

After more than 40 years of import substitution and 20 years of interventionist policies, the government embarked on a free trade, liberalisation and privatisation programme, similar to ones being implemented in most other Latin American countries, in order to make the economy more efficient and competitive. The number of people working for the public sector tripled to 165,213 between 1968 and 1989 and the public sector's share in the economy tripled to around 30 per cent of GDP. The Endara government cut 7,000 jobs in

With its skyscrapers glinting in the sun, the centre of modern Panama City resembles a miniature Manhattan

its first year of office but then the number began to grow again and reached close to 161,000 at the end of 1992, roughly one-fifth of Panama's total employment. Since then it has begun to decline.

But it is less easy for Panama than other Latin American countries to become more competitive. As the World Bank[13] has pointed out, "Panama cannot devalue its currency, since the US dollar is the *de facto* legal tender, so the inflexibility of prices for goods and services that was created through state intervention reduced economic efficiency, decreased Panama's international competitiveness, and restrained growth potential, including export growth."

Panama's monetary regime requires price and wage flexibility to effect adjustments, but the rigid price controls, labour laws, and other public sector interventions prevent mobility of resources. This was not such a problem in the past because the resulting high unemployment was absorbed by the expanding public sector (70 per cent of all new jobs in the 1970s), regardless of need or budgetary constraints. But Panama could not carry on like this for ever. The government also began to look at how Panama can best use the land and buildings that are being gradually turned over under the terms of the 1977 Canal Treaty. A Regional Interoceanic Authority (ARI) was set up. Many of the buildings are connected with US military bases. The total value of the assets along the near 50-mile canal to be turned over to ARI by the end of 1999 has been put as high at US$30 billion, just over four times the country's GDP.

The Endara administration, however, did not live up to expectations. The economy began to boom – from a very depressed base – and the state was put on its financial feet after inheriting empty coffers from the Noriega regime, but progress on structural reform was very slow, the coalition government quickly fell to partisan bickering (the Christian Democrats abandoned their partners) and corruption scandals dogged the administration. It is an open secret that much of the money invested in the high-rise apartment buildings that have sprouted in the exclusive Punta Paitilla area is drugs-related. After an attempt was made to kidnap the wife of a US diplomat living in the area, the US Embassy investigated the owners of the apartments and found that many names were on its lists of wanted individuals or those suspected of criminal activities. Endara's image was as a do-nothing president and by the time he left office in 1994 he was suffering from single digit approval ratings.

The Revolutionary Democratic Party (PRD), created by Torrijos in 1978, began to regroup, after the US invasion, around Ernesto Pérez Balladares, a former PRD secretary general, and campaign manager in the 1989 fraudulent elections of Carlos Duque, Noriega's man for the presidency. The burly Pérez Balladares, popularly known as *El Toro* (the bull), began to pick up where Torrijos had left off, returning the PRD to its broad base and drawing in workers, peasants and businessmen to form an essentially social democratic party. Pérez Balladares, holder of a Master's Degree in business from Wharton School and a former executive with Citibank, was Finance Minister (1976–81) and then Planning Minister (1981–82) under Torrijos. In 1983 he was director of the Institute of Hydraulic Resources (IRHE). He himself comes from a wealthy family and has married into the Boyd family, one of the country's richest and most illustrious.

Endara's coalition had never gained working-class support and by the time of the elections in May it was bitterly divided and failed to present a common candidate. This worked to the PRD's benefit and helped it to rise from the ashes. Pérez Balladares harked back to the golden days under Torrijos and *torojismo* (a play on Pérez Balladares nickname) as opposed to *torrijismo* became the new political buzzword. Pérez Balladares won one-third of the vote and the PRD gained 31 of the 72 seats in the Legislative Assembly and, with the support of three other parties, has a majority.

The Pérez Balladares administration

The political hallmark of the Pérez Balladares government, which took office in September 1994, has been national reconciliation. Pérez Balladares appointed Guillermo Chapman, a widely respected private sector economist and non-PRD member, to the key post of Planning Minister; Gabriel Lewis Galindo, a former ambassador to Washington at the time the Panama Canal Treaty was being negotiated who later led the political struggle against Noriega from his US exile, became Foreign Minister (his brother Samuel, a businessman in the brewery industry, ran against Pérez Balladares in the elections as the candidate for the National Consensus Alliance); José Sossa, a lawyer linked to the opposition Christian Democrats was named attorney general, and Victoria Figge, former head of the private sector organisation APEDE was appointed to run the Colón Free Zone.

PRD leftists from *la tendencia* (the name given to ex-communists who joined the PRD in its early days) were appointed to "social" areas such as the Labour and Health ministries, for example. Mitchell Doens, the Labour Minister, had links with guerrillas in Colombia and in 1995 was still barred from visiting the United States.

Significantly, the pragmatic Pérez Balladares remained the party's secretary general in order to have full control and move it into the centre ground. Soon after taking office he pardoned 217 people closely identified with the Noriega regime, including Colonel Eduardo Herrera Hassan, who was jailed in 1990 after he led a coup plot against the Endara government, and Colonel Guillermo Wong, head of Noriega's secret police. "It is my responsibility as a leader to lead a national reconciliation and look to the future", Pérez Balladares told reporters at the time.

Most Panamanians approved of the pardon, but there are fears that the government could become corrupted by its association with Noriega's former allies. Only a handful of people accused of the most serious human rights violations were not covered by the pardon. They are either in jail or in exile. Some repentant Noriega supporters such as Major Fitz Gibson, a member of Noriega's intelligence service, even found jobs in the government (in his case as deputy director of the La Joya prison). When a member of one of Panama's richest families congratulated Pérez Balladares in 1994 on his appointments and asked him what he intended to do with the "gangsters" from the past, he replied that he would "give them a job and fire them if they step out of line".

Pérez Balladares declared 20 December a national day of mourning to mark the 1989 US invasion and capped five years of debate over how best to observe the anniversary. The Endara government called it a "day of reflection" to the anger of the 20th December Movement of Families of the Dead.

If the 1980s were a "lost decade" for almost all of Latin America, few countries suffered as much as Panama. Its economy, political system and national pride were all severely wounded. Pérez Balladares, acutely aware of the need to quickly recover lost ground, wasted no time in launching initiatives on several fronts to transform Panama and its service-driven economy into a kind of Singapore, the economic model that the government aspires after. Negotiations were at an advanced stage in the middle of 1995 for Panama to join the World Trade Organisation (WTO), formerly known as GATT (the country is almost the only one in Latin American not a member of the WTO), a Brady-style foreign debt rescheduling agreement was reached in May 1995, and anti-monopoly, tax incentives and labour reform and privatisation legislation were due to be approved by the Legislative Assembly. The vested interests resulting from the distortions produced by the interventionist policies of the previous 20 years have created a strong lobby against reform. WTO membership is a *sine qua non* for Panama's bid to join the North American Free Trade Agreement or negotiate a bilateral deal with the United States.

Efforts also began to be made to clean up Panama's image of corruption, money laundering and drug trafficking, serious problems that did not abate during the Endara government. One change promoted by Pérez Balladares is to make Panamanian lawyers bear responsibility for shell corporations used by drug traffickers. In 1994 Panama was given a qualified certification by the United States for its efforts in fighting the drugs trade. Since 1986 the US government has annually passed judgement on 26 countries receiving US aid that it says are important in drug producing and trafficking. They may be considered clean, or not certified (which means a country loses trade benefits and "non-humanitarian aid), or given a qualified certification that carries no punishment but is a slap on the wrist. In 1995 Panama was certified clean, though this does not mean that the drugs problem has disappeared. One of the many ironies of post-invasion Panama is that under Noriega Panama did not have a very serious hard drugs consumption problem of its own. Most of the drugs were shipped through the country. In January 1995 Panama's drug prevention and control department said consumption had risen so much between 1992 and 1994 that Panama City now has the second highest rate among the capitals of Central America and the Dominican Republic and drugs were being introduced to schools in rural areas.

US-Panamanian relations have improved. They became strained at the end of the Endara government because Panama first accepted and then refused to take up to 10,000 Haitian refugees. Endara took the oath of office on a US military base, and remained ever-sensitive to the charge that he was in the pocket of the Americans. The refusal to take the Haitians was an attempt to mark a distance. On taking power, Pérez Balladares moved swiftly to accept Cuban refugees, but only if they were kept on US bases, and offered asylum to Lt.-General Raoul Cedras, the former Haitian army chief.

By the end of this government in 1999, Panama will be very close to assuming full control of the canal. As President Pérez Balladares has said, "No other country in the world faces such a tight calendar of tasks to be done, obligations to fulfil and expectations to be materialised as Panama does in carrying out the Torrijos-Carter Treaties and the reversion of the former Canal Zone, including the military bases."

The next four years are a once-in-history period when crucial decisions will be made that will determine whether the government's ambition to transform the country into Latin America's "Singapore" in the maritime sector and "Luxembourg" in the financial services area is realistic or a pipedream.

Notes and references

1. David McCullogh, *The Path between the seas* (Simon & Schuster, 1977), p. 35.
2. Ibid., p. 36.
3. Ibid., p. 250.
4. Ricaurte Soler, *Panama, historia de una crisis* (Siglo Veintiuno Editores, 1989), p. 46.
5. Alma Guillermoprieto, *The heart that bleeds* (Knopf, 1994), p. 214.
6. Graham Greene, *Getting to know the General* (Bodley Head, 1984), p. 30.
7. Marco Gandásegui, *La democracia en Panama* (Editorial Mestiza, 1989), p. 113.
8. Graham Greene, *Getting to know the General*, p. 31.
9. John Weeks and Phil Gunson, *Panama, made in the USA* (Latin American Bureau 1991), p. 51.
10. R.M. Koster and Guillermo Sánchez Borbón, *In the time of the tyrants* (Secker & Warburg, 1990, page 22.
11. Kevin Buckley, *Panama, the whole story* (Simon & Schuster, 1991), p. 19.
12. Eric Hobsbawm, *Age of extremes* (Michael Joseph, 1994), p.248.
13. World Bank report, 30 January 1992, p. 2.

Chapter Two

Resources and infrastructure

Panama is the only country in the world where it is possible to swim in two oceans within the space of a couple of hours. In some parts the sun's first rays appear over the Pacific every day and disappear in fiery sunsets over the Atlantic. The tiny S-shaped country borders on the Atlantic in the north, the Pacific in the south, Colombia in the east and Costa Rica in the west. At its narrowest part Panama is less than 80 kilometres wide. Most of the country, including some 750 islands, lies below 700 metres, sweltering daily in tropical heat and high humidity.

The topography in a country of 75,517 square kilometres varies from mountains towards the Caribbean coast to small hills and swathes of savannah on the Pacific side. The mountain ranges trend north-west to south-east slightly against the lie of the country, and fragment the lowlands. At the border with Costa Rica there are several volcanic cones, the highest of which is the dormant Barú in Chiriquí (3,383 metres). While Panama City has always been immune to powerful earthquakes – one reason why the area was chosen for the canal – other parts of the country have not been so lucky. The western province of Bocas del Toro was hit by an eathquake in 1990 and Darién in the 1980s. The 300-year old flat arch, made entirely of bricks and mortar and with no support, in the ruins of the Santo Domingo Church in the old quarter of Panama City has stood the test of time well.

Basins and valleys between the ranges support pockets of agriculture, and rainforests have been cleared for production of bananas, coffee, cocoa and sugar cane, for cattle ranching and for subsistence crops of rice, maize and beans. The canal runs in the gap between the Cordillera de Talamanca and the San Blas range: a whim of nature joined North and South America. To the east, in Darién, the thick jungle remains largely undisturbed and is still home to several indigenous Indian tribes.

Most of the country's 2.6 million population live within about 20 km of the Panama Canal Area (known as the Canal Zone until the 1977 treaties), a third of them in Panama City, the capital, and some 80 per cent of the US$6.9 billion GDP originates here. The contrasts are quite sharp and they stand out particularly strongly because of the country's small size: with its skyscrapers and congested traffic the bustling business centre of Panama City is a Lilliputian version of New York, while the *casco viejo*, the capital's old quarter, and particularly San Miguelito, on the outskirts, have the type of slums seen in all Latin American cities. The contrast is even more striking between the Colón Free Zone and the poverty that lies the other side of its wall.

The country has an average temperature of 27 degrees Centigrade all the year round. Nights, however, are generally cool. There are two seasons: rainy (May to December) and dry. The average population density is 33 people per square kilometre (3,890 in Panama City). The population mix is very varied and the product of the different groups of workers, most notably blacks from the Caribbean (the first ones were slaves from Africa) and Chinese, that went to Panama to work on the construction of the railroad and the canal and in the banana plantations: 59 per cent is mestizo and mulatto, 14 per cent black, 12 per cent white and 7 per cent Amerindian. Panama has around 100,000 Chinese and the embassy of Taiwan in Panama City is one of that country's most important missions in the world. Although, to a large extent, a racially harmonious society, blacks are still regarded as second-class citizens and Indians are generally marginalised. Racial segregation was practised in the Canal Zone long after it was abolished in the southern United States. (In the 1950s the US administrators of the canal pushed blacks out of the Zone to avoid civil rights protests). Of the 60 Indian tribes that inhabited Panama at the time of the Spanish conquest, there are only three of any significance left: the Kuna Yala on the San Blas islands off the Caribbean coast, the Emberá-Waunaan in Darién, and the Ngobe-Buglé, the largest, in Chiriquí, Bocas del Toro and Veraguas. The Ngobe number close to 125,000 and are one of the most rapidly increasing tribal populations in the Americas.

The official language is Spanish, though because of the heavy influence of the United States English is widely spoken among the middle and upper classes. The US influence is reflected in the Spanish spoken in Panama City which has adopted certain English words. To an English-speaking visitor with little knowledge of Spanish, this will seem like a blessing, but to a Spanish-speaking visitor with no knowledge of English it can present some problems. Panamanians, for example, turn on the "switch", go to the "newsstand" and have a "drink".

Panama's official currency is the balboa. However, the balboa only exists in the form of coins that are minted in the same size and value as US coins. The US dollar is the legal currency, and it circulates freely along with Panamanian and US coins.

Panama is an Indian word meaning "abundance of fish" and the country is rich in natural resources. Gold, basalt, manganese, lime, granite and copper have been tapped. The country is a magnificent flower garden (yellow and pink acacias, red ponciana, violet lagerstroemia and purple jacaranda); a bird-watcher's paradise (although smaller than South Carolina, Panama has 933 species, more than all of North America) and with its two oceans is also rich in marine life (lobsters, shrimps, clams and fish, particularly the black marlin for which Panama is famous). Its jungles (around 40 per cent of the total land surface is forested) are home to monkeys, pumas, armadillos, wild boars, anteaters, sloths and the harpy eagle, the national bird. The tropical forest through which the canal passes is one of the richest ecosystems on the planet.

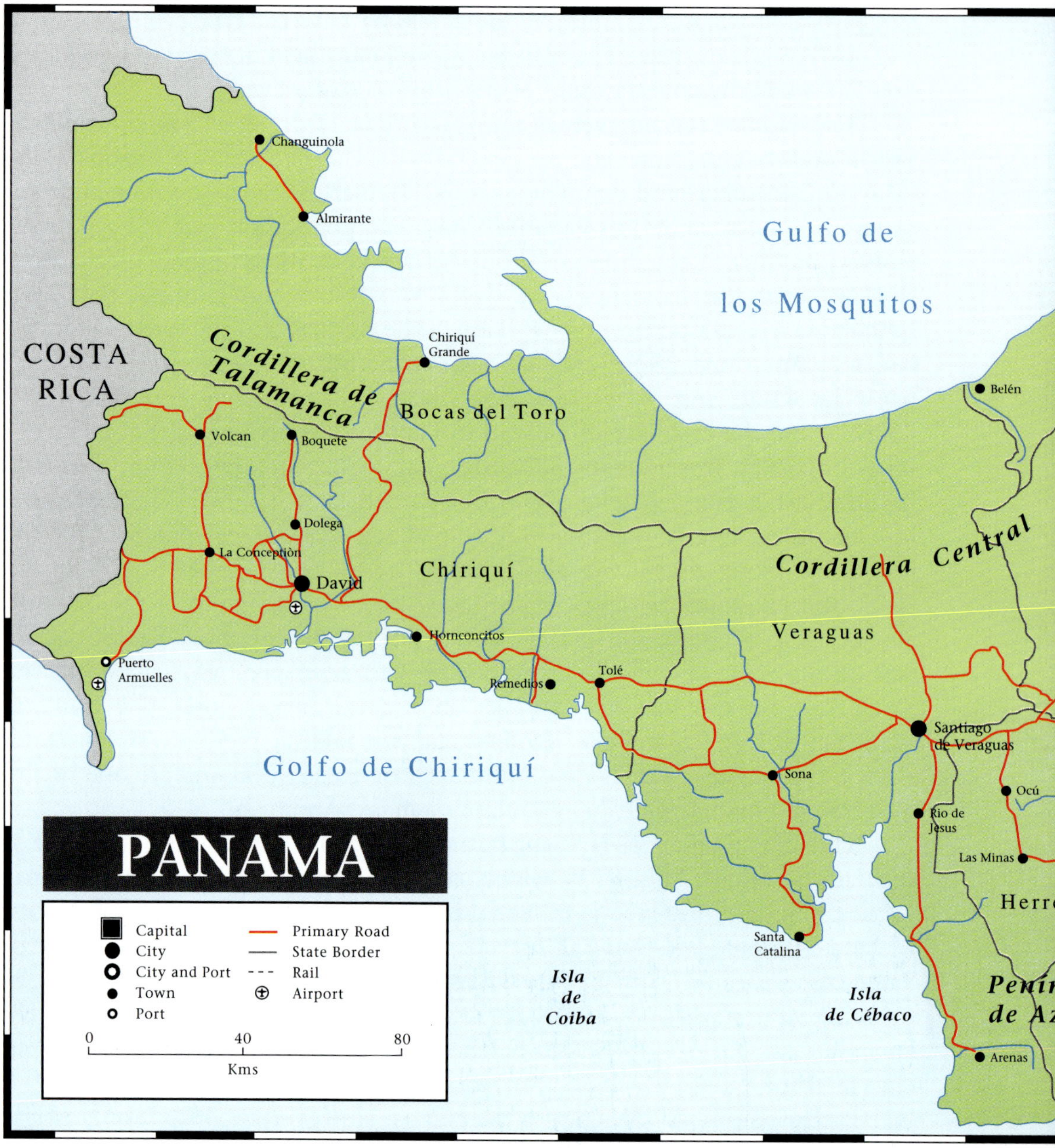

Fifty million gallons of fresh water are needed to float one cargo ship through the canal and all of it is supplied free of charge by forests on the surrounding hillsides, which capture the abundant tropical rains and feed the canal with rivers. Thanks to the Association for the Conservation of Nature (ANCON), which was founded in 1985, Panama has become much more environmentally conscious. Unleaded petrol was introduced in May 1995. Deforestation is a rising concern. In the 1980s over 39,000 hectares of forest were lost each year, while only 3,600 hectares were replanted annually. Between 1947 and 1991 ANCON estimates Panama lost 42 per cent of its forests, and if the current rate of destruction continues, by the year 2000 80 per cent will have disappeared.

Panama is divided into nine provinces (see Exhibit 2.1): Panama, Colón, Chiriquí, Los Santos, Coclé, Veraguas, Bocas del Toro, Darién and Herrera. The

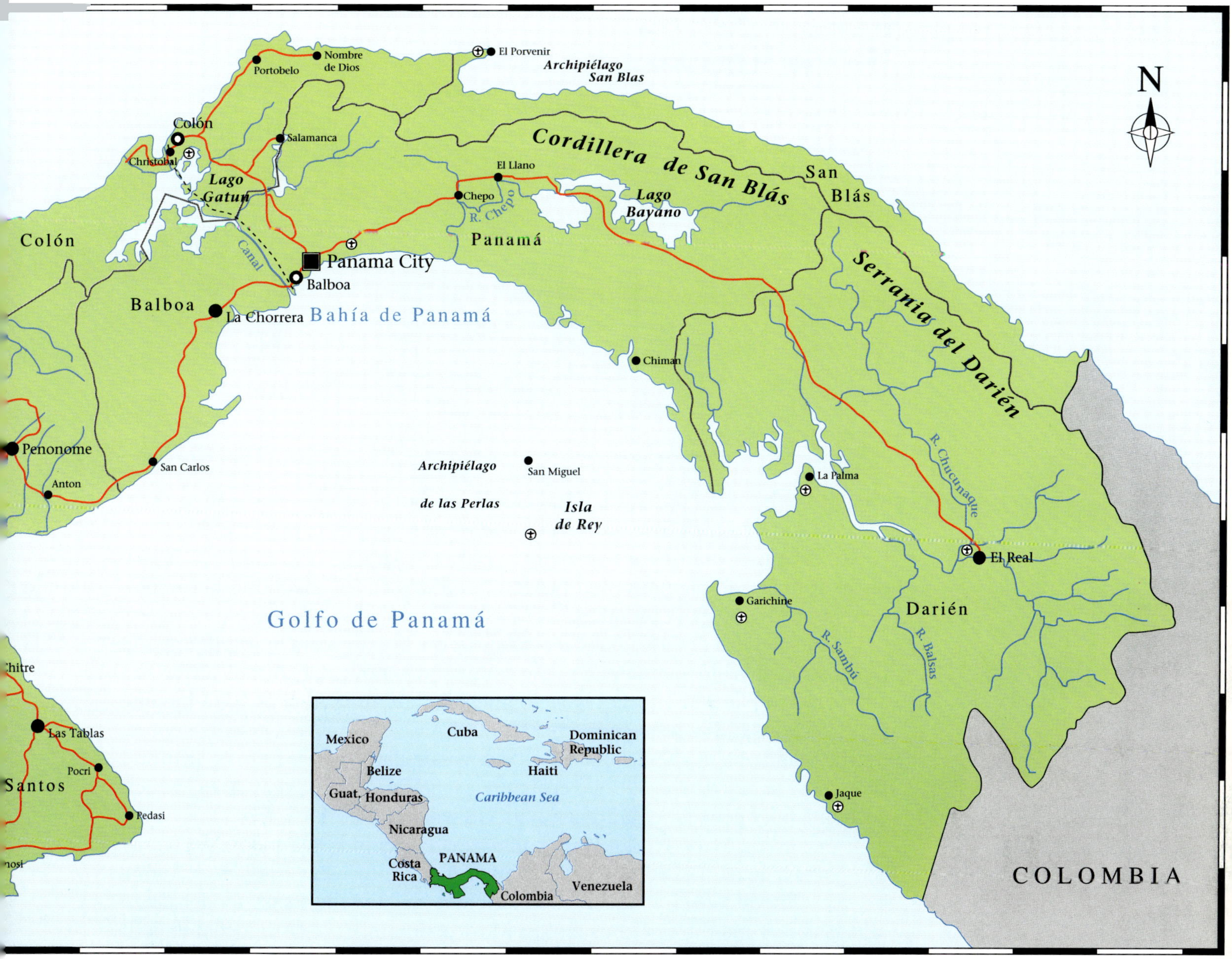

provinces, in turn, are divided into 65 districts and then subdivided into 505 *corregimientos* or subdistricts. San Blas is not a province but a government administered Indian reservation. Panama is the largest province, with 40% of the population. It comprises the districts of San Carlos, Chame, Capira, Chorrera, Arraijan, Taboga, Panama, San Miguelito, Chepo, Chiman and Balboa. The great bulk of economic activity is concentrated in the province of Panama including the financial centre, the canal, several US military bases, shrimp farming in Chame and fruit farms in Capira. Colón is best known for its free trade zone, the second largest in the world after Hong Kong; Chiriquí is Panama's breadbasket as much of the food is grown here and there is also cattle farming; Los Santos has salt, corn and cattle-raising as well as a famous carnival at Las Tablas; the principal activity at Coclé is cattle and handicrafts;

Exhibit 2.1

Population by provinces

Province	*Population*	*Inhabitants per square km*
Bocas del Toro	93,361	10.7
Coclé	173,190	35.1
Colón	168,294	34.4
Chiriquí	379,227	42.8
Darién	43,832	2.6
Herrera	93,681	40.0
Los Santos	76,947	20.2
Panamá	1,072,127	90.2
Veraguas	203,626	18.1
San Blas	34,044	14.4

Source: 1990 population census.

Veraguas, the only province with coasts on both oceans, has coffee, rice, tobacco and livestock; Bocas del Toro, the wettest province, produces bananas, cocoa, coconuts, oranges and grapefruit; Darién is largely jungle, though it produces timber and plantain, and Herrera produces shoes, alcoholic beverages, leather goods and dairy products.

Considerable progress has been made in the last 30 years in improving the living standards of Panamanians. The country was ranked 47 out of 173 in the 1994 United Nations Human Development Index. Annual per capita income was US$2,640 in 1994, the highest in Central America, but this is still very low by the standards of the developed world, particularly when bearing in mind that those employed in US government agencies in the Canal Area, which accounts for 9 per cent of GDP, are paid US wage rates.

According to the World Bank, half of the households in Panama are below the poverty level (i.e. do not have enough income to meet their basic living needs). Critical poverty (income insufficient to buy the basic food basket) affects about one-third of households. Most poor families experience diet deficiencies both of quantity and quality, with particular deficits in calories, proteins, vitamin A, calcium, iron, riboflavin and folic acid.[1] Census figures in height from the Ministry of Health show that in 1988 about one-fifth of school-age children suffered from moderate malnutirition and 6 per cent from severe malnutrition. There has been a dramatic increase in crime since the economy's profound recession and the US invasion in 1989. The number of police arrests per 1,000 citizens rose from six in 1989 to 16 in 1993, according to government figures, and in Colón, parts of which are a virtual ghetto, the rate jumped from five to 66 during the same period.

When the Pérez Balladares government took office in 1994 it admitted that Panama's income distribution was one of the most skewed in the world. According to the 1994 United Nations Human Development Report (UNHDR), between 1980 and 1991 the poorest 40 per cent of households had 8.3 per cent of national income and the income of the richest 20 per cent of the

Exhibit 2.2

Basic social indicators

Access to drinking water[1]	*Access to health services*[2]	*Newspapers per 100 inhabitants*[3]	*TV sets per 100 inhabitants*[3]	*Telephones per 100 inhabitants*[4]
84%	89%	7	16.5	11

[1]1988–91. [2]1985–91. [3]1992. [4]1990–92.
Source: 1994 United Nations Human Development Report.

population is 45 times greater than that of the poorest 20 per cent. Fewer than 20 families control the bulk of Panama's wealth and they are largely interrelated through marriage and constitute a very closely knit group. One of the main complaints of employees in the banking sector is that once they reach a certain level they cannot rise any further unless they are a member of or related to the families running the bank, or marry their boss's daughter.

Average life expectancy has risen from 60 years in 1960 to 73 years today, while the infant mortality rate has dropped to 20 per 1,000 live births from 69 in 1960; but several regions (such as Darién, San Blas and Bocas del Toro) have levels as high as 40–50 per thousand. The adult literacy rate (over the age of 15) is 90 per cent for the country as a whole, but the 1990 census showed a rate (for those over the age of 10) of only 30 per cent in the province of Bocas del Toro and 40 per cent in San Blas. Only 1 per cent of the population lives in conditions of extreme poverty (as defined by the United Nations), compared with 14 per cent in neighbouring Colombia. In 1990 there were 840 people per doctor, better than the average 1,320 in the most developed countries.

The population is currently growing at 1.6 per cent and is officially forecast to reach 3.7 million by 2025 (see Exhibit 2.3). The labour force is growing at 3.8 per cent a year. The pace of urbanisation has been fast. In 1992 54 per cent of the population lived in towns or cities, up from 39 per cent in 1960. By the year 2,000 close to 60 per cent of the population will be urbanised.

Uniting the Americas

The Pan-American highway runs from the Costa Rican border to within 100 km of Colombia through the Darién National Park (see Exhibit 2.4). But for this gap it would be possible to drive from Alaska to Patagonia. A planned extension to the highway has been on the drawing boards for more than 60 years but nothing has been done because of environmental concerns and a lack of funds.

In 1971, when the United States signed agreements for the completion of the highway with Colombia and Panama, the Colombian section was expected to cost US$60 million. At that time, technical rather than environmental problems worried planners, especially the 20 km section across the River Atrato wetlands and the 1.3 km bridge over the river. The Inter-American Development Bank approved a loan in 1994 for outlining the terms of reference for an

Exhibit 2.3

Demographic indicators

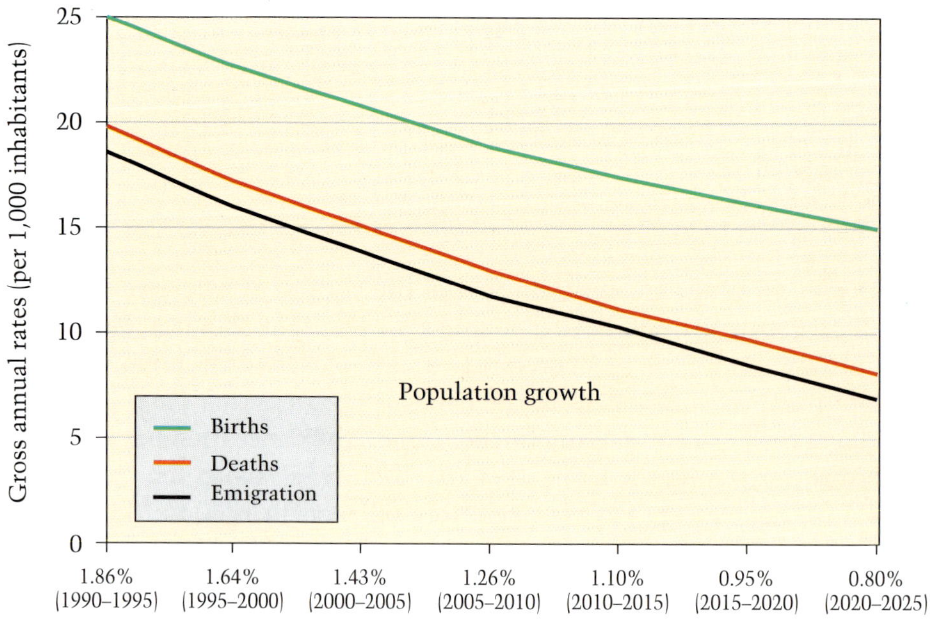

Source: INDESA.

environmental study. The estimated cost of completing the road is more than US$300 million.

Indians whose lands would be opened up by the road and environmental groups are opposed to the link. The isthmus is the key transition area for flora and fauna between North and South America. The Katios park on the Colombian side and the Darién National Park on the Panamanian side were created as buffer zones to protect Central and North American countries from hoof and mouth disease. The Panamanian government, fearing that it would bring more illegal immigrants and make drug trafficking easier, is less enthusiastic about the idea than Colombia. A thrice weekly Colombia–Panama ferry service between Colón and Cartagena began in 1994.

More pressing is the need for a decent road between Panama City and Colón, the two largest cites in Panama, and an agreement to build one was finally reached at the end of 1994 between the government and a Mexican company. The 80 km journey along the pot-hole strewn, largely single-lane road is the bane of drivers who commute daily. The road will be a toll concession and will have a big economic impact. Another major project for the near future is a bypass (known as the "Southern Corridor") around Panama City which will ease the capital's congested traffic.

The railroad, built in the 1850s between Panama City and Colón, and which ferried thousands of miners and speculators from the US east coast to California before there was a safe overland route within US territory, was closed to passenger traffic several years ago and now only moves cargo.

The Pan-American Highway: uniting the Americas

Exhibit 2.4 **Pan-American Highway**

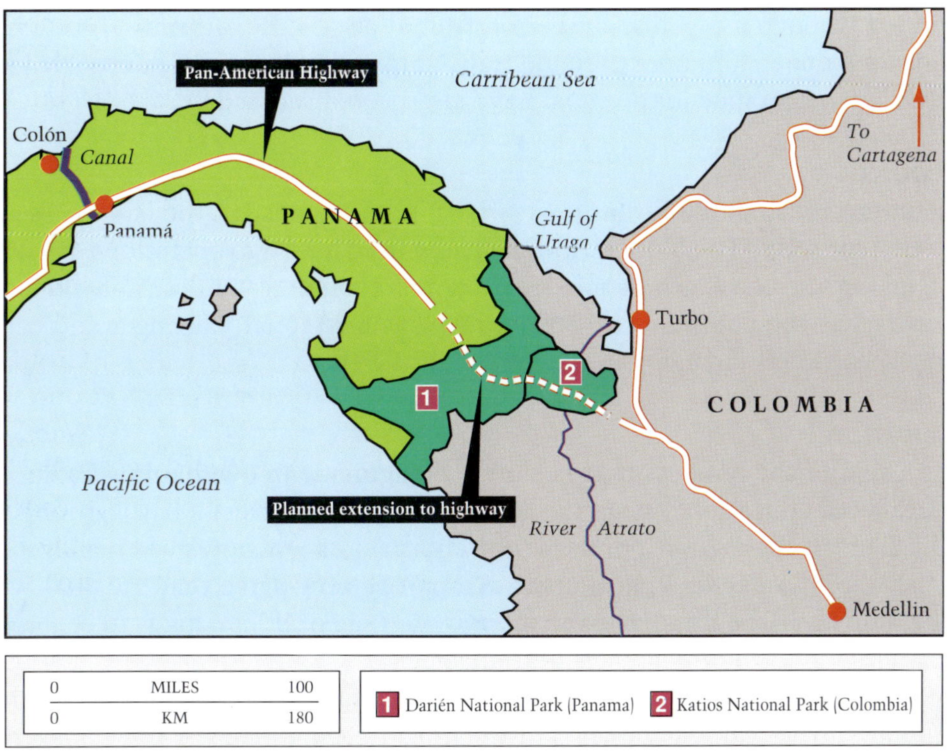

Ports

Panama has 13 ports and those of Balboa at the Pacific entrance to the canal and Cristobal at the Atlantic entrance are by far the most important for international shipping. The port of Cristobal, which is to be privatised, handles around two-thirds of Panama's container cargo and one-third of all cargo tonnage.

The great bulk of Cristobal's containerised cargo is destined to or originates from the Colón Free Zone. The National Port Authority has failed to exploit fully its geographically advantageous ports because of poor management, overemployment, high operating costs and inadequate maintenance. In the words of the World Bank[2] its services are "expensive, unreliable and inefficient". Freight rates to and from Panama are consistently higher than those to and from major US ports and about one-third higher than competing regional ports such as Jamaica. This resulted in some large container companies moving their hub operations away from Panama to geographically less advantageous locations in the Caribbean. As well as privatising Cristobal, the government is stimulating competition by promoting the building of ports by the private sector. The costs of the new port run by MOINSA at Coco Solo near Colón – which exports Lada cars to Latin America – are said to be half those of Cristobal. In January 1995 Taiwan's Evergreen Corporation announced a US$150 million investment to build a container port at Coco Solo. The Evergreen line called at Panama until the mid-1980s when it moved its operations to the Kingston, Jamaica, container port.

Construction of additional general cargo handling facilities at Petroterminal's Chiriquí Grande port on the Atlantic coast was due to begin in 1995. The new facilities will be for products other than Alaskan oil which has been pumped through a pipeline by Petroterminal across the isthmus since 1982. Plans for a major container port and trans-shipment centre on Telfer's Island at the Atlantic entrance to the canal have also been discussed.

Airports

Tocumen is the main international airport. It was opened in the late 1970s and has two runways. The older terminal is now used for cargo operations. Because of Panama's strategic geographic location and Tocumen's underutilisation, the country has the potential for development as a regional passenger and cargo hub, a position it did enjoy in the 1960s and 1970s.

Education

It is a sign of the progress that is slowly being made in overhauling Panama's deteriorated educational system that education is no longer a battleground for politicians trying to score points off one another and win votes when budgetary matters are discussed in parliament. All parties now agree that the quality of education has to be improved and more money spent if Panama is to become a more efficient economy and egalitarian society.

The first attempt at a comprehensive reform was in the mid-1970s, after General Torrijos came to power; but the programme, funded by the US Agency for International Development, came to grief on the rocks of the Roman

Catholic Church in alliance with conservative political forces trying to weaken the government. The reform, despite the backing of the US government, was viewed as "communist" and was abolished in 1979. Millions of dollars had been spent on new courses and textbooks – which were burned. In some areas Panama today is still using textbooks that have not been changed since the 1950s.

The annual budget for education accounts for around 20 per cent of public spending. Over 95 per cent of primary and secondary school students successfully complete their education, although only about 60 per cent finish their studies in the scheduled length of time. Average schooling is close to seven years, as against an average of 10 in the most developed countries. Of the total students enrolled in 1993, 10 per cent were in higher education. One of the most important changes underway concerns the training of teachers which has long been regarded as woefully inadequate. Between 1986 and 1991, according to the United Nations Human Development Report (UNHDR), Panama had 20 primary school students per teacher and 19 secondary students per teacher, ratios that compare well with average for the most developed nations. Panama's problem is one of quality. The quality of teachers – as in so many Latin American countries – is widely recognised as low. Only one in every four students at the Technological University passes all three levels. The previous system for training secondary school teachers, which was abolished for no good reason, has been restored. Training is now geared on how to teach subjects and not first learning the subjects and then taking a teaching course.

The main universities are the University of Panama, established in 1935 and the largest, and the Technological University, both state owned, and the private Roman Catholic Santa María La Antigua University. There are also half a dozen other private universities. Families who can afford it, send their children to universities in the United States.

R&D in universities is becoming much more practically oriented towards society's needs and in a major new development the University of Panama set up a foundation in 1995 to capture private sector funds and involve companies more in the field of education.

Panama needs more well-trained scientists and technicians. The country had eight of them per 1,000 inhabitants between 1986 and 1991, as against 23 in Singapore, the government's role model.

Social Security

Panama's social security system, established in 1943, was facing a critical situation because of an ageing population, high unemployment and insufficient contributions until several reforms became effective at the beginning of 1992 and modified the pension plan of the Caja de Seguro Social (CSS).

But, as a study points out,[3] "The modifications of both eligibility requirements and of pension benefits did not reach the levels recommended by international financial institutions, and still exceed the provisions existing in the majority of the countries of the region." The government admitted in its economic policy programme that, "There is a very serious problem in the CSS retirement programme whose financial viability is seriously threatened, while the majority of the population is unaware of this and expects retirement conditions to be improved."

In 1995 there were close to five social security contributors for every pensioner, compared with 12 in 1976 and 15 in 1970. The number of pensioners increased to 95,100 in 1993 from 11,425 in 1970 (see Exhibit 2.5).

The CSS provides pensions for insured retirees, disabled persons and for close surviving relatives upon the death of an insured participant. Comprehensive medical care, including hospitalisation and drugs, is provided to subscribing workers and their families and to the uninsured through the Ministry of Health facilities. In 1993 469,316 employed people were paying social security, nearly half the labour force of 941,107; and including covered dependants the CSS provided benefits for 1.4 million people (more than half the population). Despite quite high contribution rates – 7.25 per cent paid by employees and 10.75 per cent by employers – the system's funds are stretched.

The 1992 reforms were:

- The early retirement provision was eliminated as of January 1993.
- The retirement age for men was increased from 60 to 62 and for women from 55 to 57 as of January 1995.
- The benefit formula has been reduced from 60 per cent of the base salary plus 1.25 per cent after 10 years and 1.5 per cent after 20 years to 60 per cent plus 1.25 per cent after 15 years of service.
- The salary used to calculate the pension is the highest seven years of working life prior to retirement instead of the previous system of the best three years of the past 15.
- Continue the practice of not revaluing pensions for domestic inflation, except for minimum pensions which are adjusted every three years provided CSS's finances permit it.
- Shift 0.5 per cent of workers' contributions from the medical scheme to the pension scheme.
- Manage investment funds more profitably.
- No increase in contribution rates for employers.

In August 1992 the government suspended the transfer of one-third of the 13th month bonus of public and private sector employees (equivalent to 0.8 per cent of GDP) to the social security system, which was one of the reforms approved to stem the CSS's deficit. To compensate partially for the loss of revenue, the legislature approved applying the regular social security contribution rate (0.3 per cent of GDP) to this bonus and increasing by 2 percentage points the interest rate on bonds issued by the government to the CSS.

The reduction factors were applied to pensions from the date of the law's passage and did not include thousands of anticipated pensions in process which were applied for before that date, and which were computed on the more generous actuarial bases.

Demographic projections indicate that the relation between retirees and workers will remain at 22 per cent until 2001, given the decrease in the requests for new pensions (after the rush for pensions before the reforms came into force, the elimination of early pensions in 1993 and the increase in the retirement age from 57 to 62 years). The ratio will begin to increase again as of 2001.

Exhibit 2.5

Social security protection 1989–93 (thousands and %)

	1989	*1990*	*1991*	*1992*	*1993*
Total pop.	2,349	2,397	2,442	2,488	2,535
Labour force	888	820	856	920	941
Pop. protected[1]	1,052	1,218	1,264	1,327	1,422
As % of total pop. protected	44.8	50.8	51.8	53.3	56.1
Contributors	451	480	504	531	548
As % of the pop. protected	42.9	39.5	39.9	40.0	38.5
Jobholders[2]	372	398	417	439	469
As % of the labour force	42.0	48.6	48.8	47.7	48.1
Pensioners	78	82	87	91	95
Dependents[3]	601	737	759	796	873

[1]Contributors (current and pensioners) and their dependents.
[2]Contributors working.
[3]Dependents of contributors.
Figures are rounded up.
Source: Caja de Seguro Social.

The most critical part of the pensions system is the Complementary Fund established in 1965 for public sector employees. In 1993 155,996 people were contributing to this scheme which gives them a higher pension in return for greater contributions (eligible employees contribute an extra 2 per cent of their wages and the government puts in 0.3 per cent). But design faults, insufficient contributions and benefits that are too generous make it unsustainable in the long term. This is a political hot potato that has been passed from government to government. The problem is particularly sensitive because the distinction between covered and non-covered public sector employees creates a social inequality.

The scheme was established without making a sufficient initial capital contribution in order to amortise the initial liabilities of the programme. In the absence of this initial capital, financing rates were insufficient to cover actuarial costs, creating an increasing deficit as of 1981, which adversely affects public sector finances. Projections show that by not modifying the legal statutes which govern the Complementary Fund, actuarial costs will increase substantially in the future. According to a study,[4] the deficit will rise to US$63 million in the year 2000 and US$136 million in 2010 from US$32 million in 1992.

The elevated level of income substitution, the tax exemption of pensions and the feasibility of continuing to work after retirement provides in many cases a post-retirement income (under the special laws) which is greater than that earned when the individual was working. This in turn is an incentive to retire, which distorts and cuts short the careers of qualified personnel in the public sector, creates a negative redistribution of income, and adversely affects the job market.

Similar benefit levels are not offered in the private sector.

Despite the weakness of the social security system, the government does not plan to replace it with a Chile-style pension scheme. A law was approved in 1993 allowing private pension funds in addition to the state scheme but regulations had still not been drawn up by mid-1995. The government believes that the combination of cuts on the spending side and a more profitable investment policy (for example, the CSS is now allowed to allocate a certain amount each year for mortgages and not keep so much in low yield government paper) will guarantee the system's survival.

Family code

Substantial changes were made at the end of 1994 to Panama's outdated laws on marriage, divorce, adoption and protection for minors. They were the first changes since 1917 and brought Panama more into line with the situation in developed countries and the more socially progressive ones in Latin America.

Couples who have lived together for five years, for example, have the same rights if they split up as those married in the church or in a civil ceremony. There are equal rights to all goods acquired within the marriage irrespective of whose name they are in, and the right to keep the family home is for the wife and children. Another important change is that the adopted children of parents who die have to be looked after by other members of the family and cannot be returned to an orphanage.

Labour market

The rigid Panamanian labour code, introduced by General Torrijos in 1972 and long a sticking point with the IMF and the World Bank, was reformed in 1995 amidst intense opposition from unions. Over-regulation of hiring and firing practices seriously impaired job creation and mobility. Because the US dollar is Panama's legal tender (it is the only country in Latin America not to have its own currency) the government cannot devalue to increase competitiveness. In a region where free-market reforms are increasingly taking hold and giving foreign investors a much wider choice of countries, Panama's lack of flexibility has been a serious obstacle to making the economy more competitive. The urban employment rate more than doubled between 1979 and 1989 to 20.4 per cent (see Exhibit 2.6), largely because of the severe recession of 1987–89 but also because of labour laws that employers view as biased in favour of workers and that discouraged job creation. Including under-employment, close to half the labour force still does not have regular work.

The economy's capacity to create new jobs has significantly declined in the past 20 years and the public sector has become bloated by absorbing much of the new employment. The economy was recovering from the recession but growth between 1990 and 1994 was almost entirely due to fuller use of existing capacity rather than a function of increased investment. A study of Panama's labour situation[1] points out that

> since many companies shed jobs during the economic crisis, the increase in output was achieved by using labour more intensively. Clearly, a further sustained improvement in output and employment will depend heavily on increases in investment.

Exhibit 2.6

Urban unemployment (average annual growth rates)

1986	12.7
1987	14.1
1988	21.1
1989	20.4
1990	20.0
1991	16.1
1992	14.2
1993	12.5
1994	12.0

Note: 1991–94 national level and before that the metropolitan region.
Source: CEPAL.

New investment, and hence the ability to provide jobs to a growing labour force, can only be attracted by more flexible labour market regulations.

Some companies already in Panama have learned to live with the labour code and to jockey, with the help of smart lawyers, in which Panama abounds, within the administrative processes to protect their interests. Indeed, some lawyers are privately against the labour reforms because it will deprive them of lucrative business. But new companies, in particular, interested in establishing themselves in Panama have been scared away by the labour code.

The proposed reforms, vehemently opposed by the unions, included:

- the introduction of the concept of functional and geographic mobility;
- in exceptional circumstances, which a company's viability is threatened, employers can reduce wages (restoring the levels when business picks up);
- economic reasons for job cuts have been amplified and dismissal costs in these cases and for unjustified dismissals are limited to a maximum of three months' pay;
- the administrative processes are more agile and resolving labour law issues has been taken out of the hands of the Labour Ministry and placed in the courts in order to eliminate the incidence of political factors;
- greater flexibility in collective bargaining;
- short-term jobs for specific tasks without incurring excessive termination costs; and companies have to set up independently managed unemployment funds to cover contingencies. Payments to the fund are tax deductible and profits earned are tax free.

The minimum wage was US$211 a month in 1995, which is relatively high by the region's standards. It does not apply to people working for US government agencies, inside and outside the Canal Area. The lowest-paid workers in US government agencies receive around US$700 a month, while a Panamanian policeman earns not much more than US$300 a month. Such differences, which will most probably continue after the canal reverts in its entirety to Panama at the end of 1999, although US wage laws cease to reign in the Canal Area after this time, have created wage distortions (see Exhibit 2.7).

Non-wage costs are quite high. Social security tax is 18 per cent (10.75 per cent is paid by the firm) and the number of non-working days (holidays and days off) in a year is higher than in other countries in the region: 85 for Panama in 1994, compared with 63 in Mexico, 67 in Honduras, 77 in Costa Rica and 71 in Chile. In a move to increase the number of working days per year a national holiday was abolished in 1995, and taking Monday as a holiday when an official holidays falls on a Sunday was ended.

Overleaf: Panama is the only country in the Americas that has five national parks less than two hours' drive from its capital city

Exhibit 2.7

Average monthly nominal salary by sectors (US$)

	Total	*Private*	*Public*	*Canal Area*
1991	485.9	388.3	458.1	1,741.3
1992	488.6	400.4	464.3	1,838.5
1993	510.5	416.9	488.3	1,912.7

Source: Comptroller General's Office.

The political scene

The US invasion of 20 December 1989 marked a brutal break with the regime established in 1968 by General Omar Torrijos and which gradually fell apart after his death in 1981 (see Chapter 1) under General Manuel Noriega.

One of the first acts of President Guillermo Endara, sworn into office on a US military base, was to abolish the Defence Forces, which encompassed both the army and the police, and replace them with a new Public Force (largely the same people as only the high command was purged) under the supreme command of the president. The largest element of the Public Force – which introduced a new beige uniform with no camouflage, fatigues or any other trappings of militarism – is the 11,000 strong US-trained National Police.

There was an attempted coup against Endara in 1990; in 1992 a referendum called by the government to forbid Panama constitutionally from having an army was defeated. In January 1995 the government claimed to have uncovered a plot to assassinate President Pérez Balladares. About 50 people were arrested, including a number of junior and non-commissioned national police officers.

Panamanians have shown themselves to be remarkably resilient, overcoming the trauma of the invasion and building a multi-party democracy. It should be remembered, however, that the country has never enjoyed democracy in the generally accepted sense of the word; between 1903 and 1968 Panama was ruled by a series of governments (factions of the Liberal Party) representing the interests of the oligarchy, none of which undertook social reforms and were little more than private clubs.

The ADOC alliance, headed by Guillermo Endara, won the May 1989 elections on the back of a massive protest vote. Their victory, however, was denied when Noriega annulled the results of the election. Following the departure of Noriega in December 1989 the original result was reinstated and Endara was duly inagurated. The ADOC alliance, a coalition of small conservative parties, the best-organised of which were the Christian Democrats, in many ways represented a return to the pre-1968 political *status-quo*. Endara laid the foundations of a liberal democracy, got the economy back on its feet and presided over the country's cleanest ever elections, but its support quickly evaporated and it was swept out of office in the May 1994 elections. The right was taken aback by the size of its loss. The number of seats in parliament held by the Christian Democrats dropped to one from 28 and this party looks as if it might disappear. The largest number won by the eight parties opposing the Democratic Revolutionary Party (PRD), a social democratic party founded by Torrijos in 1979, was 15 by Endara's Arnulfista party. The PRD rose from the ashes to win 31 of the 72 seats in the Legislative Assembly (see Exhibit 2.8) and its secretary general, Ernesto Pérez Balladares, became president with one-third of the vote. The eight conservative parties were heavily punished for failing to unite behind a common presidential candidate and their only chance of success in the future is to form a single party.

For a country of its size, Panama has far too many political parties and this makes the political scene extremely fragmented, particularly on the right. Reading the programmes of the eight parties at the conservative end of the polit-

Exhibit 2.8

Distribution of seats in the Legislative Assembly

Pro-government		*Anti-government*		*Independent*	
PRD	31	Renovación Civilista	3	Papa Egoro	6
Solidaridad	3	Anulfista	15		
Partido Laborista	1	Molirena	5		
Liberal Republicano	3	Democrata Cristiano	1		
		Morena	1		
		Liberal Autentico	3		
Total	38		28		6

Source: Tribunal Electoral.

ical spectrum it is difficult to perceive what are their basic ideological differences. Such a large number can only be put down to personal rivalries – the cult of *personalismo* which plagues the politics of so many Latin American countries. The odd-ball party is Papa Egoro – "mother earth" in the Emberá language – headed by the singer and composer Rubén Blades which won 17 per cent of the presidential vote. Papa Egoro attracted disenchanted leftist votes from the PRD as well as people who wanted to break the mould of Panamanian politics.

Conscious of the narrow margin of his victory as president, Pérez Balladares has moved politics more into the centre ground since taking office. The PRD's comeback is partly due to the party's moderated traditional left-of-centre stance with regard to economic policy, which won it business support. The PRD is also the only one of the 13 parties with a solid working class base and the support of the trade unions which Torrijos nurtured in the 1970s and Noriega in the 1980s. To this extent, the PRD's relatively broad support makes it still resemble the Mexican Institutional Revolutionary Party (PRI), the world's longest-ruling party (66 years in power in 1995), on which the PRD was modelled when it was founded. But just as the PRI's days looked numbered, so the PRD will have to continue to reform itself.

Pérez Balladares made a promising start by greatly reducing the number of government jobs for PRD stalwarts (almost an automatic perk in the past) and appointing people on their merits. As part of his policy of "national reconciliation", about one-third of cabinet posts are filled by non-PRD figures and 217 people closely identified with the Noriega regime were pardoned in September 1994. Many people have changed their political colours with remarkable ease: José Blandon, for example, was a close adviser of Noriega for many years who turned against his master, later becoming an adviser to Ana Mae, the wife of Guillermo Endara, who stood as a candidate for mayor of Panama City in May 1994, and in the Pérez Balladares government he is an adviser on Asian affairs.

Pérez Balladares has also moved to stamp out corruption in the party. A PRD deputy was gaoled at the end of 1994 after he was caught in a bribery scam. After the monstrous level of corruption during the Noriega regime, and with some of its stalwarts back in government, Pérez Balladares knows that this issue could be the PRD's Achilles heel. The right-wing parties, desperate for issues on which to attack the government – whose conservative economic policies have robbed it of ammunition – will seize on any scandal they can. As their detractors point out, such moral scruples did not stop members of the Endara government in their last year of power dipping their hands into the till and earning the nickname of "Ali Baba and the 40 thieves". If the PRD is capable of holding the centre ground, rooting out corruption and narrowing the chasm between rich and poor many political analysts believe it could be in power for a long time. The main resistance to the government is likely to come from its own PRD members as the economic policies run counter to the interests of the labour movement, which historically has constituted the party's backbone. Parallels have been drawn between President Pérez Balladares and President Carlos Menem of Argentina, and it is possible that like him, Pérez Balladares will hold a referendum to allow him to run for a second presidential term in 1999.

The large number of decentralised government entities and semi-autonomous institutions gives the president enormous power of patronage. Decentralised entities which fall under the responsibility of a ministry and follow the government's policies include: the Banco Nacional de Panamá (the largest Panamanian bank and the maximum monetary authority in the absence of a central bank), the Caja de Ahorros (a savings bank), CSS (the Social Security Agency), the National Lottery, the Colón Free Zone; IRHE (the Hydroelectric and Electric Energy Resources Institute); INTEL (the National Telecommunications Institute); and the Universidad Nacional. Semi-autonomous institutions include IPAT, the tourist bureau; the National Port Authority; the National Culture Institute, and several agricultural institutes.

"Non-political" forces

The media

Panamanians may not be avid newspaper readers – seven in every 100 people bought them in 1992 – but they have a wide choice, and all but one – *La Estrella*, owned by the family of Vice-President Tomás Altamirano Duque – is anti-government, although it too has taken a fairly neutral stance. The military regime owned three newspapers, none of which survives today. The most outspoken and generally regarded as the most objective newspaper is *La Prensa*, founded in 1980 by Roberto Eisenmann, one of Panama's most powerful businessmen. The paper was closed for several months in 1982 by General Paredes and by General Noriega in 1989. The daily was a rallying point for the opposition and played an important role in Noriega's overthrow. Other newspapers include *El Siglo*, *Crítica Libre* and *Panamá América*, the oldest. There are also six TV channels: Canal 13 and Canal 4 have national coverage; Canal 8 is administered by the US Southern Command; Canal 5 is an educational channel and belongs to the Roman Catholic Church; Canal 11 is run by the University of Panama and the Education Ministry; and Canal 2 is run by a group of businessmen. Many middle-class Panamanians have satellite TV and access US stations.

The port of Colón, home of the largest free trade zone in the Americas and the largest in the world after Hong Kong

Trade unions

It is estimated that less than 10 per cent of the labour force is unionised. The largest and oldest confederation is the Panamanian Workers Federation (CRTP) whose main members are Local 907 (Panamanian workers in US Army installations); the Federation of Workers of the Central Provinces (mainly sugar workers); the Industrial Federation of Food, Beverage and Hotel Workers (FITAHBA); the National Union of Bank Employees (SINABAN); and SITRACHILCO (banana workers of the Chiriquí Land Company). Almost all CRTP members work in private sector companies. The CRTP is allied to the Democratic Revolutionary Party and funding by the US AIFLD was cut off shortly before the US invasion because the CRTP refused to support Washington's policy against Noriega. Aniano Pinzón, the CRTP secretary general, stood as a candidate for the PRD in the 1994 elections but was not elected.

Other labour organisations include the National Central of Panamanian Workers (CNTP), which groups together workers in the textile, food and construction sectors as well as many working in Colón; the Authentic Workers Central, the most Marxist orientated; and the General Central of Panamanian Workers (CGTP), which was founded in 1990 and is linked to the Christian Democrats. CGTP leaders backed the Democratic Alliance of Civic Opposition against Noriega. Most Panamanian workers in the Panama Canal Area belong to US unions affiliated to the AFL-CIO.

The manufacturing sector led the union movement in the 1960s and 1970s, but increased unemployment, the decline in this sector's relative share of the economy and the growing trend of agreements at company level, instead of collective bargaining, offering job security in return for wage restraint, has weakened its position.

Business organisations

The private sector has a powerful lobby through the Panamanian Association of Company Executives (APEDE), the National Council of Private Companies (CONEP), the Chamber of Commerce, the Chamber of Construction (CAPAC), the National Union of Small and Medium-Size Companies (UNPYME), the American Chamber of Commerce and Industry (AMCHAM), the Banking Association (ABP) and the Colón Free Zone Users' Association.

US–Panama relations

Panamanians have had a love–hate relationship with the United States since the middle of the 19th century when the transisthmian railroad was built and later the canal (see Chapter 1). US intervention in Panama began with its domination of the means of transport. No other country in Latin America has been treated so much as if it was an appendage of the United States, suffering numerous interventions, culminating with the 1989 invasion, and interference in its domestic politics. "Not a single leaf falls in Panama without the US Embassy knowing about it", said a European ambassador.

US influence is pervasive: the dollar is Panama's currency, US television, radio and magazines are all available and upper class Panamanians frequently travel to the United States to go on holiday, study and do business. Roberto Eisenmann, the owner of *La Prensa*, defined the relationship well,[6] "The love part of our relationship has to do with the advantages our unique association brings: the canal, our trade situation, and so on. The hate part is like what a teenager feels about his overprotective father: he knows he should love him, but he wishes that his father would just leave him alone for a while."

Panama will come of age and stand on its own feet on 31 December 1999 when the canal and all property and surrounding land that has not already been returned to Panama under the Torrijos-Carter Treaty that went into effect on 1 October 1979 are handed over. All US troops attached to the US Southern Command must also depart. The withdrawal of troops will mean a large loss of income (US military operations constitute more than 5 per cent of GDP) and jobs, but full control of the canal and the area by it give Panama increased revenue possibilities, as well as major new responsibilities (see Chapter 10).

The number of Americans born in the former Canal Zone who work for the Panama Canal Commission – known as "Zonians" – has dwindled to several hundred from more than 4,000 at its peak. The Canal Zone, as it was called until 1979, had its own US governor and police force. Although part of Panama, the strip of land slicing the country in two administratively belonged to the United States. It was a separate and privileged world of neat homes and manicured lawns that was in stark contrast to the slums of El Chorillo only a few metres away on the other side of the fence. The Zonians had their own schools, shops and hospitals in a bastion of colonialism. It was not uncommon for second and even third-generation Zonians to speak no Spanish; after all they had little need to leave their cosy world and deal with the rough and tumble of Panama the other side of the fence. To do so meant risking the loss of their identity. The remnants of this class feel much the same about the collapse of their world as the British who were in India or whites in South Africa.

Buildings, houses and land in the Canal Area have gradually been returned to the government of Panama since 1979. The 193rd Infantry Brigade pulled out in 1994. Because of Panama's lack of funds, some of the buildings abandoned and not immediately used, for example at Coco Solo near Colón, have fallen into a considerable state of disrepair. The US forces, which were reduced to fewer than 6,000 by the end of 1995 from 10,000 in 1993, have a significant impact on an economy the size of Panama's (GDP of US$6.9 billion in 1994). Besides the approximate US$110 million in salaries and benefits paid by the US military to its 5,000 Panamanian workforce, the military organisations make direct purchases of goods and services from the Panamanian economy. Individual service members and their families also purchase goods and services locally. The military also generate economic activity for countless taxi drivers, restaurant, hotel and other service industry employees. The total impact of the military presence has been estimated at over US$225 million per year. The gross income flow to Panama from the Panama Canal Commission and the US military and civilian employees stationed in the country is around US$700 million per year. Panamanians working for the Panama Canal Commission and the US Department of Defense in the Canal Area are a privileged group as they are paid US wages. There is growing uncertainty among Panamanian employees of US government agencies over their fate after the year 2000 and among Panamanians in general about the impact of the US withdrawal and the government's ability to assume the new responsibilities.

After the invasion, which caused an estimated US$1 billion of damage, US troops, under Operation Promote Liberty, went out into the countryside to win hearts and minds, upgrading roads; repairing bridges; refurbishing schools and health clinics; drilling water wells and constructing or repairing sewage and water supply systems.

Although nationalistic sentiment can run high, opinion polls consistently show from 60 per cent to 70 per cent in favour of the bases staying in Panama, but the US Department of Defence is adamant that it will fulfil the terms of the canal treaties. Washington is also keen to pull out for budgetary reasons. The US Southern Command at Quarry Heights, which is responsible for all US military activities in the Southern Theatre (Central America below Mexico and South America), will be relocated in Miami. The School of the Americas, the US military's controversial training centre for Latin American armies for decades, was closed in Panama in 1984 and transferred to Fort Benning, Georgia in the United States. The school was the centre of a US hemispheric military strategy aimed at fighting communism.

With rapid deployment forces and much more sophisticated technology for war, some of which was tried out during the invasion of Panama, the United States no longer needs a large and permanent presence in Latin America. It would not be surprising, however, if the US and Panamanian governments reached an agreement to keep a small force in Panama. This would assuage any fears Washington may have about security in Panama post the year 2000 and have a high psychological value for foreign investors who may be anxious about the future. In May 1995, a draft resolution was circulating in the US Senate, urging the US president to renegotiate a post-2000 bases agreement. The Panamanian government has said it would look favourably at any such request. Washington is hoping that Panama will ask first, but Panama is waiting to be asked as this would strengthen its bargaining position.

Notes and references

1. World Bank document, 30 January 1992, p. 88.
2. Ibid., p. 15.
3. Hernando Perez Montas, *Panama's Social Security: impact of the new legislation on the actuarial projections of the disability, death and old age retirement programme* (Devtech, July 1992), p. 1.
4. Hernando Perez Montas, *Study and actuarial projections of the complementary fund and special retirement laws of Panama's public sector* (Devtech, December 1992), p. 2.
5. Peter Gregory and Alberto Davila, *An evaluation of the Panamanian labour code* (Devtech, April 1993), p. 1.
6. Quoted in Alma Guillermoprieto's *The heart that bleeds* (Knopf, 1994), p. 232.

Chapter Three

The economy

In 1995 Panama embarked on the most important change of direction in the predominantly service-based economy (see Exhibit 3.1) in more than 45 years. Reform of tax incentives and exemptions, labour market reforms (see Chapter 2), privatisation (see Chapter 8) and membership of the World Trade Organisation (formerly known as GATT) – *a sine qua non* for Panama's aspiration to join the North American Free Trade Agreement (NAFTA) – represent a complete break with the interventionist policies that have kept Panama isolated from the free-market changes sweeping through Latin America. It remains to be seen, however, whether these orthodox policies will improve Panama's skewed income distribution. At the same time, a Brady-style foreign debt agreement enables the country to resume payments on its commercial bank debt for the first time since 1988 and normalise its relations with external private creditors.

Singapore is to some extent the Panama government's role model, and there are quite a few similarities, as well as many differences, between the two countries which make this aspiration more than wishful thinking. Singapore's population of 2.8 million is not much more than Panama's, the racial mix is also very varied (in Singapore's case there are Chinese, Malays, Indians and Eurasians) and, like Panama, the tiny City state is an important junction for world trade. Singapore, too, has a large banking centre.

The economy grew at an exceptionally strong average yearly rate of 7.6 per cent between 1990 and 1993 (see Exhibit 3.2), but this was from a very depressed base, following the profound recession of 1988 and 1989, and was largely due to a boom in residential and commercial construction, stimulated by repatriation of capital and to the dynamism of the Colón Free Zone, helped by the recovery of Latin American economies. Growth dropped to 4.7 per cent in 1994 and in 1995 slowed down to 2–3 per cent. GDP surpassed the 1987 historical peak in 1992 but only in 1994 did real per capita GDP overtake the all-time high reached in 1982 of US$933 in 1970 dollars (see Exhibit 3.3). Most of the growth outside the construction sector (which reached the peak of its expansive cycle in 1992) and the Colón Free Zone has come from fuller use of existing installed capacity and not from new investment. Panama began a new economic cycle in 1995 when expansion will depend much more on investment. This, in turn, hinges to a large extent on the success of the reforms.

Exhibit 3.1

GDP by sectors (in millions of 1970 US$ and %)

	GDP (US$m)		Contributions to GDP (%)	
	*1994**	*1993*	*1994**	*1993*
Agriculture	246.0	236.8	10.1	10.2
Manufacturing	227.7	217.8	9.3	9.3
Utilities	80.2	75.8	3.3	3.3
Commerce, restaurants and hotels	284.4	275.0	11.6	11.8
Transportation, storage and communications	630.0	593.3	25.8	25.4
Colón Free Zone	225.7	204.1	9.2	8.8
Oil pipeline	17.8	19.5	0.7	0.8
Panama Canal	205.3	196.8	8.4	8.4
Finance and real estate	368.5	347.7	15.1	14.9
Government services	250.9	254.0	10.3	10.9
Other components	535.4	504.8	21.9	21.6
Total	2,441.9	2,332.3	100.0	100.0

*Provisional figures.
Source: Comptroller General's Office.

Exhibit 3.2

Sectoral performance of GDP (% change in real terms)

	1991	*1992*	*1993*	*1994*
GDP	9.6	8.5	5.4	4.7
Agriculture and fishing	5.0	6.7	0.6	3.9
Mining	50.0	40.0	19.0	12.0
Manufacturing	8.7	8.1	7.0	4.5
Construction	117.0	55.4	31.5	6.5
Commerce	10.8	8.1	5.4	3.4
Financial services	7.4	7.8	7.6	6.0
Transport and communications	13.7	7.9	2.7	6.2
Colón Free Trade Zone	35.9	27.3	14.5	10.6
Oil pipeline	–6.2	–29.3	–46.7	–8.7
Canal Commission	6.0	0.8	–4.1	4.3

Source: Comptroller General's Office.

Exhibit 3.3

Real GDP per capita 1982–94 (in 1970 US dollars)

	GDP ($bn)	*Per capita GDP ($)*
1982	1.90	933
1983	1.91	919
1984	1.91	895
1985	2.00	914
1986	2.06	928
1987	2.11	931
1988	1.78	769
1989	1.77	751
1990	1.86	770
1991	2.03	835
1992	2.20	889
1993	2.33	920
1994	2.44	945

Source: Comptroller General's Office.

The 1989–94 Endara government that took power after the US invasion got the economy moving again but did little in the way of the much-needed structural reform which was left to the Pérez Balladares administration. The greatest efforts were directed towards advancing the trade liberalisation programme and the organisation of an autonomous government entity known as the Inter-Oceanic Region Authority (ARI) (see Chapter 10), whose task it is to develop the assets in the Panama Canal Area already returned to the government and those to be handed over by the year 2000. It also launched the privatisation process with the auction sale of Cítricos de Chiriquí for US$5.6 million, the first transaction completed by ProPrivat created in late 1992. Through partial privatisation of telecommunications, electricity, water and ports the government hopes to make Panama's prices in these areas – among the highest in the region – more internationally competitive.

The government's task is a difficult one. The 1980s were very much a lost decade for the Panamanian economy and not much progress was made in the first half of the 1990s. Aware that time is not on its side, the Pérez Balladares government did not delay and presented most of its major legislation in the first half of 1995.

One of the obstacles to making the economy more efficient is the privileged position of significant parts of the private sector which has developed behind high tariffs (Panama's trade protection was the highest in Latin America) and generous tax exemptions and incentives since the 1950s that have been abused. For example, companies in the Cólon Free Zone paid a maximum corporate income tax rate of 8.5 per cent on income derived from exports and re-exports, while firms in the rest of the country paid a top rate of 34 per cent. In 1995 a uniform rate of 30 per cent was established (the Free Zone companies pay 15 per cent on exports and re-exports and 30 per cent on domestic transactions). The incentive system which sprang up in an *ad hoc* fashion over the years violated all sound fiscal criteria. It encouraged industrial and agricultural activities in which Panama does not have a comparative advantage, deprived the Treasury every year of a large volume of tax receipts, stimulated tax evasion and was inequitable. "The result has been the production of high-priced goods and services and reduced ability to provide employment to a growing labour force", the World Bank said in a report on Panama.[1] Examples abound of the Panamanian economy paying high prices for staple foods (see below) and other goods, such as cement, fertilisers and the ex-refinery price of petroleum products.

The incentives were so attractive that many companies' investment decisions were made more for reasons of tax savings than for productivity. Manufacturing companies, for example, were able to deduct from their tax base all investments and generously depreciate fixed assets. Added to this, they paid only a 3 per cent duty on imports of capital goods. The "cost" of these exemptions (income tax reductions and lower import tariffs) for more than 25 activities ranging from construction to tourism, reforestation, and even cars bought by members of the Legislative Assembly (zero tariff on imported cars), was US$213.3 million in 1992 (3.7 per cent of GDP), according to the Planning Ministry.

The tax exemptions policy has been a bad business for the state: the incentives, for example, granted every year under Law 3 of 1986 represented 40 per cent of the investment of manufacturing companies whose share of GDP (10 per cent) is declining. Less than one-third of total tax revenue comes from direct taxes, a very low figure by international standards, and tax receipts still only represented 13 per cent of GDP in 1993, though this was a significant improvement over 8.8 per cent in 1989. The policy of tax exemptions and high

There has been a boom in residential and commercial construction in recent years stimulated by repatriation of capital and the dynamism of the Colón Free Zone

tariffs resulted in the production of high-priced goods and services and reduced ability to create jobs for a labour force growing at 3.8 per cent a year in the 1990s.

Panama needs a higher level of investment than most other Latin American countries to create jobs. The Planning Ministry estimates that US$3 billion of investment (almost half of GDP) is needed to create 100,000 jobs (a little over one-tenth of the labour force).

The Law on the Universalisation of Tax Incentives, a central plank in the government's economic programme, replaced tax exemptions with tax credits for specific productive activities deemed to be beneficial to the economy as a whole, extends some incentives and eliminates others. The result should be a substantial increase in direct tax revenue.

The biggest evaders of income tax are companies in the Cólon Free Zone, which generates around 9 per cent of GDP. Some firms are also suspected of money-laundering activities. A favourite technique is to over-invoice goods. The government had hoped to levy a 1.5 per cent tax in the middle of 1995 on the CIF value of goods which enter the Zone, but firms kicked up such a fuss – claiming the move would ruin businesses – that it backed down and settled for a much less ambitious and more complicated tax formula (see Chapter 9), which will collect substantially less than the originally envisaged revenue. The 1.5 per cent tax would have fulfilled two purposes: to generate more tax revenue and to discourage money laundering.

Dollar-based economy

The US dollar has been Panama's currency since 1904, although it is called the balboa for nationalistic reasons. Consequently, fiscal policy is the government's principal macroeconomic policy instrument. Because Panama does not have a central bank to print its own currency, government spending and investment are strictly bound by tax and non-tax revenues and the government's ability to borrow. Creditworthiness is linked directly to public finances. In 1994, the non-financial public sector deficit on an accrual basis (i.e. interest payments due but unpaid) was 1.1 per cent of GDP. In 1995, a similar outcome was expected, with a central government deficit of about 5 per cent of GDP, financed by surpluses in decentralised entities such as INTEL, the telecommunications company, and IRHE, the electricity company, as well as loans from IFIS. Budgetary control has been greatly aided by the gradual computerisation of public sector accounts (a US AID-financed scheme which Panama has pioneered in Latin America). This enables the Comptroller General's Office to know the exact state of public finances every day.

The disadvantage of not having an independent monetary or exchange-rate policy is not a serious problem for an economy the size of Panama; the advantages of the dollar more than outweigh the inconveniences. This point was driven home in early 1995 when Panama was basically not affected by the meltdown in the Mexican currency which sent tremors through most Latin American countries. The country's inflation is broadly in line with that of the United States (see Exhibit 3.4) and there is complete freedom of capital movements. The inability to devalue, however, has meant that the inflexibility of prices for goods and services that was created through interventionist policies in the past reduced economic efficiency, decreased Panama's international competitiveness and restrained growth potential. This is one of the reasons why economic and labour market liberalisation is important for Panama. In the words of the World Bank,[2] "Decreased production costs, which are passed on to consumers in reduced user charges, imply a real devaluation and thus increased international competitiveness."

Panamanian economists point out that the mere mention by a government of the introduction of a national currency would produce a massive run on deposits in the banking system.

Exhibit 3.4

Consumer prices, 1989–94 (year-end % change)

1989	0.1
1990	0.9
1991	1.1
1992	1.8
1993	0.5
1994	1.3

Source: Comptroller General's Office.

Agriculture

Panamanian peasants were the "favourite sons of the revolution" according to a much publicised government slogan during the 1968–81 Torrijos era. There was an agrarian reform programme in the 1970s which benefited landless peasants – much of the expropriated land belonged to multinational companies such as United Brands and the Coconut Boston Company – and infrastructure was improved. Over 16 per cent of Panama's farm land changed hands between 1969 and 1973 and more than 200 *asentamientos* (settlements) were established. They were a showpiece of General Torrijos, himself a country boy from the poor province of Veraguas, who liked to be photographed at the *asentamiento* he nurtured at Coclesito, where he had a house; but the subsidies were costly, mechanisation saddled peasants with debts and production was low.

While the *asentamientos* may have been socially desirable, the programme sapped the previously buoyant private agricultural sector. Prior to 1970 growth in the agricultural sector was export-led. The amount of time put into them by the government was out of all proportion to their role in the economy. It was estimated that officials spent three-quarters of their time on the *asiementos* but since they had neither the expertise nor the necessary technology their efforts were not rewarded with higher output. Peasants also tended to spend more time on land which was their own rather than on the co-operatives. Instead of encouraging production by settling the problem of land ownership, a volatile issue in Latin America, the government left it alone. General Torrijos probably found it easier to maintain political control by not granting land titles, as by that way the authorities had more leverage over peasants. The 1990 census revealed that 53 per cent of the land is occupied without titles by 63 per cent of farms. Close to half the 280,000 farming units had less than one hectare and three-quarters less than five. Just over 70 per cent of farmers occupy 4 per cent of plots of less than five hectares, and 2.4 per cent have 51 per cent of the plots of more than 100 hectares.

The import-substitution strategy which followed made Panama self-sufficient in rice, poultry, potatoes, onions and tomatoes but at a considerable financial cost, and real per capita agricultural output has gradually declined by 18 per cent between 1980 and 1992, according to the Food and Agricultural Organisation. In all cases except sorghum, yields in Panama are lower than the international average, and in all cases except potatoes less than the South American average. As the World Bank pointed out,[3] "These results reflect the poor quality of most of Panama's soils as well as inappropriate policies which have concentrated in areas which do not coincide with the country's comparative advantage."

Panamanian prices for many basic products, such as beans (see Exhibit 3.5), are higher than in many other Latin American countries and often well above international prices. The purchasing power of Panama's minimum salary is half that of its neighbour Costa Rica. The Planning Ministry believes the price of the basket of basic foods is around 40 per cent higher than it would be without the distortions. The most scandalous situation is that of the rich rice-producing companies whose prices for the main staple in the Panamanian diet are generally higher than international ones and who still benefit from tax exemptions because they are regarded as "poor" farmers. Membership of the World Trade Organisation will generate downward pressure on prices. Not surprisingly, resistance to Panama's entry into the World Trade Organisation came from such sectors.

Agriculture's share of the economy (excluding cattle and fisheries) has been declining over the years and by 1993 was down to 5.7 per cent from 7 per cent in 1987. About one-quarter of the labour force is employed in the agriculture sector (41 per cent in 1970 in the fullest sense of the word) and produces 10 per cent of GDP. While tax exemptions for the agricultural sector, price controls and high tariffs have depressed food production and resulted in Pana-

Exhibit 3.5

Price comparison between some basic products (prices in US$ per pound or litre)

	Costa Rica	*Mexico*	*Panama*
Black beans	0.35	0.53	0.64
White sugar	0.23	0.29	0.31
Potatoes	0.20	0.53	0.38
Tomatoes	0.34	0.53	0.69
Milk	0.43	0.58	0.74
Eggs	1.29	1.16	1.85

Prices at November 1994.
Source: Planning Ministry.

Exhibit 3.6

Agricultural exports 1990–94 (US$m)

Commodity	*1990*	*1991*	*1992*	*1993*	*1994*[1]
Bananas	212.8	196.5	198.0	201.2	146.5
Shrimp	44.3	50.4	53.9	56.9	48.9
Raw sugar	36.8	24.4	20.0	21.8	15.7
Coffee	13.8	13.0	10.8	11.6	5.9
Meat	6.6	12.2	4.7	16.0	4.6
Fresh fish	11.3	11.3	12.7	18.5	13.5
Hides & skins	6.6	6.4	9.4	8.0	6.7
Fresh tropical fruits	2.8	6.3	9.8	14.8	12.8
Tobacco	3.4	5.4	5.3	5.6	1.3
Tropical fruit jams	6.7	5.2	3.4	4.9	5.3
Cut flowers	0.7	1.0	1.6	1.5	1.1
Mayonnaise	2.0	2.0	2.1	2.9	2.5
Cheese (American type)	1.3	1.5	2.1	2.8	1.9
Alcohol	1.2	2.1	2.6	1.9	2.1
Condensed milk	3.4	3.0	2.8	4.1	2.9
Evaporated milk	1.3	1.0	0.9	1.1	1.2

[1]January–September.
Source: Comptroller General's Office.

manians having to pay a premium for home-grown produce, the cattle sector has fared better (with or without tax exemptions Panama has a comparative advantage in this area).

Panamanians like their beef steaks and consume per head twice as much as people in neighbouring Costa Rica. They can afford to, for Panama is more than self-sufficient in beef (a lot is exported to Mexico and exports to Japan began in 1995) which is mainly provided by large private ranches in the provinces of Chiriquí and Veraguas where Brama and Indo-Brazil bulls and cows graze.

Government policies so far have not done a great deal to encourage

Panama has produced high-quality coffee for many years and more modern farming practices have improved yields

exports of agricultural products other than the traditional ones of bananas, coffee, sugar and shrimps (see Exhibit 3.6). Production of bananas, the principal agricultural export, is located in the eastern provinces of Panama near the Costa Rican border and has been traditionally dominated by the Chiriquí Land Company. Dole Co. has been exporting bananas bought from independent producers through Costa Rican ports since 1991. Panama was the world's fifth largest banana producer in 1994 when it sold a record 41.1 million boxes. The bulk of banana exports are shipped to Germany and Italy. The plantations provide jobs for more than 16,000 people, the largest single employer.

Coffee is produced in the central and western provinces and has benefited from higher world prices. Panama has produced high-quality coffee for many years and more modern farming practices have greatly improved yields. Sugar output has been hit by a world surplus and consequently depressed prices. The area planted has fallen from some 40,000 hectares in the early 1980s to around 25,000 hectares. Non-traditional fresh produce exports have a largely unexploited potential, particularly melons for the US winter market where some success is beginning to be achieved. Other products are okra, cassava, cucumbers, strawberries and eggplant. Cut flowers from the Chiriquí area have potential, but access to appropriate air transport remains a problem.

Panama's forestry potential lies in industrial hardwood, especially the growing of teak. It is estimated that some 30 per cent of land cannot be used productively for any activity other than forestry because of the poor quality of the soil and degradation of land by traditional farming methods. Panama has to be careful, however, because the canal is a rain-fed waterway and exploitation without sufficient controls could cause substantial ecological damage.

Shrimp and fresh fish industry

Panama has been quite successful in developing a shrimp and fresh fish industry in controlled conditions along the lines developed by Taiwan and Ecuador in the 1960s (on-shore ponds built in the tidal zone). This is a much more reliable and productive system than the hit-and-miss business of fishing from boats.

Ralston Purina, a US company, set up a Panamanian subsidiary, Agromarina, in the 1970s for the purpose of raising salt water shrimp in a controlled aquaculture environment. They installed a hatchery at Vera Cruz and ponds at the mouth of the river at Aguadulce. Shrimp boats were used to gather the gravid shrimp from the sea. The egg-bearing shrimp were then taken into the hatchery where the eggs were hatched through 11 larval and post-larval stages and reared in a controlled environment. This was said to be the first commercial venture of salt water shrimp aquaculture in the Western hemisphere. Many followed their lead and large tracts of marsh areas and mangrove went into production. Unchecked expansion can have serious environmental consequences.

Mining

Panama was the main route for shipping precious metals from Latin America to Europe after the Spanish conquest, but little of it came from the country

Panama's mining sector has the potential for substantial growth

Exhibit 3.7

Investment in mining, 1990–94 (US$m)

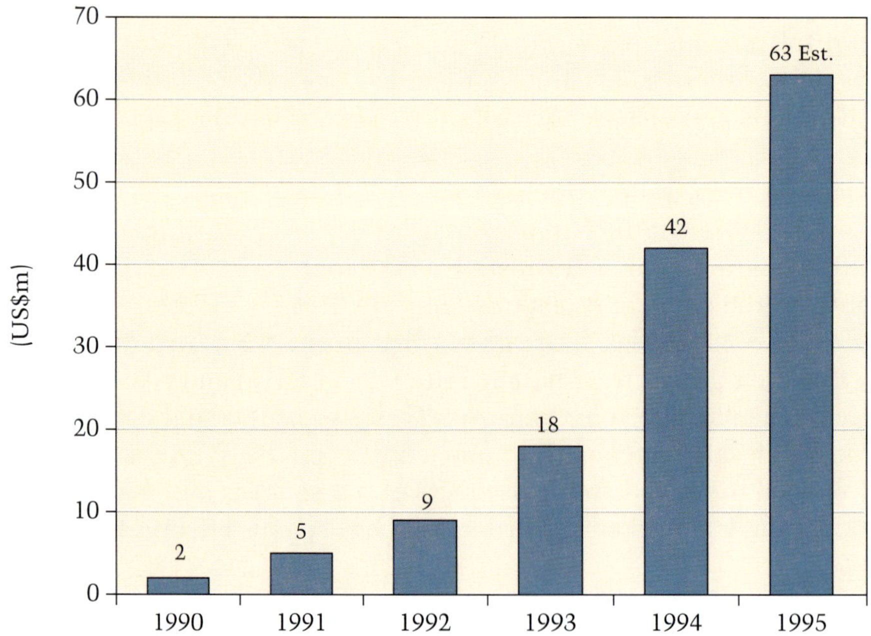

Source: MinAmerica.

itself. Panama's mining sector, none the less, has the potential for substantial growth and it is the most promising new area of the economy (see Exhibit 3.7). The country has two of the largest undeveloped copper deposits in the world. Other minerals with commercial potential are gold, silver and manganese. Mining investments are aided by a favourable mining law, which encourages foreign investment (see Chapter 11).

Until recently, Panama's mining sector was best known for the hugely ambitious Cerro Colorado (literally the "red mountain") project, 250 km west of Panama City near the Gulf of Chiriquí, but the project turned sour. This was the great project of the Torrijos and subsequent governments which was supposed to have resulted in the construction of one of the world's largest copper mining and smelting complexes, providing more than 2,000 jobs and, assuming copper prices held, US$500 million in exports. Rodrigo Gonzalez, the chairman of Cerro Colorado, said in the late 1970s that the project would bring so much wealth to the area that Guaymi Indians living there, who would have been displaced, "instead of dying of worms would die of indigestion." But copper prices collapsed and the financing for the US$1.6 billion project could not be obtained.

None the less Panama still has mineable reserves of 1.4 billion tonnes grading 0.7 per cent copper. Rio Tinto Zinc transferred its 49 per cent holding to the government in 1994 and the state now fully owns Cerro Colorado. The government wants private mining companies to exploit the richest and most accessible part of the area which has estimated reserves of 60 million tonnes of 0.9% grading.

Mining optimists claim that by the beginning of the 21st century Panama will be exporting more than US$400 million of minerals a year, compared with US$4 million in 1994. The Remance gold mine, which started in 1990, has proven reserves of 200,000 tonnes with 6.5 grams per tonne of gold (gpt). Potential reserves are put at 3 million tonnes. Production capacity is 300 tonnes a day and exports are worth around US$12 million a year. The Santa Rosa gold mine, the largest in Central America, has 6.5 million tonnes of reserves with 1.8 gpt. It is a wholly owned subsidiary of Greenstone Resources of Canada and was due to begin operating in 1995. Its exports will generate around US$30 million a year and, together with Remance, are worth about the same as coffee and sugar exports combined.

Cerro Quema is a third gold mine developed by Cemsa of Panama and Cyprus/Amax of the United States. It is expected to come into production in 1997 and its exports are estimated at US$60–70 million a year. If all goes well Panama would be exporting US$100 million of minerals in 1998, roughly the same as the value of shrimps, sugar and coffee in 1993.

The largest project is Cerro Petaquilla, 120 km west of Panama City and close to the Caribbean coast. An expanding mining district embracing at least eight separate deposits, Petaquilla and its satellites rank as the third largest copper and gold-ore complex in the world. Since 1992 exploration and drilling have been in the hands of Canada's Adrian Resources which has a 52 per cent interest in Petaquilla Mining Property. The other 48 per cent is in the hands of Metall Mining Corp of Canada. The Panamanian company MinAmerica has 20 per cent of Adrian Resources Ltd, Canada. Petaquilla's reserves were discovered at the end of the 1960s during a United Nations programme. The Japanese company Mitsui explored the area in the 1970s and abandoned it in 1980.

According to a preliminary feasibility study by Kilborn the Petaquilla deposit has a mineable reserve of 495 million tonnes grading 0.53 per cent copper and 0.124 gpt gold at a 0.195 copper equivalent cut-off. At a 0.5 per cent copper equivalent cut-off, the mineable reserves drop to 287 million tonnes grading 0.7 per cent copper and 0.14 gpt gold. The study proposed a production rate of 60,000 tonnes per day over 22 years. The annual production of copper in concentrate would be about 110,000 tonnes while that of gold would be about 57,000 oz. per year at an average copper cost of US$0.34 per pound net of credits.

Adrian's finds have attracted the interest of a Who's Who of international mining majors. Canada's Teck Corp signed an agreement with Adrian in November 1994, whereby Teck will become the operator. Teck exercised an option to buy half of Adrian's interest in Petaquilla, and it has the financial capacity to organise the US$485 million investment necessary to fully exploit Petaquilla. It also agreed to fund Adrian's ongoing exploration costs on other major copper deposits in the same area.

According to reports by Wood Gundy and MinAmerica, the Petaquilla and Botija mineable reserves still have room to grow through exploration. Both deposits cover surface areas of around one mile by half a mile. The deposits contain uniform, blanket-like mineralisation averaging in excess of 500 feet of thickness with very low anticipated stripping ratios. The actual thickness of large portions of the two deposits is not yet defined as certain drill holes terminated in strong copper mineralisation that was in excess of 800 feet in thickness. Work on the other copper deposits is intended to both expand resources and attempt to link all the deposits together into potentially one large deposit. The feasibility study only looked at the Petaquilla and Botija pits, but there is the possibility that some of the other exploration areas may be linked with these two pits.

Petaquilla's exports are estimated as high as US$450 million a year. All told, revenue from mining exports could more than replace the income from military spending that Panama will lose when the United States pulls out of its bases in the country at the end of 1999.

Transisthmian oil pipeline

The 131 km long pipeline across lowland pastures, banana plantations and swamps which pumps US oil between the Pacific and Atlantic coasts is known as Panama's "second canal". The pipeline was opened in October 1982. Supertankers from Valdez, Alaska, offload their crude oil at Petroterminal's terminal in Puerto Armuelles on the Pacific coast and it is pumped to the other coast at Chiriquí Grande.

Petroterminal is a joint venture between Northville Industries, the Chicago Bridge and Iron Company (together they own 60 per cent), and Corporación Financiera Nacional, the Panamanian government's economic development agency, which has a 40 per cent stake. The terminal is managed by Northville Industries, the largest independent oil storage and distribution company on the East Coast of the United States.

Both the Puerto Armuelles and Chiriquí Grande terminals have total storage capacities of 2.5 million barrels, ballast water treatment facilities, and fire and environmental protection systems. Supertankers up to 265,000 dwt can be accommodated at the Puerto Armuelles facility which is equipped with three berths. The oil is offloaded at a maximum rate of 100,000 barrels per hour, and is either temporarily stored or immediately pumped across the isthmus in the 40-inch diameter pipeline. Oil tanks at the Chiriquí Grande facility are located on a hillside 3.5 km from the shoreline and 250 metres above sea level, to allow the gravity flow of oil to awaiting tankers. Ships can be loaded at the rate of 50,000 barrels per hour. The Alaskan crude goes to refineries on the East and Gulf coasts and in Puerto Rico.

Pipeline revenues have gradually declined over the past seven years (see Exhibit 3.1), reflecting a decrease in Alaskan oil production, an increase in consumption of Alaskan oil in California and some competition from US pipelines. The outlook is for further declines. The contribution to GDP was less than 1 per cent in 1994, down from 3 per cent in 1990.

In a bid to boost revenue general cargo handling, facilities began to be built at Chiriquí Grande in 1995 for products other than oil. This should benefit exporters of bananas, coffee, sugar and other products and spur development in the area. The project includes the rehabilitation of the road from the Interamerican Highway to Chiriquí Grande (95 km). A 600 feet long by 80 feet wide pier, capable of handling vessels with up to 32 feet in draft, is to be built. A nearby container yard will be equipped with lighting and electrical and gas connections for artificial environment, dry storage warehouse facilities for bulk cargo, sugar and fertilisers.

Foreign trade

Panama emerged from trade isolation in 1995 and was poised to join the World Trade Organisation (WTO). Negotiators were seeking to gain acceptance of a proposal that would lower Panama's highest tariff rate to 40 per cent from the maximum rate of 60 per cent for industrial products and 90 per cent for agricultural products. It was almost the only Latin American country not to be a member of the world's trading club. Until the 1990–94 Endara government began to dismantle the complex trade protection system, traditional policies on trade and economic incentives directed agricultural and manufacturing production toward import substitution.

Before the introduction of the first phase of the trade reform in August 1991, the average production-weighted nominal protection equalled 51 per cent for the whole economy, 57 per cent for agriculture and 50 per cent for manufacturing. Panama's average nominal tariff duties were still the highest in the region in 1994: 40 per cent as against 20 per cent for other Central American countries.

WTO membership, however, will bring limited benefits to the country in

Some analysts believe Panama has the potential to become a major oil and downstream products distribution centre

the form of a significant increase in exports. Its importance is more as a passport for the Pérez Balladares government's aspiration to join the North American Free Trade Agreement (NAFTA) (Panama will play its "strategic card" here) and sending a positive signal to foreign investors. Sandwiched between Mercosur in South America, the developing world's largest customs union, and NAFTA, the government believes it must belong to a large trading bloc (Panama has never shown much interest in the Central American Common Market). But by reducing the anti-export bias of the economy there will be a shift of funds from formerly protected industries to exportable activities and efficient import-substitution. The World Bank estimated in its 1992 report, on the basis of GDP growth projections that turned out to be too conservative for 1992 and 1993 and too high for 1994, that in response to trade reform and deregulation, the share of exports of goods and non-factor services would grow from 38.5 per cent of GDP in 1990 to close to 43 per cent in 1995 and 48 per cent in 1999. It estimated that non-traditional exports would increase their share of the total from 48 per cent in 1990 to 55 per cent in 1995 and close to 56 per cent in 1999. Panama has no comparative advantages for exporting raw materials and unprocessed food within Central America, but it does have better prospects in tropical fruits, meat and some light manufacturing in large markets like the United States and Mexico.

As the economy opens up, imports of goods could increase from 37.3 per cent of GDP in 1990 to some 40 per cent in 1995 and 43 per cent in 1999. The composition of imports would also change. Imports of consumer goods and intermediate goods would increase, as the share of imported capital goods declines in response to the growth in labour-intensive production.

WTO membership will mean dismantling the tax credit system for exports known as CAT, which was introduced in 1974. The certificates were redeemable in payment of direct taxes and customs tariffs and were given for non-traditional exports. Thanks to their introduction, non-traditional exports grew between 1975 and 1982. The amount of the CAT was equal to 20 per cent of local value added and was granted provided the export had a local content of at least 20 per cent of the gross value. The long-term balance, however, was not so favourable: according to the planning ministry the "cost" of the incentive between 1980 and 1993 (excluding 1990, an abnormal year after the US invasion) was US$113 million for generating yearly funds of less than 1 per cent of GDP, while non-subsidised exports during the same period contributed the equivalent of 30 per cent of GDP.

Exports

Panama is not a strong exporter of goods and has traditionally registered a trade deficit (see Exhibit 3.8). Where it does score is when non-factor services are added (principally the re-exports of the Colón Free Zone) which makes export earnings among the largest in the world relative to GDP (see Exhibit 3.9). The country has profited from its geographical location and dollar-based economy

Exhibit 3.9

Volume of exports, real effective exchange rate and terms of trade

(Index 1980 = 100)

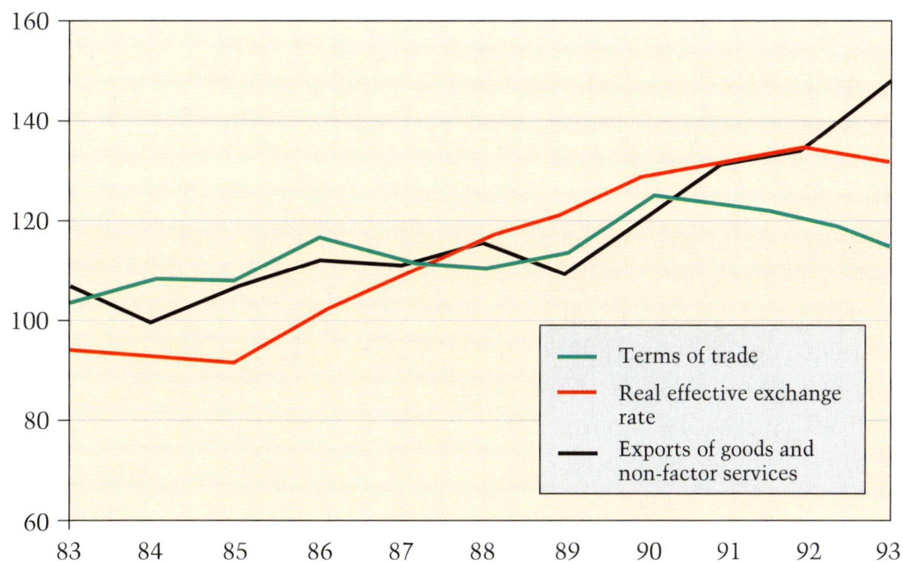

Source: Inter-American Development Bank.

Exhibit 3.8

Exports and imports of goods 1984–94 (US$m)*

	Imports (FOB)	*Exports (FOB)*	*Trade deficit*
1984	1,319.5	461.7	857.8
1985	1,300.9	476.6	824.3
1986	1,158.7	481.8	676.8
1987	1,219.4	510.8	708.7
1988	785.6	464.2	321.4
1989	941.0	484.7	456.4
1990	1,382.0	540.6	841.4
1991	1,581.8	540.6	1,041.2
1992	1,825.4	480.9	1,344.5
1993	1,979.6	507.6	1,472.0
1994	2,202.6	531.8	1,670.8

*Excludes imports and re-exports of the Colón Free Trade Zone.
Source: Inter-American Development Bank and Comptroller General's Office.

to develop a strong services sector (Canal, offshore banking centre and Colón Free Zone). Non-factor services surpluses have long helped to finance the large trade deficits.

Traditional products (see Exhibit 3.6), mainly bananas, sugar, coffee and shrimps, account for some 60 per cent of total merchandise exports and other than shrimps they have not grown substantially over the last decade. Non-traditional exports include fresh fish, tropical fruits, particularly melons, leather and men's shirts. Exports of melons have increased from US$700,000 in 1990 to more than US$5.5 million.

The United States is the principal export market and also Panama's largest supplier of goods.

Panama has changed its international trade classification system from the Customs Cooperation Council Nomenclature (CCCN) to the Harmonised System (HS). WTO membership will also provide a customs valuation system that conforms to international standards.

Flag registry

Panama overtook Liberia as the world's leading register of ships in 1994 when income from this activity amounted to US$44.6 million, up from US$39 million in 1993 and US$34.5 million in 1990. Of the 12,870 ships flying the Panamanian "flag of convenience" about 40 per cent are of Japanese origin, 20 per cent European (most of them Greek) and the rest US, Korean and other nationalities. Ships join Panama's flag registry, started in 1925, because of tax exemptions (earnings generated are not subject to income tax), wages and benefits are lower than rival countries and registry fees are up to 50 per cent lower than those of Norway, Japan and the United Kingdom, for example. Panamanian registered ships can use crews of any nationality, although there is a theoretical requirement that they hire a tenth of their crews from Panama. But since there are not enough Panamanians to go round this is not rigidly enforceable. Panama's geographical location is also a point in its favour as it is a cross-point between several shipping routes. The flag registry business is also very lucrative for Panamanian law firms.

Notes and references

1. World Bank report on Panama, 30 January 1992, p. 2.
2. Ibid., p. 13.
3. *Panama structural change and growth prospects* (World Bank, 1985), p. 57.

Chapter Four

Tourism

The English Romantic poet John Keats got it wrong. "Stout Cortez" never climbed a peak in Darién or any other province of Panama. Had he done so, however, he would have been ideally placed to see the country's tremendous potential for tourism spread before him: Atlantic and Pacific beaches, exotic jungle and spectacular wildlife.

Tourism contributes 4–5 per cent of GDP (see Exhibit 4.1), roughly the same as exports of bananas, shrimps, sugar and coffee, and provides employment, directly and indirectly, to 30,000 people. After the Panama Canal and the Colón Free Zone, tourism is Panama's largest foreign currency earner. The potential for increased earnings is substantial if Panama succeeds in opening

Exhibit 4.1

Tourism revenue, 1990–94 (US$m)

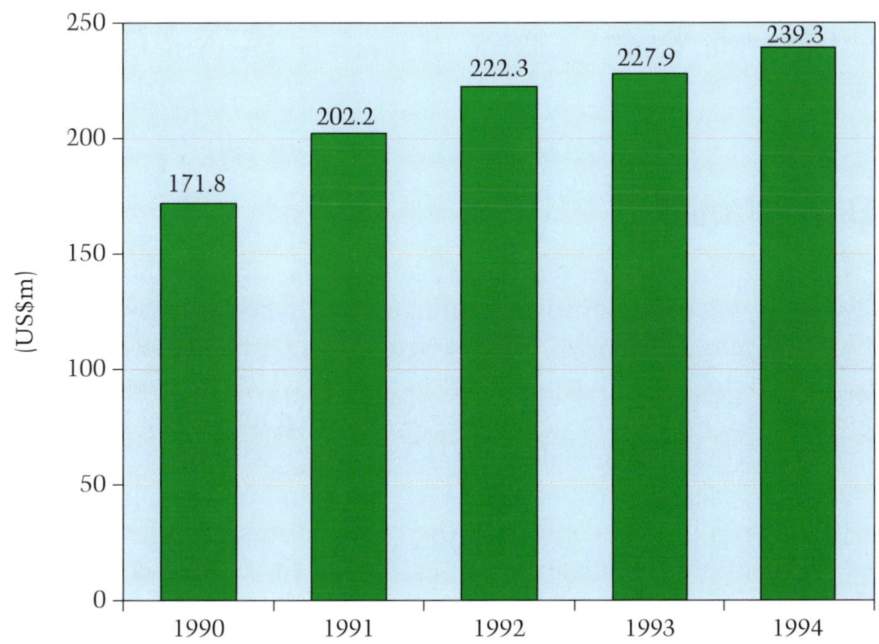

Source: IPAT.

Opposite: Darién National Park is an ecological bridge between North and South America

up new areas. A new Tourism Law came into force in 1994 which offers tax incentives and other benefits for local and foreign investors. The country received 422,000 visitors in 1994, up from 380,000 in 1993, 80 per cent of whom came for business reasons. Panama has close to 7,500 hotel and other guest rooms, 4,000 of which are in Panama City.

One of the changes taking place is the building of more hotels equipped for businessmen in the capital so that the older hotels, such as the Hotel El Panamá, can be freed largely for tourists. Rooms of one type or another are scarce in most areas outside Panama City, except for places like Contadora Island (17 minutes by air from Panama City); nearby beautiful Pacific beaches like Rio Mar; the enchanting Isla Grande, off the Caribbean coast (only reachable by motorised dugout); and other spots. The luxury Hotel Contadora Caesar Park, the only one on the island of Contadora, was bought by a group of Spanish businessmen in 1993 and 180 rooms were added to the 150-room resort property, which has its own nine-hole golf course, tennis courts and large swimming pool.

The great majority of people who come to Panama stay in Panama City and see little if anything of the country. They come for the duty-free stores in Panama City or the Colón Free Zone which sell imported Japanese, European and US goods. Some also come to buy the *panamá*, the famous Panama hat known for its tight weave and light weight, although it is in fact made in Ecuador. (The name goes back to the 1880s when Ferdinand de Lesseps, who liked wearing the hat, came to Panama to oversee the building of the canal, a project he had to abandon after several years). Panama does, however, produce its own hat, the *montuno*, at a much lower cost than its famous cousin, and the *guayabera* (loose-fitting shirt) which is ideal for the humid climate.

"Panama is more than a canal" ran an old slogan of the Panamanian Tourism Institute (IPAT) and nothing could be nearer to the truth. The "eighth wonder of the world" is still a great tourist attraction, but there are many more places to see.

San Blas islands

As the launch pulled into the old rickety jetty of the tiny Caribbean island of WichubWala, young Indian boys swimming in the crystal-clear water began to chant: "Money, money, money". Tourists from the mainland had arrived to see and endlessly photograph (for a price) one of the few remaining pieces of indigenous Panama. The 360 islands of San Blas which stretch along 320 km of coastline, only 50 of which are inhabited, are home to the Kunas. They were there long before the Spaniards arrived. The reefs surrounding San Blas are among the last living ones in the world with their original marine life. The women still dress in their traditional clothes of mainly red and orange skirts and wear head scarves to protect themselves from the fierce sun, a golden ring in their nose and bands around their ankle.

The islands, reached by 30-minute flights departing daily from Panama City's Paitilla airport, are world famous for the multi-coloured *molas* which the Kunas produce. In the Kunas' language, *molas* means dress; they are intricately hand-sewn multi-layered inlays, usually depicting the islands' animal life, mainly birds, fish and monkeys. Legend has it that the *molas* were the Kunas' imitation of the Scottish tartans brought to Panama when a group of Scots attempted to establish a colony in Darién at the end of the 17th century. Guided by their elders, Kuna girls learn to make *molas* from an early age. They can be bought for as little as US$5.

Each island has its own chief or *sahila* who settles any differences that might arise among villagers. No land is individually owned, but the coconut trees are. Even on uninhabited islands a "caretaker" guards the coconut trees and their precious crop, which is the basic livelihood of the Kunas. The *sahilas* of all the islands meet occasionally to handle matters affecting the whole tribe. In addition, the Kunas have an *intendente* who acts as the governor and liaison between the government and the tribe.

Overleaf: "Panama is more than a canal" – the country offers beautiful beaches and has enormous potential for ecotourism

Panama Canal

There are many ways to see the canal. Richard Halliburton swam its length in 1928 and it cost him 38 cents after his displacement tonnage was calculated. Until recently there was a scenic railway trip between Panama City and Colón along the railroad built in the 1850s when it was the easiest route from New York to San Francisco before the interior of the United States was opened up. Today the track is used to move cargo. One of the best spots to view the canal is Miraflores Locks where ships coming from the Atlantic are lowered to the level of the Pacific or begin their journey by being raised up in two stages. Maintained at a cost of US$100 million a year, the original machinery is still used to operate the locks.

Ecotourism

Panama has enormous potential for ecotourism. The pristine Darién jungle near Colombia, inhabited by the Emberá-Waunaan, is only a 50-minute flight away from the traffic congestion and shopping malls of Panama City. There is a small runway very close to the River Sambu and you can head off into the jungle in a motorised dugout with the permission of the Indian authorities. As Michèle Labrut points out in her definitive guide to Panama,[1] the country has 12 "life zones", according to the classification of the US botanist L. R. Holridge. A life zone in ecology is defined by climatic and soil conditions that create the type of forests growing in those regions. More than 12 per cent of the land area is in 15 protected national parks (see Exhibit 4.2). The flora is abundant with 10,000 species of plants – almost eight different species per square kilometre – including 1,200 varieties of orchids, as well as 687 species of ferns and 1,500 varieties of other trees. In the province of Chiriquí alone, there are 13 kinds of snakes and 13 kinds of lizards. The Chiriquí highlands are the easiest place in the world to see the famed resplendant quetzal.

Darién is an ecological bridge between South and North America and it is protected by a national park, the largest in Panama and the second biggest in Central America. Construction of the Pan-American Highway as far as Yaviza in the Darién has produced deforestation, but the Darién Gap still stands untouched between Yaviza and Colombia. This region of tropical rainforests is the heart of the national park, which UNESCO has declared both a World Heritage Site and a Man and the Biosphere Reserve. Travel and tourist infrastructure is fairly primitive, as befits ecotourism, with the exception of the luxury fishing lodge at Pinas Bay on the Pacific coast. The road as far as Yaviza is driveable during the dry season (January–April) but not recommended at the height of the rainy season (August–December).

Panama is the only country in the Americas that has five national parks less than two hours drive from its capital city, and it is the only one with a park within the perimeter of the city itself (Metropolitano). The parks are protected by the government and private organisations such as Panama's ANCON and the United States' Smithsonian Tropical Research Institute which runs the Barro Colorado National Monument, an island formed in Gatun Lake when the canal was built.

Nearer to Panama City is Taboga island, a short boat ride, which for centuries has been known as the "isle of flowers". Jasmine, oleander and hibiscus bloom everywhere and create a vivid backdrop for holidaymakers. Thousands of pelicans nest on the back of the island which was a favourite hideout for buccaneers and pirates and where the Spanish *conquistador* Pizarro planned his search of Peru. The bell tower of the island's church, built in 1550, is believed to be the second oldest in the Western hemisphere.

The 1993–2002 tourism master plan

The Endara government approved a US$685 million master plan in 1993 which provides the broad framework for tourism's future growth. While the number of visitors has been steadily growing since the 1988–89 crisis period, the figure is still far from the more than 600,000 that Panama was attracting in the late 1970s. One key issue is Panama's tarnished image (due to its drug trafficking and money-laundering problem). Another problem is the lack of government promotion of the country, although this too is improving, thanks to the greater marketing efforts of the Panamanian Tourism Institute (IPAT).

The plan divides the country into nine tourist zones and aims to more than double the number of rooms to over 18,000 by 2002. Planners believe that if all goes well Panama could be attracting 1.5 million tourists a year by 2002. Of the 10,900 new rooms, 6,400 would be specifically built in areas that need them in order to be able to participate in the tourism industry and the rest would be induced growth (see Exhibit 4.3). Envisaged expansion for some areas is quite significant: for example, the goal is to have 1,059 rooms in San Blas, as against today's 45, and 737 in Darién (37 at the moment).

It is envisaged that of the US$685 million total investment, US$23.5 million would come from the government and the rest from the private sector (see Exhibit 4.4). The bulk of the investment (40 per cent) would be in Las Perlas, the beaches in the Contadora island area and those nearest to Panama City.

Investment in the capital itself (Metropolitana zone) would account for just over a quarter. One of the proposals for this zone is a theme park in the Panama Canal Area.

Exhibit 4.2

Panama's national parks

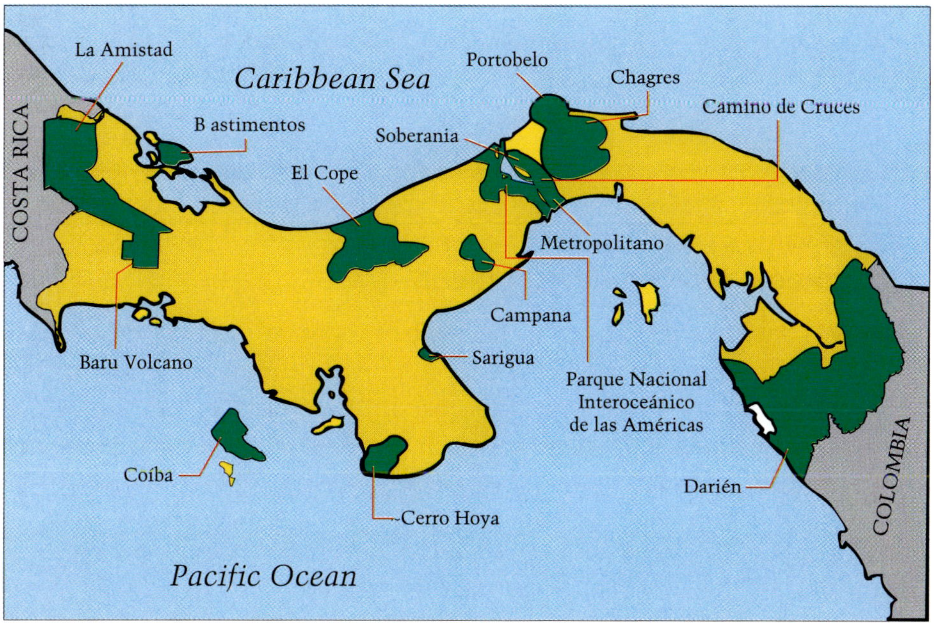

Source: INRENARE.

Exhibit 4.3

Hotel rooms in 2002

Zone	*Plan*	*Induced growth*	*Total*	*Number in 1992*	*Overall total*
La Amistad	150	400	550	233	783
Bastimentos	600	–	600	43	643
Arco Seco	500	100	600	282	882
Farallón	450	350	800	193	993
Metropolitana	115	2,285	2,400	4,235	6,635
Portobelo	900	250	1,150	45	1,195
San Blas	1,000	–	1,000	59	1,059
Las Perlas	2,500	–	2,500	151	2,651
Darién	185	515	700	37	737
Other areas	–	600	600	2,064	2,664
Total	6,400	4,500	10,900	7,342	18,242

Source: Tourism Master Plan IPAT.

Exhibit 4.4

Investment by tourist zones (US$m)

Zone	*Public*	*Private*	*Total*	*% share*
La Amistad	3.5	21.3	24.8	3.6
Bastimientos	1.8	31.4	33.2	4.9
Arcos Seco	1.6	21.0	22.6	3.3
Farallón	1.4	61.2	62.6	9.2
Metropolitana	2.7	177.8	180.6	26.4
Portobelo	5.6	43.1	48.8	7.1
San Blas	2.4	10.1	12.6	1.8
Las Perlas	2.4	273.0	275.4	40.2
Total	23.5	661.7	685.2	100.0

Source: Tourism Master Plan IPAT.

Law to promote tourism development

This law was approved in June 1994 and one of its most important novelties is that a maximum 60-day period is set for approval of projects. Prior to that it took up to a year and some investors lost interest during the cumbersome bureaucratic procedures and withdrew their projects. The very generous incentives and benefits include:

Hotels

When the investment is more than US$300,000 in the metropolitan area of Panama City and more than US$50,000 in other areas, excluding the value of the land and not including bed-and-breakfast establishments, for which the minimum investment is set by IPAT, the following incentives are granted:

- full exemption for 20 years from import duties, payments, levies, or fees of any kind paid for imports deemed by IPAT as indispensable for tourism activities;
- exemption from real estate taxes for 20 years;
- depreciation of fixed assets is allowed at a rate of 10 per cent a year excluding the value of the land; and
- interest earned by creditors from investments is exempt from income tax.

To foster investment in hotels outside the metropolitan area, developers can issue paper until 1 January 2000 to finance development. Investors acquiring the paper who are not in any way involved in the development are able to deduct 50 per cent of the amount acquired for income tax purposes.

Convention centres, recreational parks, zoos, ecotourism and marinas

The following tax incentives are granted: three-year exemption from import duties on materials and equipment used in the building; depreciation over a period of 10 years and exemption from property taxes on improvements for 20 years.

Convention facilities

The largest convention centre is in Panama City at Atlapa. The 18-acre complex can cater for 10,500 people. There is a 34,445 square foot exhibit hall free of columns.

Note

1. Michèle Labrut, *Getting to know Panama* (Focus, 1993).

Chapter Five

The banking sector

With its skyscrapers glinting in the intensely bright sun, the centre of modern Panama City resembles a miniature Manhattan. The 30 foreign banks conducting offshore business and 64 local and foreign banks with a general licence had total assets of US$32.8 billion at the end of 1994, close to five times Panama's GDP. This was a sharp rise over 1993 (see Exhibit 5.1) and a considerable recovery from the crisis of 1988 and 1989, but total assets of the banking centre, the largest in Latin America, are still well below the peak of US$49 billion in 1982.

Growth in total assets was considerably faster than that of nominal GDP and thus the banking centre's relative importance in the economy increased (see Exhibit 5.2). The ratio between assets and GDP in 1994 was close to that reached before the 1988 crisis. The funds of banks with a general licence increased by US$5.15 billion in 1994, 35.6 per cent of which came from international interbank deposits.

The cornerstone of Panamanian banking – and happily in place before the post 1973 Euromarkets boom – is the 1970 law. This exempts offshore business conducted from Panama from income tax, frees from tax all interest earned on domestic savings accounts and all offshore transactions and permits the setting up of accounts in any currency as well as numbered accounts.

The total assets of the 23 banks operating in Panama were US$854 million in 1970 and the centre went from strength to strength until 1982 when banks began to withdraw deposits and stop booking loans out of Panama because of Mexico's foreign debt crisis and the attraction of International Banking Facilities (IBFs) in the United States. IBFs offered similar advantages to Panama: deposit and loan business can be conducted with foreign residents and foreign banks without being subject to reserve requirements, interest rate ceilings and FDIC insurance requirements. IBFs effectively allow a bank to conduct business in a Eurocurrency environment without establishing an offshore facility. (Panama authorised IBFs in 1989 and then stopped them in 1994. Banks appealed against the measures and in 1995 operations were reviewed and approved on a case-by-case basis). Assets dropped from US$49 billion in 1982 to US$31.4 billion at the end 1987, the last "normal" year (they halved to US$14.8 billion in 1988). In 1987 Panama's share of loans booked out of six major centres – Hong Kong, Singapore, Grand Cayman, Bahamas and Bahrain – dropped to 3 per cent in 1987 from 9 per cent in 1980.

A major advantage of Panama's banking centre is that the US dollar is the legal tender, though for reasons of national pride it is referred to as the balboa in book-keeping. The country also has no controls on the movements of capi-

Exhibit 5.1

Total assets of foreign and Panamanian banks 1982–94 (US$m)

	Banking system[1]	*International banks*[2]	*Total*
1982	32.5	16.4	49.0
1983	30.1	12.6	42.7
1984	27.8	10.1	37.9
1985	28.2	10.6	38.9
1986	30.1	9.4	40.3
1987	22.1	9.2	31.4
1988	11.5	3.3	14.8
1989	11.1	4.2	15.3
1990	13.0	5.3	18.4
1991	15.2	5.4	20.6
1992	17.1	5.9	23.0
1993	21.3	4.7	26.0
1994	26.5	6.2	32.8

[1]Banks with a general licence for domestic and international operations.
[2]Banks with only an international licence for offshore business.
Source: Panama Banking Association.

Exhibit 5.2

Ratio of banking assets to GDP

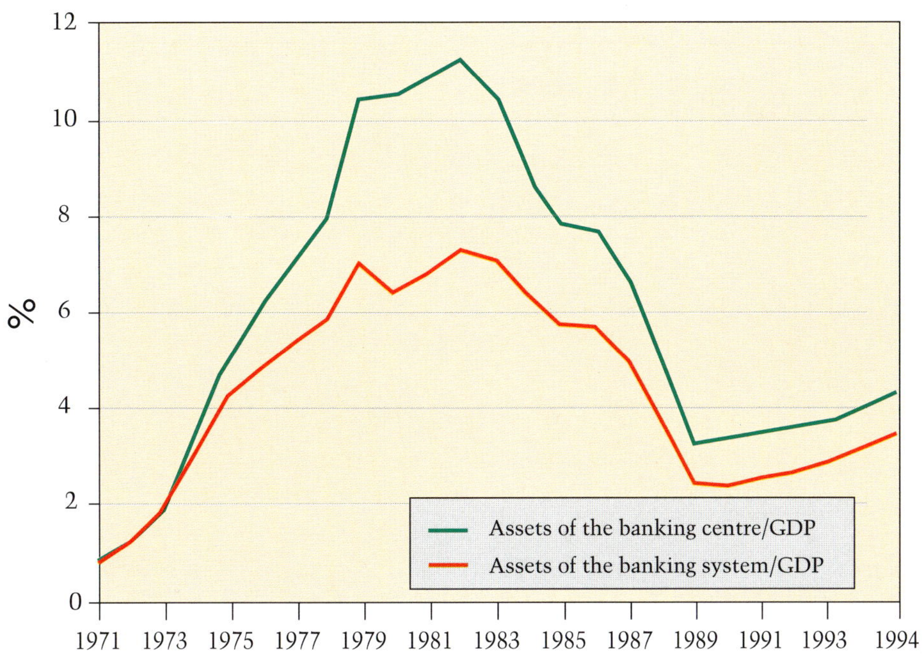

Source: Panama Banking Association.

tal, and Colón on the Atlantic coast houses the second biggest free trading zone (after Hong Kong) in the world. The monies, however, an economy the size of Panama can generate itself are tiny compared to those "booked" by the big international banks through their Panamanian branches and subsidiaries. Like other non-oil exporting countries of the Third World, Panama is essentially a taker of funds from the international money-go-round and not a giver and for this reason it will never be on a par with the world's financial capitals. The real banking centre for Latin America is Miami and the day it provides offshore facilities will be a worrying one for Panama. Despite its limitations, Panama is a significant funneller or recycler of funds from international markets plus private capital from Latin America, a region where capital flight has traditionally been very high because of political turbulence.

The 110 banks are not all chasing the same business, which is just as well since there are so many of them in a highly competitive market. Of the 110 banks, 64 have a general licence (for domestic and international business), 30 for international business only and 16 have representative offices. Bankers reckon Panama has reached saturation point, though a few continue to set up each year, mainly small ones from Latin America. Just over half the banks in Panama are Latin American. The Panamanian market is served not only by the country's own banks, whose numbers have grown considerably in the past few years, but also by some major international banks. Citibank (which arrived in 1904) and Chase Manhattan (1915) came with the Stars and Stripes to the Canal Zone and stayed to set up networks of retail branches around the country. Chase opened in 1950 the first branch of a foreign bank in David, the capital of the province of Chiriquí. At one point six foreign banks had branches in David, an agricultural centre, as well as two Panamanian banks. Chase (which has since withdrawn from the countryside) was the first to take banking to rural Panama and start farm credit programmes.

Lloyds (previously known as Bank of London and South America) is essentially there in pursuit of trade finance linked to Panama's location and the Colón Free Zone. Many Latin American banks are there to tap the international money markets from Panama or to funnel funds into their national systems, while some US and European ones find Panama conveniently placed to service the whole of their South American Euromarket portfolios. Even in an era of instant telecommunications it is still easier to deal with clients in the same Western hemisphere time zone, and not five hours ahead as in the case of Europe, or nine hours behind as in the case of the Japanese, who are a growing financial and commercial presence in Panama. (See Exhibit 5.3.)

The National Banking Commission, an agency of the Ministry of Planning and Economic Policy and chaired by the minister, vets all new applications, checks international licence banks to ensure that they have a clean record and have a physical presence in the country – and not just a name plate – and supervises general licence banks to ensure they comply with the not very burdensome reserve requirements. The legal reserve for demand deposits is 10 per cent; for savings deposits 5 per cent, and for time deposits of less than one year, 5 per cent. These deposits pay zero interest, to the annoyance of bankers. In the absence of a deposit guarantee fund, however, which is a normal safe-

Exhibit 5.3

Ranking of banks with general licence by total assets (US$m)

	1994	*1993*
Banco Latinoamericano de Exportaciones	4,022	3,118
Banco Nacional de Panamá	2,664	2,520
Banco de Brasil	2,420	1,320
Deutsch-Sudamerikanische Bank	1,847	1,503
The Bank of Tokyo	988	816
Banco General and subsidiaries	950	867
Banque Sudameris	804	643
The Dai-Ichi Kangyo Bank	789	765
Banco del Istmo and subsidiaries	766	566
Chase Manhattan	735	703

Source: KPMG Peat Marwick.

guard in a mature banking system, these reserve requirements do represent an element of security. Failure to maintain the reserve levels acts as an early warning system for the authorities of possible problems in a bank. At least 30 per cent of the reserve must be in cash.

As Panama does not have a central bank, the Commission is responsible for establishing reserve levels and interest rates. Other central bank functions, such as receipt of tax revenue, holding of reserves and short-term loans to the government, are carried out by the Banco Nacional de Panamá (see below) which is also the country's largest commercial bank.

Getting to grips with the money-laundering problem

During the 1983–89 Noriega regime Panama's banking centre was known as the "washing machine" because of money-laundering activities. The country, run by a group of officers as if it was a private fiefdom, was ripe for money laundering: it is close to Colombia, one of the world's largest cocaine producers, the US dollar is the currency, there are no controls on capital movements, it is easy to set up shell corporations and more than 100 banks are chasing funds.

Since the US invasion at the end of 1989 – one of the reasons for "Operation Just Cause" was the drug-trafficking and money-laundering problem (Noriega was sentenced to 40 years' jail by a Miami court) – Panama has taken several steps to clean up its bad image, which still sticks to the country. Bankers feel the magnitude of the problem is still exaggerated by US authorities and their stance is hypocritical, given the problems on its own doorstep. There was outrage among the banking community when the US Drug Enforcement Agency (DEA) said in 1990 that 22 banks in Panama were responsible for laundering around US$1 billion a year. Bankers see Panama as a tiny cog in an enormous worldwide machine and that the country's importance in drug trafficking is much more as a transit point than a money-laundering centre.

The irony of the subsequent arrest of one of the DEA agents, who accompanied Noriega to Miami, on drug-trafficking charges did not escape the banking community. No one, however, has ever been brought to trial in Panama for money laundering and this illustrates two problems that have yet to be resolved: the difficulty of proving cases and the inadequacy of the Panamanian legal system.

Panama was singled out by the US State Department in March 1994 as a problem country in the drugs field, but was given a clean bill in its last annual review in March 1995. After the US invasion Panama had to sign a Mutual Legal Assistance Treaty with the United States as part of the aid package. This commits the government to supplying documentary and other evidence required in drugs cases. The Panamanian Legislative Assembly ratified the treaty in 1990 but the US Senate did not ratify it until May 1995 and then placed limitations on it (see Chapter 1).

Tighter controls have been put on banks to curb money laundering: banks have to report all deposits and withdrawals of more than US$10,000, as done in the United States. These forms are then kept in the bank and are at the disposal of the National Banking Commission's inspectors. The volume of forms is enormous and moves were afoot in 1995 to computerise this information. One of Panama's problems is that the Banking Commission is seriously understaffed and does not have the human or technological resources to supervise the system adequately, though this too is improving. The Commission has only some 40 auditors for the whole banking system and bankers say many are little more than secretaries.

Bankers' awareness that Panama has to clean up its image is also making them more thorough about checking the credentials of new customers, particularly those who roll up with cash in suitcases. The "get to know your customer" policy includes tighter reference requirements; new clients have to produce a certificate from their embassy vouching for their passport as some in the past were opening accounts with false passports. Co-operation between the Panamanian and US governments is also much greater since the downfall of Noriega, as one would expect. Banks sent a circular, for example, requesting information on the Zimar jewellery company in the Colón Free Zone, closed down for drug-trafficking activities, complied without complaint, although some thought it violated Panama's banking secrecy laws.

The government is adamant that it will not lift its banking secrecy laws. Some bankers view the dissatisfaction in certain quarters in Washington at Panama's progress as a Machiavellian plot to kill the banking centre. But the more bankers complain, the more suspicious US authorities become that Panama has something to hide. This is a vicious circle which is difficult to break.

It is widely acknowledged that drug traffickers have greatly benefited from Panama's corporate law, unchanged since 1927, which makes it easy to set up shell corporations. Shell corporations can be bought for as little as US$500. Both bearer and nominative shares can be issued. The details of shareholders are a private matter recorded only in the books of the company and there is no obligation to file such information with any institution or government department. Panama is by far the most popular offshore company location, with an estimated 750,000 in 1994, compared to 95,000 in the British Virgin Islands, the next most favoured place, which was put on the map for this kind of business during Panama's crisis in 1988 and 1989 when activity moved to other areas. "It's not right for lawyers to be able to set up these corporations, and then sell them to anyone, without bearing any responsibility for their end use", said President Pérez Balladares in 1994.[1] Laws concerning lawyers' responsibility were being changed in 1995.

Panamanian banks

For a country of its size, Panama has a remarkable number of banks of its own. Between 1984 and 1994 the number of banks virtually doubled to 20. The largest is the state-owned Banco Nacional de Panamá (BNP) with assets of US$ 2.6 billion at the end of 1994 and 49 branches (see Exhibit 5.4). BNP is the government's fiscal agent. The Caja de Ahorros, a savings bank, Banco de Desarrollo Agrícola, the agricultural development bank, and Banco Hipotecacio Nacional (mortgages) also belong to the state. The rest are privately owned. Most analysts believe there are too many banks and that some will have to merge.

Lending to the different sectors of the Panamanian economy increased 10.4 per cent in 1994 to US$6.52 billion (see Exhibit 5.5)

Banco Nacional de Panamá (whose funds in US banks were frozen during the final part of the Noriega regime) was technically insolvent at the time of the US invasion and is now back on its feet. All banks were closed between 3 March and 3 May 1988 and restrictions on operations remained in force until

Exhibit 5.4

Ranking of Panamanian banks by total assets (US$m)

	1994	*1993*
Banco Nacional de Panamá	2,664	2,520
Banco General and subsidiaries	950	867
Banco del Istmo and subsidiaries	766	566
Primer Banco de Ahorros and subsidiaries	654	574
Caja de Ahorros	477	446
Banco Continental de Panamá	411	353
Banco Comercial de Panamá	359	320
Towerbank International and subsidiary	250.7	227
Banco Internacional de Panamá and subsidiaries	250.3	211
Banco Panamericano	185	118

Source: KPMG Peat Marwick.

Exhibit 5.5

Lending to the Panamanian economy by sectors (US$m)

	1994	*1993*
Total	6,524	5,908
Public sector	1,104	1,185
Private sector	5,420	4,723
Finance & insurance companies	215	184
Agriculture	124	108
Cattle	144	117
Fisheries	25	17
Commerce	2,394	2,086
Industry	286	263
Housing	1,334	1,183
Construction	150	125
Consumer loans	748	640

Source: Panama Banking Association.

July 1990. Luis H. Moreno, who was BNP's general manager during the Endara government, presented 22 criminal charges for fraud, embezzlement and other irregular activities after he took over. The bank's equity was US$1.2 million negative, 35 per cent of the portfolio of loans to the private sector were non-performing, and cash and marketable securities represented 13.4 per cent of total deposits, a very low liquidity ratio by international standards. Re-valuation of the loan portfolio, cleaning up the balance sheet, restoration of confidence and the return of deposits and prudent management have produced a turnaround. Although its pre-tax profit in 1994 of US$30.1 million was lower than 1993's US$38.2 million, it was 47 per cent higher than the budgeted estimate. Total assets rose 5.7 per cent to US$2.6 billion and the liquidity ratio improved to 65.4 per cent from 58.9 per cent in 1993. Equity grew 18.8 per cent to US$189.8 million.

BNP is responsible for the clearing system which some banks complain is slower and more cumbersome than if the banks had their own system. BNP is fully computerising the system which will stay in its hands and be located in a separate building to be constructed.

The Caja de Ahorros has 37 branches and would have collapsed in 1988 had it been a privately owned bank. It took four years to restore its health but now it is in better shape. The Caja has been particularly aggressive in installing ATMs, and planned to double its network to 28 by the end of 1995 as well as open four new branches. This bank is theoretically a candidate for privatisation, but its managers believe that this will not be necessary as long as it continues to improve.

Probably the most aggressive and successful newcomer is Banco del Istmo, the third largest, whose business has grown considerably through judicious acquisitions. The bank was harassed during the downfall of the Noriega regime because of its links with the opposition. Samuel Lewis Galindo, one of the original owners, is the brother of Gabriel Lewis Galindo, the Foreign

Minister in the Pérez Balladares government who was ambassador to the United States at the time the Panama Canal Treaty was negotiated, and led the political struggle against Noriega from his US exile.

Founded in 1984, Istmo's first two branches were in rural Panama and it was not until it purchased Bank of Colombia in 1986 that it acquired a network in Panama City. In 1992 it acquired Banco Santander-Panama, the subsidiary of Spain's Banco Santander, which specialises in corporate business and renamed it Banco Mercantil del Istmo. Istmo's credit card business came from the purchase of Banco Sur and ended Chase Manhattan's virtual monopoly in Panama.

The Panamanian market has reached saturation point, though this may not prevent the establishment of more banks. The minimum paid-in capital requirement is still the US$1 million laid down in the 1970 law which is very low. The National Banking Commission does not look at an application unless the bank is prepared to put down at least US$3 million. Many bankers believe the minimum requirement should be increased to more than US$20 million. There are bound to be mergers.

Note

1. *Miami Herald*, 6 June 1994.

Chapter Six

Foreign debt

Panama began to normalise relations with its commercial bank creditors in May 1995 when it reached a Brady-style agreement in principle on restructuring some US$2 billion of defaulted debt and US$1.5 billion of overdue interest.[1] Interest and principal payments were suspended at the end of 1987 during the regime of General Manuel Antonio Noriega, which was severely battered by US economic sanctions (see Chapter 1) and heading for a deep recession. The deal was expected to be finalised in time for Brady bonds to be issued at the end of 1995 or early 1996. An International Monetary Fund (IMF) programme was also being negotiated to facilitate the Brady programme.

The agreement offers four options for the exchange of eligible debt: a Par Bond with below-market coupons; a Discount Bond with floating-rate coupons; an Interest Reduction Bond and a New Money Option (see below). Both the Par and the Discount Bonds have full principal collateral. All the bonds will be denominated in US dollars: in addition, a rolling-interest guarantee will be phased in, starting with the coverage of nine months of interest. By the second anniversary of the debt, 12 months of interest will be secured. Brazil is the only other Brady country to have a phase-in. The Discount Bond option carried a 45 per cent forgiveness element applicable to the face amount of the eligible debt.

Unlike other Brady agreements, in which creditors had to accept a mix of fixed- and floating-rate bonds with different maturities whether they wanted to or not, this agreement gives the banks more flexibility. Each of the options was freely available to creditors on a voluntary basis, and the options chosen will not be subject to reallocation. A debt-equity option was not possible because Panamanian legislation virtually prohibits the use of debt paper for privatisations.

The collateralised options are more onerous to Panama in the short term, since the collateral guarantees must be delivered by the closing date. In order to make the non-collateralised options more attractive to creditors – and minimise the cash outlay on the closing date – Panama and its bankers structured the conversion alternative so as to make the Interest Reduction Bonds (IRB) the most attractive option: the IRBs are to be issued in bearer form, while the Par and Discount Bonds will be issued in registered form.

Partial payments of eligible interest began to be made in cash at the rate of around US$2 million per month from January 1995 through the closing date, plus an additional payment of US$100 million at the closing date. Interest on eligible debt denominated in US dollars is calculated at US$ Libor plus 13/16 per cent per annum. Interest on non-US$ debt was among the remaining matters to be negotiated. After the cash payments, the remaining eligible interest should amount to around 66 per cent of the eligible debt and will be exchanged for past-due interest (PDI) bonds. The PDI bonds closely resemble the structure of the Ecuador PDI bonds. The most noteworthy feature of this structure is that Panama has the option to capitalise a portion of the accrued interest for the first six years. Panama will probably take advantage of the cash-flow relief provided by this option.

The deal was struck after many months of hard bargaining, as Panama held out for the best possible terms. Its total foreign debt of US$5.5 billion (78 per cent of GDP) at the end of 1994 gives the country one of the highest per capita debts in the world (US$2,115). Including domestic dollar debt, total debt is US$7 billion. The Endara government (1990–94) came close to a deal with commercial bank creditors towards the end of its term of office which resembled a "classic" Mexico-style Brady, in terms of debt reduction. But the incoming Balladares government indicated that the 1994 Ecuador deal set a precedent for Panama and it pushed for more favourable terms so that it has a little more leeway to allocate more funds to education, health and other welfare items. Also, the Balladares government had a relatively freer hand to negotiate a deal, as the next elections are not until 1998.

Exhibit 6.1

Brady bond debt service projections, 1996–2025 (US$m)

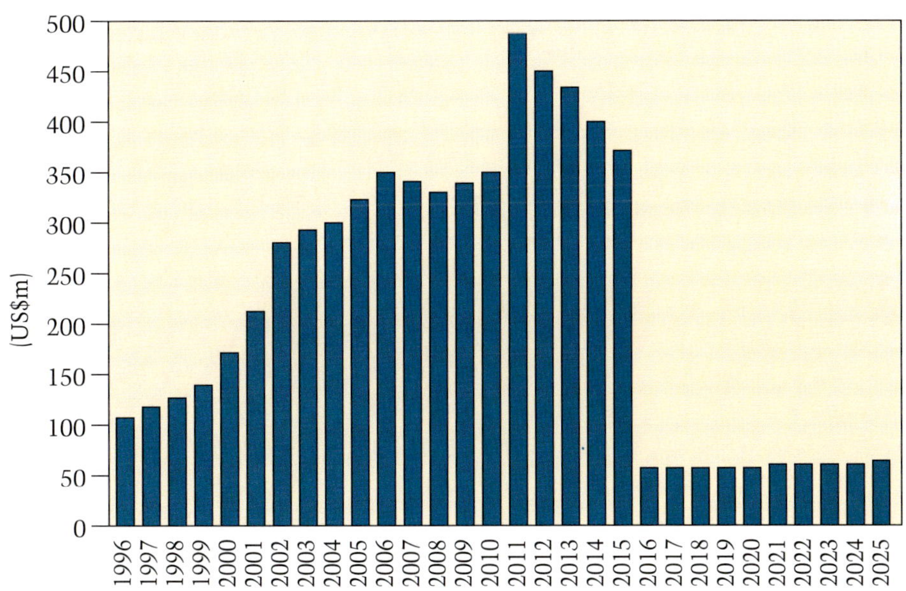

Assumes creditors swap 40% of their loans for par bonds, 40% for IRBs, and 20% for discount bonds.

Source: ING Securities.

Because the US dollar is Panama's currency, Panama's situation, unlike that of other Latin American debtors, boils down to the availability of government funds and not the availability of foreign exchange. The country's creditworthiness is similar to that of a local government, in which the key factor is the sustainability of a given fiscal policy in a given macroeconomic environment. Therefore, traditional yardsticks like the debt service ratio, which is a balance of payments indicator, are less useful for Panama than for other countries, which may have the local resources but lack the foreign exchange. The cost of servicing the commercial bank debt will be US$120–140 million a year for the first four years – which is fiscally manageable – and then it rises significantly. (See Exhibit 6.1).

The Endara government reached agreements to restructure debt owed to multilateral creditors, Paris Club creditors and external and domestic bond holders. In April 1994, the government restructured US$452 million of fixed and floating rate notes issued in US dollars, Ecus and yen. Payment of 25 per cent of past due interest arrears was made in cash. The agreement included an exchange of the principal into a new bond on a one-for-one basis plus 75 per cent of past due interest arrears with an eight-year maturity. The dollar and Ecu notes were exchanged for a new Eurodollar floating rate note paying interest semi-annually at 100 basis points over six-month Libor. The yen notes were exchanged for a new Euroyen note that carries a fixed coupon of 3.75 per cent paid semi-annually. In August 1994 Banco Nacional de Panamá (BNP) agreed to pay US$102 million in money market facilities owed to commercial banks which fell due between that month and November. The decision was controversial since the debt was originally included as part of the commercial bank obligations and was honoured before the remaining public sector commercial bank debt. The last government also restructured US$70 million of domestic bonds.

Panama, however, did not receive about US$200 million of the multilateral and US$44 million of the bilateral financing it had expected for 1994, because of non-compliance of the conditions necessary for the release of the

Exhibit 6.2

Central government fiscal accounts (US$m)

	1993	*1994*	*1995f*
Current revenues	1,352	1,367	1,504
Current expenditures	1,314	1,430	1,627
Debt service (including principal)	369	449	645
Education	287	307	312
Health	257	267	272
Capital expenditures	186	225	237
Balance	−148	−287	−361
Memo			
Central government balance/GDP (%)	−2.3	−4.1	−4.9
Public sector balance/GDP (%)	1.0	−1.1	−1.3

Source: Comptroller General's Office and ING Securities.

loans.

While the debt agreement will reduce Panama's foreign debt burden from 78 per cent of GDP in 1994 to an estimated 71 per cent at the end of 1995, the servicing of that debt will still consume a large portion of the Panamanian budget. In 1995, the central government's budget included US$645 million for external and domestic debt service, 35 per cent of cash expenditures. (See Exhibit 6.2). The reverted areas (see Chapter 10) could be used to reduce the country's debt burden via debt–equity swaps, but this course of action has been ruled out by the Privatisation Law of 1992 and the law incorporating ARI, the body responsible for the reverted areas.

The debt burden will severely constrain the government's flexibility in meeting the demands placed upon its scarce fiscal resources and leave no room for populist policies. President Balladares came to power promising an ambitious social investment programme and he could come under pressure to meet the promises more fully. The government plans to use the revenue generated by the reverted areas to capitalise a Social Investment Fund, but such funds had not amounted to much by 1995. As well as the spending pressures, important sources of revenue will decline – the withdrawal of US troops will result in the gradual loss of US$300–400 million in yearly income, and privatisations, assuming they are successful, will produce large one-off payments but the stream of income passed on every year will fall or disappear.

Note

1. Most of the details are drawn from the ING Capital's Emerging Markets Weekly Reports of 12 and 25 May 1995.

Panama Brady exchange options

Exchange of principal

Discount Bonds

Discount:	45 per cent.
Interest rate:	Six-month US dollar Libor + $\frac{13}{16}$ per cent per annum.
Tenor:	30 years.
Amortisation:	Bullet repayment at maturity.
Principal collateral:	Payment of principal upon maturity would be secured in full by the pledge of US Treasury zero-coupon bonds delivered on the closing date.
Interest collateral:	The payment of nine months of interest would be secured on a rolling basis by the pledge of cash or permitted investments delivered on the closing date. The Republic will pledge additional cash or permitted investments in two approximately equal annual instalments so that, on the second anniversary of the insurance of the Discount Bonds, the payment of 12 months of interest would be so secured.
Form:	Registered.

Par Bonds

Interest rate:	Year 1	3.00 per cent.
	Year 2	3.25 per cent.
	Year 3	3.50 per cent.
	Year 4	3.75 per cent.
	Year 5–6	4.25 per cent.
	Year 7–8	4.75 per cent.
	Year 9–10	5.25 per cent.
	Year 11–30	5.50 per cent.
Tenor:	30 years.	
Amortisation:	Bullet repayment at maturity.	
Principal collateral:	The payment of principal upon maturity would be secured in full by the pledge of US Treasury zero-coupon bonds delivered on the closing date.	
Interest collateral:	The payment of nine months of interest would be secured on a rolling basis by the pledge of cash or permitted investments delivered on the closing date. The Republic will pledge additional cash or permitted investments in three equal annual instalments so that, on the third anniversary of the issuance of the Par Bonds, the payment of 12 months of interest would be so secured.	
Form:	Registered.	

Interest Reduction Bonds

Interest rate:	Year 1	3.50 per cent.
	Year 2	3.75 per cent.
	Year 3	4.00 per cent.
	Year 4	4.25 per cent.
	Year 5	4.50 per cent.
	Year 6	4.75 per cent.
	Year 7	5.00 per cent.
	Year 8–18	Six-month US dollar Libor + $\frac{13}{16}$ per cent per annum.
Tenor:	18 years.	
Amortisation:	27 equal semi-annual instalments, commencing five years following issuance.	
Interest collateral:	Until the seventh anniversary after the closing date, the payment of six months of interest would be secured on a rolling basis by the pledge of cash or permitted investments delivered on the closing date.	
Form:	Bearer.	

New Money Option

Creditors who elect this option will receive Debt Conversion Bonds equal to the full face amount of principal tendered in the exchange, and will also commit to purchase an amount of New Money Bonds equal to 10 per cent of the Eligible Debt exchanged for Debt Conversion Bonds.

Debt Conversion Bonds

Interest rate	Year 1	4.50 per cent.
	Year 2–4	4.75 per cent.
	Year 5–7	5.75 per cent.
	Year 8–20	Six-month US dollar Libor + 13/16 per cent per annum.
Tenor:	20 years.	
Amortisation:	22 equal semi-annual instalments, commencing 9½ years following issuance.	
Form:	Bearer.	

New Money Bonds

Interest rate:	Six-month US dollar Libor + 13/16 per cent per annum.
Tenor:	15 years.
Amortisation:	16 equal semi-annual instalments, commencing 7½ years following issuance.
Form:	Bearer.

Exchange of past-due interest

Past-Due Interest Bonds

Interest rate:	Six-month US dollar Libor + 13/16 per cent per annum.	
Tenor:	20 years.	
Amortisation:	21 semi-annual instalments, commencing 10 years following issuance.	
	Instalments 1–8	2.00 per cent.
	Instalments 9–11	3.00 per cent.
	Instalments 12–21	7.50 per cent.
Capitalisation:	During the first six years from the closing, the Republic will have the option to capitalise a portion of accrued interest in an amount up to the difference (if positive) between six-month US dollar Libor + 13/16 per cent per annum and 4 per cent per annum.	
Form:	Bearer.	

Chapter Seven

Securities market

Equity market

Panama has a fledgling equity market today, but during the mid and late 19th century two world class projects were undertaken and both turned to the international capital markets. First, there was the construction of the Panama railroad and then the unsuccessful building of the Canal by the French engineer Ferdinand de Lesseps. Both the Panama Rail Road Company and the Compagnie Universelle du Canal Interocéanique de Panama were public companies. Both stocks traded frequently among Panamanians and foreign investors alike.

It was not until 1970 that the government of General Omar Torrijos provided the first comprehensive securities market legislation and the National Securities Commission (whose acronym in Spanish is CNV) was created, and 20 years later the Lilliputian Panama Stock Exchange (PSE) began to operate.

It is the only US dollar-based exchange in Latin America and the benefit of this was clearly driven home at the end of 1994 and in early 1995 when Panama hardly felt the so-called "tequila impact" – the fall-out from the meltdown of the Mexican currency which rocked many markets in the region. Use of the US dollar and Panama's location give the PSE potential to develop a niche regional role and become a "Luxembourg" in Latin America. For example, the cost of a US$10 million bond issue is around US$15,000 in Panama, much lower than in New York or London.

Only 13 shares from banks, breweries, insurance companies and conglomerates are regularly traded (see Exhibit 7.1). Only two foreign companies have listed securities on the PSE: Banco de Colombia and Label. The total trading volume of securities in 1994 was US$290 million, of which US$70 million were shares (see Exhibit 7.2).

Although still small, equity trading has been growing rapidly. Privatisations, particularly of Cemento Bayano in 1994 (sold for close to US$60 million), have had an enormous impact and but for them equity trading would have remained marginal. In 1993 equity trading was US$6.6 million and in 1992 a mere US$1.2 million. Equity trading accounted for 24 per cent of total turnover in 1994, up from 8.5 per cent in 1993 (see Exhibit 7.3). The bulk of trading was corporate bonds.

Exhibit 7.1

The five most actively traded shares on the Panama Stock Exchange, 1994

Ranking	*Company*	*Trading volume (US$)*
1	Coca Cola de Panamá	2,818,817
2	Financiera Automotriz	2,507,230
3	Empresa General de Inversiones	1,089,378
4	Cervecería Nacional	990,602
5	Capitales Nacionales	537,894

Source: Panama Stock Exchange.

Total market capitalisation grew from US$554.8 million at the end of 1992 to US$1.49 billion at the end of March 1995, of which US$737.7 million were equities (see Exhibit 7.4).

The trading system is open outcry. Brokers meet for business between 1100 and 1200 hours. All the trades are "lock in". Trade matching is accomplished on the trade date (T). Only the 17 members of the exchange (a seat costs US$100,000, the minimum capital requirement, and 250 shares in the PSE) can participate in the clearing and settlement system. The exchange uses three different rolling settlement periods: same-day settlement, which takes place before 1500 hours on the trade date; regular settlement, which takes place two business days after the trade date (T+2), and period settlement in which both parties agree on a future settlement date.

The exchange uses a combination of trade-for-trade and daily netting for the settlement of trades. For the settlement of the cash side, the exchange uses daily netting. Net buyers must deliver a single amount of money, and net sellers receive a net cash payment. Securities are settled on a trade-for-trade basis. Settlement involves the physical exchange of certificates and certified cheques and by early 1996, if all goes well, a central clearing, settlement and depository institution is scheduled to be operational. Some of the 17 members of the exchange, and Panamanian and foreign banks, offer custodial and management services. Securities will be dematerialised and settlement will take place at T+3 by electronic book entry. By 1996, trades are expected to settle at T+1. An order-driven screen-based trading system is planned for 1996.

Another prospective development is that since Panama's currency is the US dollar, the exchange plans to launch a Panamanian Depository Receipt, similar to the American Depository Receipt, and targeted at medium-size Latin American companies that want to tap a larger capital market but cannot pay for the cost of an Initial Public Offering (IPO) in the United States.

The exchange's general index is a weighted average market capitalisation index, based on the Paschee Method and using the methodology of the International Finance Corporation. The base date for the index is 31 December 1992 and it comprises 10 stocks. Commissions are negotiable and range from 0.5 per cent to 2 per cent.

The average price/earnings ratio in 1994 was 11 times (see Exhibit 7.5). The ratio is based on past earnings, which makes it more conservative.

Exhibit 7.2

Trading volume (US$m)

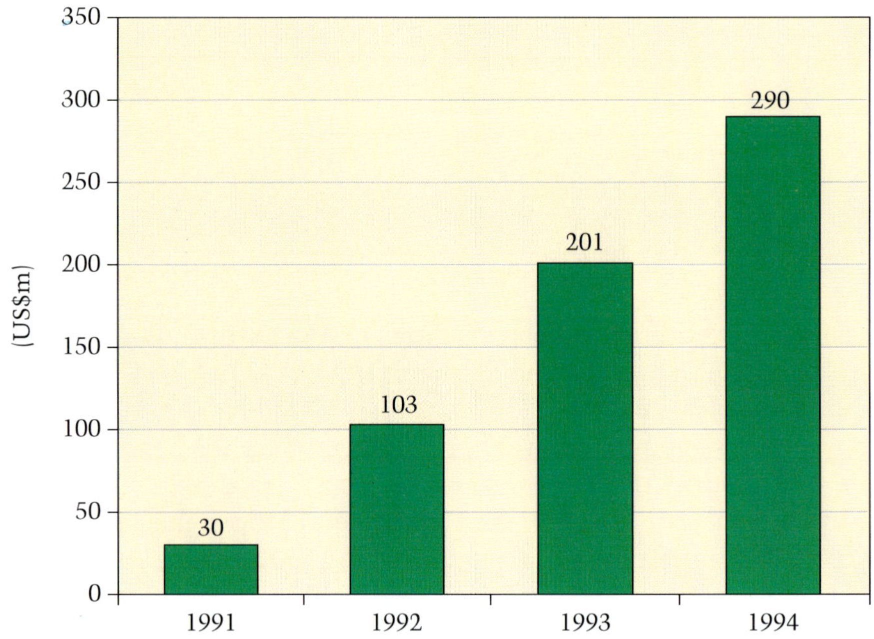

Source: Panama Stock Exchange.

Although still small, equity trading has been growing rapidly thanks largely to recent privatisations

Exhibit 7.3

Trading volumes (% breakdown)

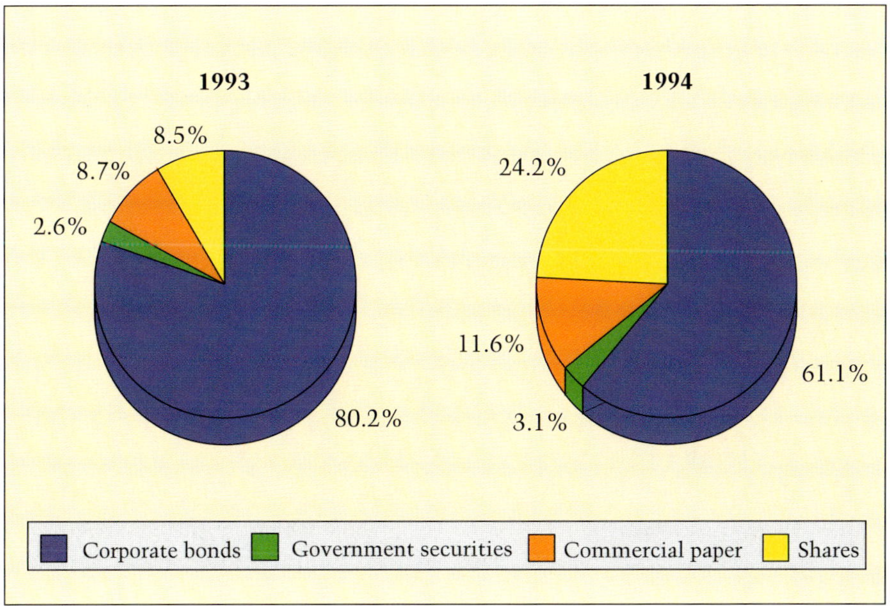

Source: Panama Stock Exchange.

Exhibit 7.4

Market capitalisation, March 1995

	US$m
Domestic equities	737.7
Foreign equities	63.9
Domestic debt	689.9
Other securities and derivatives	4.8
Total	1,496.3

Source: Panama Stock Exchange.

Exhibit 7.6

Commercial paper (US$m)

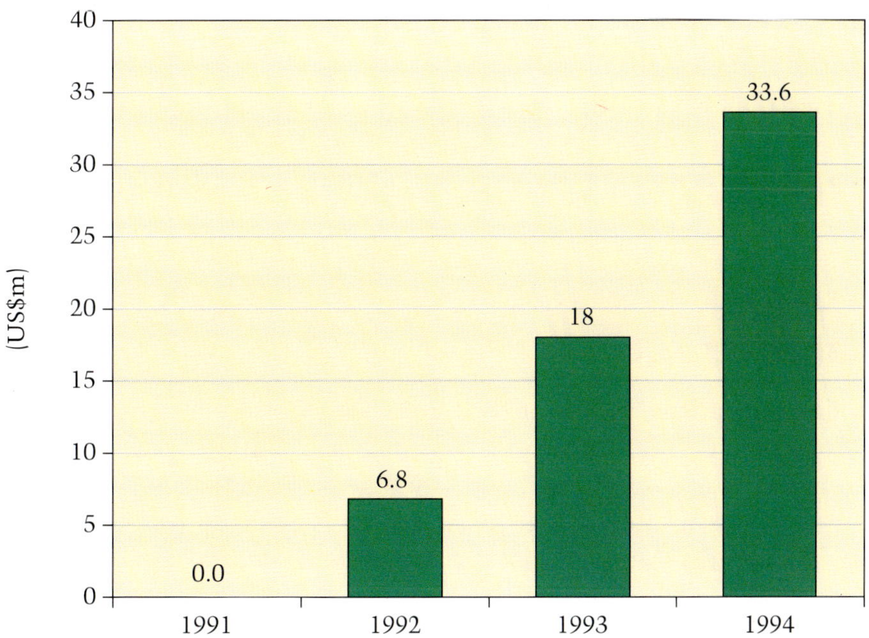

Source: Panama Stock Exchange.

Exhibit 7.5

Market data

	1992	*1993*	*1994*
Price/earnings ratio	6.75	6.30	11.01
Price/book value	1.02	1.26	1.78
Dividend yield (%)	5.40	5.56	2.80

Source: Panama Stock Exchange

Panama reached an agreement in principle with its commercial bank creditors in May 1995 and this increased demand for Panamanian paper.

The market value of domestic debt was US$689.9 million at the end of March 1995; there is no foreign debt traded through the PSE (there was US$15 million in 1992). With more than 100 banks, insurance companies and many other firms, the local debt market is quite active. The size of the secondary market at the end of 1994 was US$32.5 million. For an exotic paper, Panamanian debt is very liquid. Growth in commercial paper (see Exhibit 7.6) has been particularly strong.

Wall Street Securities, one of Panama's leading independent (i.e. non-bank) investment banking firms, launched the first Panama country fund in April 1995. The Panama Balanced Fund, a sub-fund of Interamerica's Fund Limited, incorporated under the laws of the Bahamas, is initially focusing on Panamanian corporate and government securities. The fund has a custodian agreement with Coutts apart from Panamanian assets which are the responsibility of Chase Manhattan in Panama City.

Regulations

The regulatory body is the National Securities Commission which has five members: the Minister of Commerce and Industry, the general manager of the Panama National Bank, and three representatives of the banking, industrial and commercial sectors. There are shareholder protection codes.

Anti-takeover rules

Panama has regulations governing attempts to acquire substantial blocks of voting stock in certain Panamanian companies. The purposes of decrees approved in 1977, 1985, 1986 and 1987 include ensuring adequate public disclosure in the case of offers which may lead to control, as well as protecting minority shareholders and promoting complete and accurate disclosure of transactions.

The decrees impose certain requirements when offers are made – by tender or otherwise – to acquire more than 5 per cent of any class of issued and outstanding equity security whose market value is more than US$5 million.

The requirements include refraining from acquiring any target company securities until the offer has been approved by a two-thirds shareholder vote, if the company's board of directors decides to put the question to shareholders.

Taxation

Income tax is only levied on income generated from domestic sources. Foreign income is not taxable, even if the transaction originated or was directed from Panama. Capital gains from the sale of securities registered with the National Securities Commission are tax free. Interest paid on debt securities (and bank deposits) is also tax free, provided the security is registered with the CNV and traded through a brokerage house authorised to operate in Panama. Dividends are subject to a 10 per cent withholding tax except when capitalised.

Chapter Eight

Privatisation

The public sector's share of the economy tripled between 1970 and 1990 to around 30 per cent of GDP. By the end of 1992 close to 161,000 people were employed in the public sector (one in every five jobholders). Jobs were created regardless of the need or budgetary constraints. The 1990–94 Endara government began a privatisation programme and also reduced employment as part of a reform of the public sector and this is being carried on by the Pérez Balladares administration.

The Endara government's programme for privatisation proceeded slowly and generated just over US$100 million (see Exhibit 8.1). First off the mark was the Hotel Taboga which was sold for US$560,000. The largest privatisation so far has been Cemento Bayano, Panama's leading cement producer (50 per cent market share) which was bought in September 1994 by Cementos Mexicanos, Mexico's largest cement producer and the world's fourth biggest, for US$59.6 million. Air Panama was sold but the concession was disolved because of problems between workers and the new management.

Attempts to begin the partial privatisation of the National Telecommunications Institute (INTEL), the jewel in the state's crown, under the Endara government came to nothing because of fierce opposition from

Exhibit 8.1

Companies privatised 1990–94

Company	*Date*	*Price*
Hotel Taboga	1990	US$560,000
Hotel Washington	1991	US$2 million
Citricos de Chiriquí (citric fruits)	1993	US$5.6 million
La Compañía de Palma Aceitera (palm oil)	1993	US$6.0 million
Air Panama (concession disolved by mutual agreement)	1993	
Manzanillo-Cocosolo Port	1993	US$8 million (yearly)
Corporación Bananera del Atlántico (bananas)	1994	US$6.8 million
Cemento Bayano	1994	US$59.6 million

Source: ProPrivat.

Exhibit 8.2

Impact of lower international telephone charges (US$m)

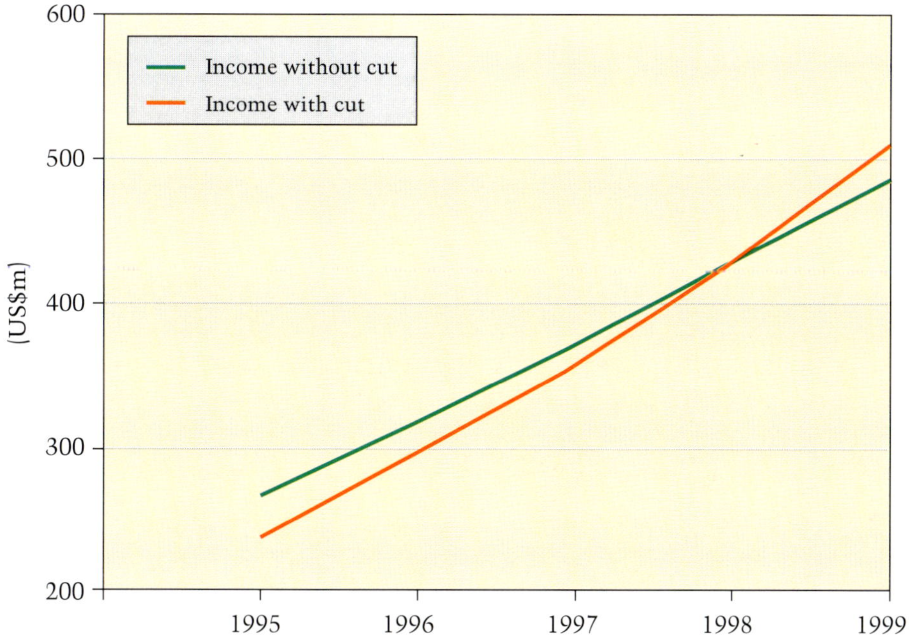

Source: INTEL.

workers. Legislation was approved in early 1995 turning INTEL into a limited company, and the regulatory framework for the telecommunications sector was expected to be approved by the end of the year, thereby paving the way for privatisation of 49 per cent of the company probably in early 1996. Some INTEL officials believe the state could obtain as much as US$1 billion from the privatisation. Prospective buyers, however, may be discouraged by the fact that the 2 per cent of INTEL that will be reserved for workers will be held in a trust whose voting rights will be retained by the government, along with the 49 per cent stake it will keep. The government will thus maintain a majority of the shareholders' voting rights. The government granted the first cellular telephone licence (band A) in 1995 and a second one (band B) could be linked to the INTEL privatisation or be awarded at the same time as band A. Panama and Haiti are the only two countries in the Western hemisphere that do not have mobile telephones and this has generated a flourishing industry in radio phones.

The other area where privatisation is taking place, apart from the plans for the land and buildings reverting to Panama (see Chapter 10) under the canal treaties, is in the electricity sector. The Hydroelectric and Electric Energy Resources Institute (IRHE) is allowed to grant concessions to private sector companies to generate between them a maximum of 20 per cent of its total power generation. This will have a beneficial impact on the tourism industry and on light manufacturing operations in remote areas. The government was also reviewing the terms of reference for the Esti hydroelectric project in

Chiriquí province which the Endara government put out to tender, but there were only two bids and it was cancelled. The Esti project has been rescheduled for 2001 and a thermal plant will be put out to tender to fill the energy gap. The government was also planning in 1995 to grant a concession for operating or administering the national racetrack and to privatise the Atlapa convention centre in Panama City.

The World Bank[1] pointed out that despite high electricity tariffs, IRHE "faces extremely difficult financial problems, because of bad management practices and high operating costs. The high operating costs resulted from over-employment, poor commercial practices, and corrupt practices".

The average 1990 tariff of 11.7 US cents/kWh was 40 per cent higher than the long-run marginal cost. The power generation system deteriorated during the Noriega regime, especially during the 1987–89 crisis, because of a lack of spare parts and postponement of maintenance. Electricity losses are estimated at around one-quarter of net generation.

INTEL

As both the operator and regulator, INTEL's monopoly has enabled it to get away with providing a bad public service for a long time and be a cash cow for the government during the 1987–89 political crisis. Privatisation will change this. INTEL prohibited other companies from providing even the complementary services it did not offer (such as cellular telephones).

INTEL had 270,000 lines in 1994 and a waiting list of 60,000. With 11 lines per 100 inhabitants, Panama compares quite well with other Latin American countries, but if it aspires to be a more developed nation it should have around 25. The company's level of labour efficiency is very low: INTEL has 14 employees for each 1,000 lines, double the Central American average. According to the World Bank, an efficient company has 10 employees or fewer per 1,000 lines, and the ratio in the United States is four employees per 1,000 lines. The company must either get rid of many workers or considerably increase the number of lines without hiring new employees. An inordinate proportion of INTEL's income – US$160 million out of a budgeted total of US$280 million in 1994 – comes from international calls whose tariffs are very high and are one factor that makes the country unattractive for foreign investors. INTEL says it lost US$30 million between 1991 and 1994 through "call-back" pirate operations (sophisticated technology used to hook up to the dialling tone of the country with whom the caller is communicating, which is much cheaper). INTEL believes that a cut in international tariffs would generate more revenue by 1999 than keeping the present rates as it would encourage greater use (see Exhibit 8.2).

Domestic tariffs are very low. The standing charge in 1995 was still only US$10.50 and there is a flat rate charge of 10 US cents per minute to almost all areas.

Although just over half of the lines are digital, INTEL has done little to promote such technologies as touchtone telephones. During peak hours

(0900–1600) callers often have to wait for a dialling tone, they are cut off during the call or they cannot get a line. Faults per line and fault repair time are twice as high as in efficient companies. Around 60 per cent of INTEL's fleet of vehicles are more than five years old and many need to be replaced urgently. Juan Porras, INTEL's general manager, lashed out at INTEL's inefficiency after taking up his post in 1994 when he said that "in an activity that today works at the speed of light, INTEL operates at the speed of the state bureaucracy".

As the state's most profitable company, INTEL was milked during the Noriega regime for a large contribution to the budget, to the detriment of much needed investment. INTEL needs to invest at least US$120 million a year and in 1994 invested around US$80 million.

The computer system for billing customers is antiquated (bills for some long-distance calls take up to four months to arrive) and customers cannot query items over the phone: they have personally to go to INTEL's offices. INTEL's workers also waste time: there is no communications system for engineers repairing and installing lines to keep in touch with their head office, so they have to keep on touching base to receive new instructions.

Note

1. World Bank report on Panama, 30 January 1992, p. 14.

Chapter Nine

The Colón Free Zone

Nowhere are the contrasts more striking between impoverished Panama and bustling business than in the Atlantic Coast port of Colón, home of the largest free trade zone in the Americas and the second biggest in the world after Hong Kong. Protected from the surrounding squalor by high walls and security guards, the Colón Free Zone, a showpiece of the economy, is an island of materialism in a sea of unemployment, poverty and crime (Colón's rates are the highest in Panama).

The crowded narrow streets of the Zone offer the latest in Asian technology and European fashion. On the other side of the wall ragged children run barefoot across unswept streets and in the decaying inner areas of Colón the largely black population live in dilapidated wooden and packing-case shacks and barracks put up early this century to house the workers that dug the Panama Canal.

Business (imports and re-exports) more than doubled to US$10.5 billion between 1989 and 1994 (see Exhibit 9.1) and the Zone's contribution to GDP

Exhibit 9.1

Imports and re-exports, 1984–95 (US$bn)

	Imports	*Re-exports*
1984	1.33	1.53
1985	1.58	1.78
1986	1.93	2.18
1987	2.00	2.27
1988	1.84	2.11
1989	2.27	2.36
1990	2.67	3.00
1991	3.68	3.95
1992	4.36	4.82
1993	4.49	5.15
1994	4.95	5.61
1995*	5.50	6.22

*Estimated.
Source: Comptroller General's Office and Colón Free Zone.

Exhibit 9.2

Re-exports, first half of 1994 and 1995 (US$m)

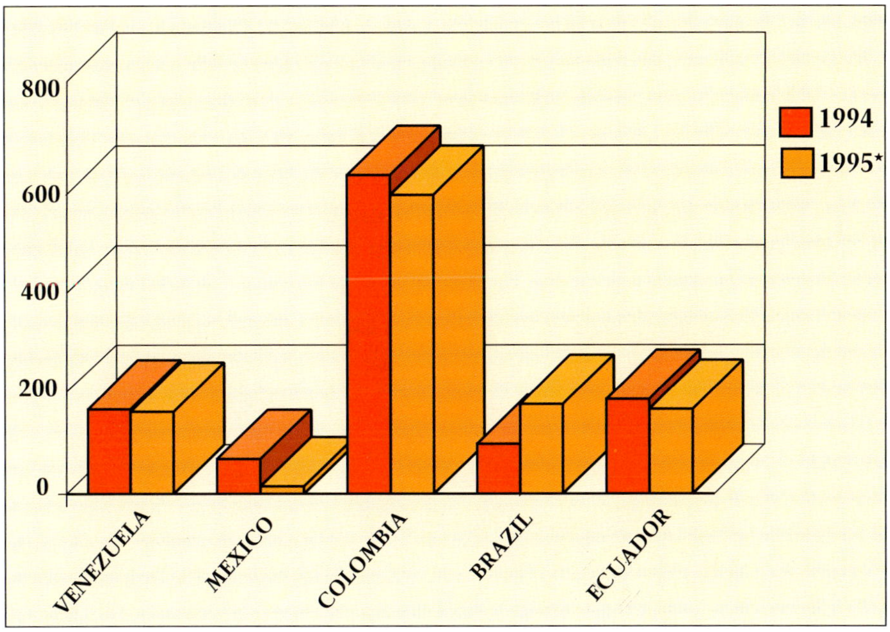

*1995 figures until 14 June.
Source: Colón Free Zone.

Exhibit 9.3

Investment in construction, 1989–94 (US$m)

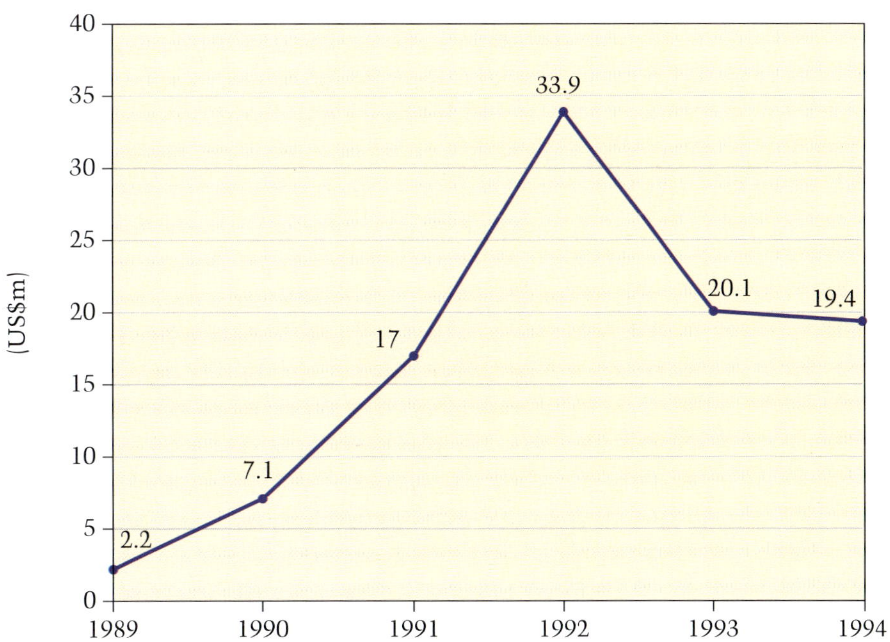

Source: Colón Free Zone.

(9.2 per cent in 1994, up from 4 per cent in 1987) is now more than the canal's. Along with the construction boom in Panama City, the Zone has been the main motor of Panama's growth since 1990. The 12,200 people employed in the 202-hectare Zone contribute almost as much to the economy as the 180,000 people working in the agricultural and fisheries sector. The Zone is so overcrowded that expansion is taking place on land reclaimed from the sea.

Some 1,500 companies (980 have physical premises and 520 are represented by agents) take advantage of the lack of import and export duties to sell everything from cars to perfumes, clothing, computers and electronic equipment. Goods are imported, chiefly from Hong Kong, Japan, the United States and South Korea and re-exported, principally to Latin American countries (see Exhibit 9.2). The biggest market is neighbouring Colombia. The number of visitors has grown from just over 40,000 in 1989 to around 100,000 in 1995. Investment in construction peaked at close to US$34 million in 1992 (see Exhibit 9.3).

Reasons for success

Established in 1948, the Zone's success is due to Panama's location at the cross-roads of the world, the fact that the US dollar is the legal tender, a large banking centre on its doorstep, a developed insurance and reinsurance industry, not very onerous business requirements and, increasingly, to the strong growth in several Latin American countries. Colón has regained the glory that once belonged to nearby Portobelo which, until the middle of the 18th century, was a major trading centre in the New World.

When the Zone was established, it was a Mecca of trade liberalisation in an area dominated by trade protection. Many users feared that as Latin America embraced economic reform, dismantling trade barriers and opening up markets, this would sound a death knell for the Zone. The reverse has happened: Latin America's trade reforms have helped to spur business. This was particularly true in 1991 and 1992. The Zone is an important wholesale site for middle to small buyers as they can fill a container with a wide range of goods without the need to buy large quantities that put a burden on their inventory.

The World Bank singled out other attractions in its 1985 report on Panama.

> The Zone links producers in North America, the Far East and Europe with the Latin American market, offering a variety of services in addition to mere commercial intermediation. Several of the larger firms' links with producers, especially in the Far East and Europe, are long established and they easily obtain credit from them. This, together with their own financial strength, allows them in turn to extend substantial credit to Latin American importers who would likely be obliged to prepay any direct purchases. Moreover, Panama's strict banking secrecy extends to the Zone and, together with a tradition of mercantile discretion, provides an attractive environment.

Some 5 per cent of the deposits in the banking system come from the Zone and around 10 per cent of loans go to it.

The Zone has held its own very well against Miami which offers other advantages over Panama: the ability to provide direct retailing services to the US market, a vastly superior transport infrastructure and cheaper, more efficient auxiliary services, particularly utilities and telecommunications. Miami's airport, the gateway to Latin America, and the city's port have provided springboards for growth in its trade zones.

Operating in the Zone

There are four ways in which a company can operate in the Colón Zone:

(1) Leasing lots on which the company builds a warehouse or other facilities. The land lease arrangements are granted for a minimum of 5 years and a maximum of 20. The cost of the lease in 1995 was US$0.50 per square metre per month in the Colón area, US$0.35 in France Field (now joined to the main area by a bridge) and US$0.20 in undeveloped areas. Alternatively, the Zone can lease its own building space to companies. The respective costs are US$2.40 per square metre per month in the Colón area, US$1.75 in France Field and US$1.65 in Coco Solo.

(2) Purchasing an existing facility from the Zone Administration.

(3) Reach an agreement with a company already established in the Zone as the operator's representative. The cost of this service is set by mutual agreement between the parties concerned. Representation agreements are subject to the approval of the Zone Administration.

(4) Leasing a warehouse operated by the Zone Administration. The firm receives its goods and stores them like any other company there. There are no fixed costs and the payment of the services is based on the weight or volume of the goods stored (0.5 per cent of the FOB value of the goods). Representation is an advantageous system for those beginning operations and not wishing to incur operating expenses. Companies operating in the Zone have to employ a minimum of five local employees and export a minimum of 60 per cent of their goods.

Companies are engaged in four types of sales operations:

(1) Foreign trade operations, involving the re-export of goods from warehouses.

(2) Internal trade operations, consisting of sales to clients in Panama.

(3) Direct sales made to foreign clients which are shipped from the manufacturing sources without physically arriving in the Zone.

(4) Transfer operations, in which sales are made to other Zone firms.

Firms in the Zone have long enjoyed the status of a privileged élite, and when the government moved in the middle of 1995 to combat the widespread tax fraud there by trying to levy a 1.5 per cent tax on the CIF value of goods entering the Zone it stirred up such a hornets' nest of complaints that it also backed down and had to settle for a less ambitious and more complicated tax formula.

The 1.5 per cent tax would have been more difficult to avoid and also would have discouraged laundering of drugs money. A favourite technique used by some money-laundering companies is to over-invoice goods, while traditional tax fraud relies on under-invoicing.

In 1991 two professors at Miami University investigating free trade zones found that razor blades made in Israel, for example, could be bought for 9 cents each on the open market while they were exported from the Colón Free Zone at US$29.35 each.

The 1.5 per cent tax was replaced by a single 15 per cent tax on exports and re-exports which is paid in advance on the basis of the previous year's exports and using a graduated scale. The previous tax varied between 2.5 per cent and 8.5 per cent. The table presented by the Colón Free Zone Users' Association was regarded as too low by the government and the tax rates were increased: firms suggested an advance tax payment of US$7,000, for example, for exports up to US$2 million and the government increased it to US$8,500. The top end was raised to US$500,000 for export orders worth over US$120 million from the firms' proposal of US$240,000 on orders of more than US$80 million. Under the new system the government will collect an estimated US$42 million a year compared with the originally envisaged amount of US$60–70 million, but it is an improvement, although far from sufficient for Colón's needs outside the Zone.

Domestic transactions are taxed at a single rate of 30 per cent (the same rate applies to the rest of the country).

The Zone's eyes are now set on becoming much more of a distribution centre which would centralise goods from the rest of the world for export. This strategy is part of the plan to enhance Panama's maritime sector, particularly within the context of the American Hemisphere Free Trade Market planned for 2005. Victoria Figge, general manager of the Zone Administration, visited Hong Kong in January 1995 and told businessmen there that as the biggest import market Hong Kong could do more to use the Zone to reach consumers "from Alaska to the tip of South America". There is, for example, scope for more assembly plants in the Zone. Attempts over the past decade to promote the Zone as a base for the manufacture of light industrial products such as electronic assembly, precision instruments, toys, cosmetics, etc have not been very successful. There are, however, some export-oriented clothing producers. Equally, Latin American countries could centralise their goods in the Zone and use it as a springboard for exporting to Europe and the Far East.

Need for further reform

However, before this can happen infrastructure needs to be improved and the Zone has to continue to clean up its image as a pivotal place for drug trafficking and money laundering, largely developed during the regime of General Noriega.

A major breakthrough on the infrastructure front came in January 1995 when the government awarded the contract for building a toll road between Panama City and Colón. The current 80-kilometre road, strewn with potholes, is the bane of commuters' lives. Very few people who work in the Zone live in Colón; many commute from Panama City. There are also plans to privatise the railway between Panama City and Colón, which stopped moving passengers after it was transferred to Panama by the US government in 1979 and fell into a greater state of disrepair. If successful, such a move would have a big impact, as would conversion of the airport at France Field, built during World War II, into an international cargo airport. A ferry service between Colón and Colombia began in 1994. The Zone will also benefit from the privatisation of INTEL, the telecommunications company, and from privatisation of the Cristobal port at Colón.

The fight against drug trafficking and money laundering is more difficult. Security has been tightened and US-trained sniffer dogs are employed to hunt for drugs in containers. The Users' Association adopted a code of ethics in 1994, and the government body that administers the Zone is being much more stringent about vetting new companies that want to set up and checking the credentials of firms already there. The Zone is applying the same "get to know your client" policy as the banking sector in Panama City. Three bank references, not only one, are now required for opening a business, and information is requested on the directors and legal representative of the company and not just the owner. The lax regulations in the past were got around by paying bribes and the dynamic Victoria Figge has also moved to stamp out this practice. The operating permit costs US$1,200; some companies paid up to US$100,000 in the past. Several companies have been closed down. Responding to criticism made to her in private that press coverage of closures was damaging the Zone's image, she told the Users Association in November 1994, "It is not the administration's statements or press release that are responsible for the bad image but the years of impunity which have earned the discredit of the national and international community."

Probably the most controversial decision taken by the government was to ban all service companies from the Zone and require all those already there to move out by 1996. Although the laws governing the Zone do not allow service companies, over the years a large number of banks, restaurants, travel agents and insurance companies have managed to establish themselves. The Users' Association was up in arms in 1995 and was fighting the decision through the courts. It is estimated that more than 80 companies are affected. Machines to take bank deposits would be allowed, but otherwise all service-related business would have to be conducted outside the Zone if the government does not give in to pressure from the Users' Association. By July no bank had made any effort to relocate and it was therefore impossible to meet the December deadline to open their operations outside the Zone. It would appear that the government would have to back down.

The move is a central plank in the government's policy of promoting economic development in the rest of Colón which has been ignored and abandoned by successive administrations who have done little more than throw populist promises at the town.

Colón is widely considered a "tinder box" that will explode one day unless something is done. Its crime rate rose twelve-fold between 1989 and 1993 when 66 in every 1,000 inhabitants were arrested by the police, more than double the rate in Panama City. Colón's infant mortality rate in 1993 was 28 per 1,000 live births, as against 17 in Panama. "For many people the Zone has stopped being of Colón and for Colón and has become something which is in Colón. And this has to stop", President Pérez Balladares told a meeting in Colón at the end of 1994. Many Panamanians consider Colón a shameful blot on the national landscape.

The government hopes the service companies will relocate in the centre of Colón, but many analysts believe they will simply close up shop or move to Panama City. Security measures and a minimum of infrastructure in Colón are needed if the move is to be successful. If service companies do move they would act as a catalyst for the development of commerce and Colón would have a chance to climb out of its slum. An important spin-off from this would be that more people who work in the Zone would be encouraged to live in Colón which, in turn, would also spur development.

The government is investing US$20 million in providing homes for 2,744 families which, in the words of President Pérez Balladares, would not be "four walls for dwarfs or pygmies". More schools are to be built.

Users are also upset by the government's attempts to fight the massive tax fraud in the Zone, potentially a major source of revenue. In 1995 the government introduced a 1.5 per cent tax on the CIF value of imported goods entering the Zone. This is much more difficult to evade and is collected in advance against the 8.5 per cent corporate tax on income derived from export sales. Again users wheeled out the argument that the government would kill the goose that lays the golden egg.

A forewarning of what could happen to Colón if users do not become less greedy and the government does not invest in the town came after the US invasion of Panama in 1989 when mobs looted the ports, but not the heavily guarded Zone. And in 1991 MODESCO, a movement of unemployed people which still exists, led riots.

Chapter Ten

The canal

Noon on 31 December 1999 will be an historic moment for Panama. At that time control of the management, operation, maintenance and protection of the Panama Canal will be transferred from the US government to the government of Panama after 86 years of US dominance.[1] By then all US troops stationed in the country must have departed and the military bases will belong to Panama.

The handover is an emotionally charged issue: the canal's history goes back to the birth of Panama as a nation (see Chapter 1). Transfer of the canal, which accounts for nearly 9 per cent of GDP and after the banana industry employs more Panamanians than any other single activity, represents a unique opportunity to stimulate Panama's economic development and partially offset the loss of income from the closure of US bases. But, by the same token, the handover puts a tremendous responsibility onto the shoulders of Panama and they are not, nor can they be expected to be, as broad as those of the world's most powerful nation. Some canal users are already concerned about the transfer as they are concerned about the future safety, efficiency and cost effectiveness of the waterway. However warranted or unwarranted the fears may be, the government knows it cannot afford to generate fears in the international trade and shipping communities as they want to be completely assured that for ships, at least, the transfer will make no difference. Otherwise they will seek alternative routes. And for the United States the canal is a symbol of its ability to live up to its international commitments. A smooth transition is in everyone's interests.

The Panama Canal Commission (PCC), the US government agency that operates the canal, will cease to exist at the end of 1999 and the body of laws under which it operates will cease to be valid. All canal employees (some 7,500 in 1995, only 800 of whom are US citizens) will cease to be employed by the PCC and the canal will begin to operate under the laws of the new Panamanian organisation. A major step was taken in November 1994 when the Panamanian Legislative Assembly approved a constitutional addition that set up a politically independent body, known as the Panama Canal Authority, to run the canal. This sent a positive message to the international community as it established the general framework for the canal's administration and operations; the Legislative Assembly is constrained as any organic law that affects the canal is subjected to tests of constitutionality. Although the supervising

Exhibit 10.1

Total oceangoing transits (1915–94)

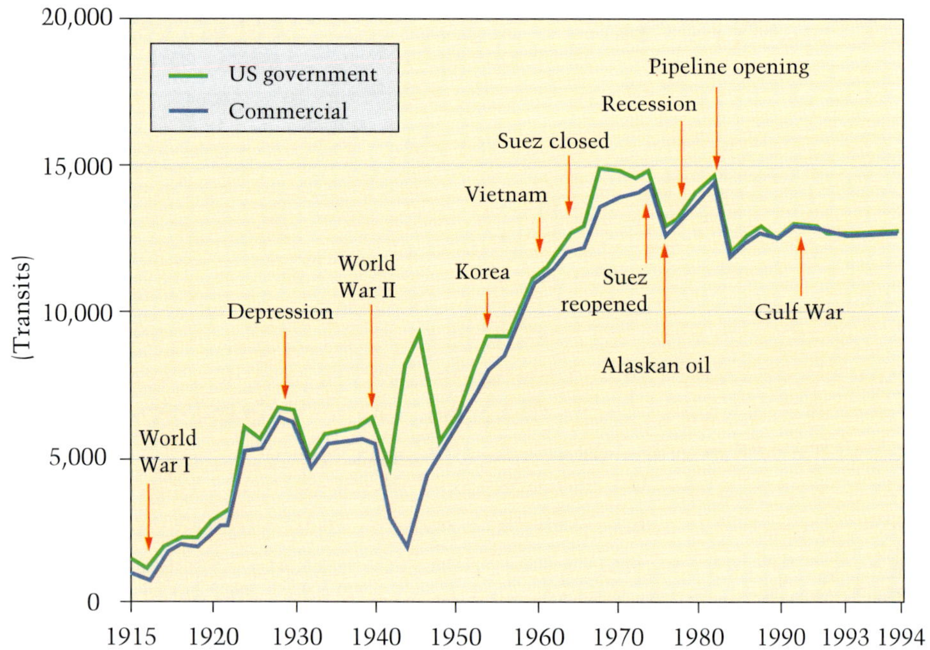

Source: Panama Canal Commission.

Exhibit 10.2

Oceangoing transits, 100 feet beam and over, 1965–94

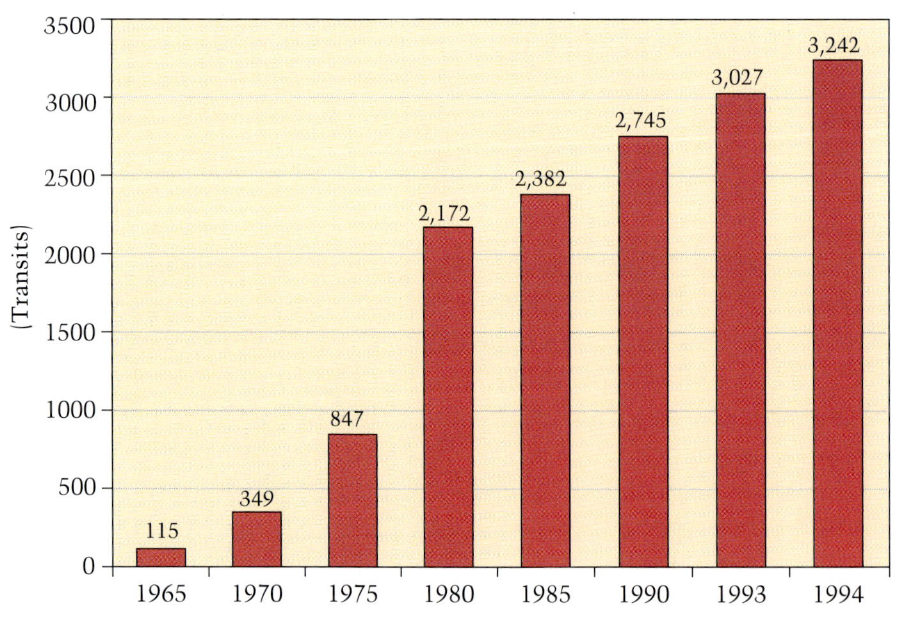

Source: Panama Canal Commission.

Exhibit 10.3

Average Panama Canal net tonnage (oceangoing commercial vessels)

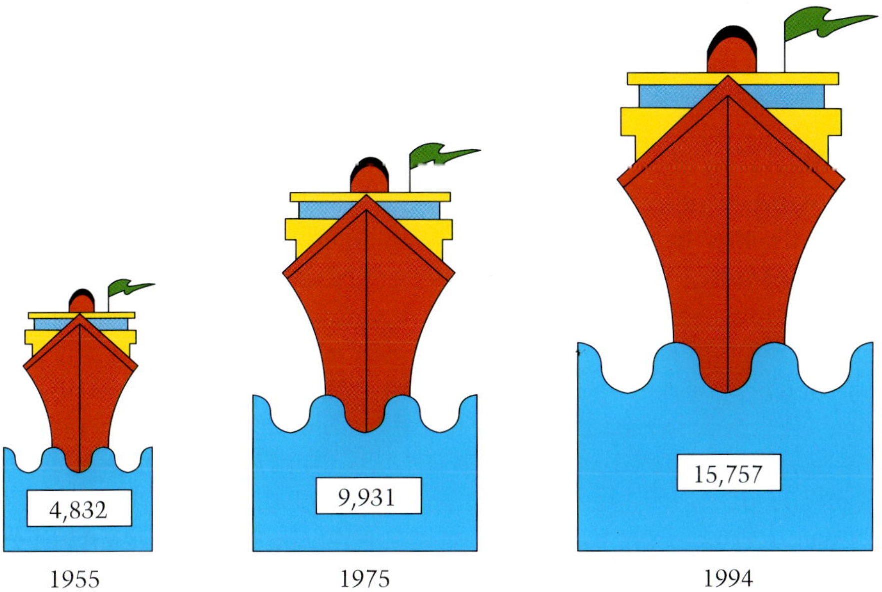

Source: Panama Canal Commission.

Exhibit 10.4

Principal commodity groups shipped through the Canal, 1994

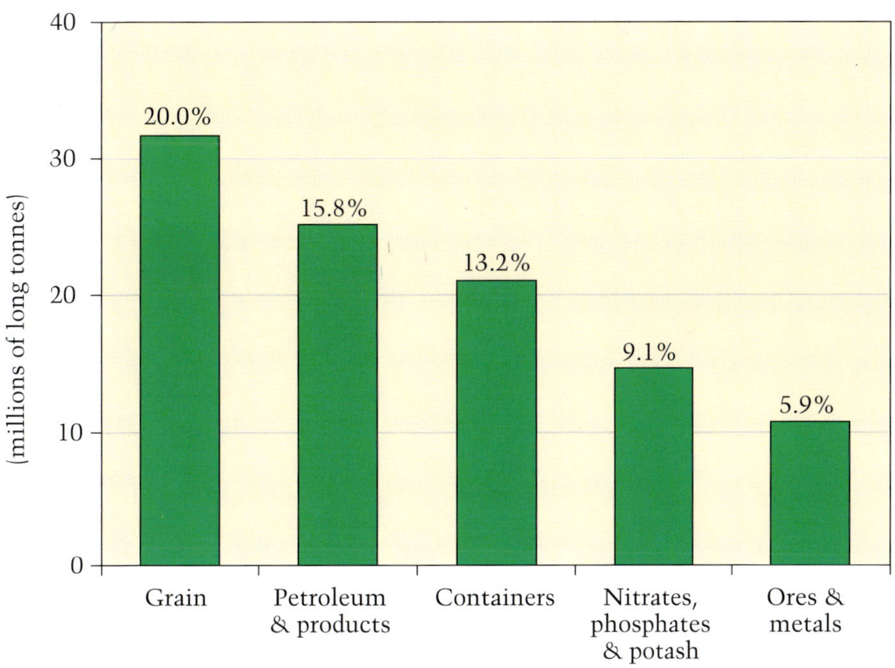

Source: Panama Canal Commission.

governments and the legal foundations will change, the structure of the Panama Canal Commission itself will continue with only those changes necessary to accommodate the new operational environment and Panamanian legal requirements.

The constitutional addition also brought relief to the canal's Panamanian employees who were concerned that the new body would be as politicised as some other parts of the civil service and that their terms and conditions of employment could be less favourable. But regulations for the Panama Canal Authority have still to be issued and many other decisions of great political sensitivity have to be tackled between now and the year 2000, and time is running out. Some require close co-ordination between the US and Panamanian governments. Key issues include: labour-management relations (for example whether to continue the present wage system based on US salaries or modify it to obtain savings), environmental policy (Panama does not yet have the necessary environmental regulations to safeguard the canal), the financial management structure, the tolls policy (maximising revenues or maximising traffic) and the canal's role in national economic development. A vital area is that the canal is not allowed to become a cash cow, like INTEL, the state telecommunications company, was to the detriment of its upkeep.

The concerns in the international shipping community about the future efficiency of the canal stem from the history of previous transfers of assets which some view as harbingers of the post-handover era. Past experience shows the vital importance of careful and early planning during a transition period leading to the transfer of operations. The most often cited example of the lack of planning and the lack of proper legislation for assuring successful utilisation of transferred assets is the Panama railroad between Balboa and Colón (opened in 1855), which was handed over to Panama in 1979. The railroad facilities were old and in need of rehabilitation at the time of the transfer, but despite this good passenger levels were maintained through cross-subsidies. The company was losing between US$1 and US$3.5 million annually in the immediate years before the transfer. When Panama received the railroad it was not prepared to undertake the required maintenance of the railroad and only moves freight, but remains a money-losing operation.

The ports in the canal area were also transferred in 1979 and, while they have remained profitable, users consider the prices high and the service levels in need of improvement (Cristobal at Colón is to be privatised). The 1979 transfers were characterised by problems that would be disastrous for an operation as important as the canal: employees going from one administrative system to up to six personnel systems; an exodus of management expertise, a lack of a pre-arranged spare parts supply pipeline and inadequate planning to assure continuing preventive maintenance and capital improvement programmes.

Canal traffic and tolls revenue improved notably in FY 1994, reversing a two-year declining trend. (The FY runs from 1 October to 30 September.) Thanks primarily to the upturn in the US economy, the sustained growth of the Pacific Rim newly industrialised economies and strong growth of some South American economies, oceangoing commercial cargo increased 8.1 per cent to 170.5 million long tonnes, the highest volume since 1982. A total of

12,478 transits, 12,337 of which were commercial (the rest were vessels owned or operated by the US government), or an average of 34.2 a day, were made (see Exhibit 10.1), 1.8 per cent higher than in FY 1993. Net tonnage rose 4.1 per cent to 195.6 million tonnes, the highest after the 1982 historical peak of 203.7 million tonnes.

The average size of commercial vessels also continued to increase, an unbroken trend. Transits by vessels with beams of 100 feet and over rose 7.1 per cent to 3,242 transits and they accounted for 26 per cent of total transits (see Exhibit 10.2). Accordingly, the average ship size in terms of net tonnage increased to 15,757 from 15,430 in FY 1993 (see Exhibit 10.3).

These upward trends continued in FY 1995. In the first half of FY 1995 the number of transits rose 8.1 per cent to 6,770 (37.2 a day). Commercial cargo grew 9.8 per cent to 93.1 million long tonnes and net tonnage rose 7.3 per cent to 106.9 million. Average net tonnage was 15,876, slightly down on the 15,976 registered in the first half of FY 1994.

Tolls revenue in FY 1994 was a record US$419.2 million, 4.6 per cent more than in FY 1993, and it looked as if this would be broken again in FY 1995. Tolls revenue in the first half was up 7.2 per cent at US$229 million.

Grains continued to be the leading commodity group shipped through the canal (see Exhibit 10.4). The 2 per cent increase in FY 1994 to 34.1 million long tonnes was solely due to a big jump in US exports of wheat to the Far East, mainly to China, and to North Africa, mostly to Egypt. Total wheat tonnage rose 32.3 per cent to 7.7 million long tonnes (shipment to North Africa rose 181.1 per cent to 1.8 million long tonnes). Corn tonnage, however, which is the largest component of the group, declined a fraction to 16 million tonnes, partly because of the flooding that hit the US Midwest harvest during the spring of 1993 and declining US shipments to Japan. Shipments of petroleum and products increased for the third year running. Crude oil flows went up 13.5 per cent to 9.8 million tonnes, mostly due to increases in Ecuadorean, Venezuelan and west coast Colombian oil.

The dominant trade route in canal traffic continued to be the US East Coast–Far East, which accounted for 29.4 per cent of total commercial cargo passing through the waterway (see Exhibit 10.5).

Although the Panama Canal's share of international seaborne trade has gradually declined over the years to less than 4 per cent (12 per cent of US trade), many countries are highly dependent on the waterway. For example, over half of all Ecuador's imports and exports pass through the canal, as does some 40 per cent of both Chile's and Peru's international trade. Without the canal, a large share of west coast South American trade would probably lose its competitive position and stop moving. Two-thirds of Ecuador's banana exports move through the canal and this is an industry upon which up to 500,000 people depend. A banana ship that leaves Ecuador for Europe saves some 5,000 miles. Unlike the United States, the largest user (14 per cent of all its international seaborne trade passed through the canal in 1992), which could adjust, over a period of time, to a closure of the canal, though it would have a major impact on some businesses in the eastern region, Latin American countries and Japan, to some extent, do not have readily available alternatives in the

Exhibit 10.5

Cargo by trade routes, 1993 and 1994 (millions of long tonnes)

	1993	*1994*
US east coast–Asia	72.1	69.6
Europe–US west coast and Canada	15.2	13.7
US east coast–west coast South America	14.9	10.6
West coast South America–Europe	9.8	8.5
Other	58.5	55.3
Total	170.5	157.7

Source: Panama Canal Commission.

event of a disruption. Latin America, where trade liberalisation is sweeping through the region, would be hard hit. While less than 5 per cent of Japan's total trade moves through the canal, the waterway is very important for certain products: the bulk of grain imports is shipped through the canal, as is more than half of all Japanese cars exported to the United States.

The canal has only been closed one day since it began to operate in 1914 (other than in 1915 when there was a major landslide), and that was when the United States invaded Panama on 20 December 1989. The Panama Canal Commission believes this sent a positive signal to the international trade community that even during a period of major internal problems the canal can operate. Ironically, one of the reasons for the creation of the Panamanian Defence Force in 1983 under General Noriega was to defend the canal after the withdrawal of US troops; it was abolished after the invasion. A referendum called by the Panamanian government in 1992 to constitutionally forbid Panama to have an army – which would have institutionalised the country's inability to defend the canal – was roundly defeated. The post-transfer defence vacuum, as it stands at the moment, worries some canal users, though the canal has always been very difficult to defend because of its very nature (a 1970 US government study said that just a guerrilla raid on the locks and dams could result in a loss of stored water that could take up to two years to replace). Also the collapse of communism in the former Soviet Union has changed US national security concerns. Perhaps foreseeing a defence problem, the Treaty Concerning the Permanent Neutrality and Operation of the Panama Canal, signed in 1977 at the same time as the Panama Canal Treaty, gives the United States the right to intervene in Panama to restore what it regards as the efficient working of the canal, though it is difficult to imagine the circumstances that would give rise to such an action in the 21st century. According to General Fred Woerner, a former Commander of the US Southern Command based in Panama, the canal requires "industrial security" protection (IDs, a good intelligence system and migration control).

The termination of the Canal Treaty is a psychological as well as an operational and defence problem. Fernando Manfredo, a former administrator of the Panama Canal Commission, noted how the accident rate in the labour force increased significantly after former US President Jimmy Carter visited Panama as part of the Treaty process and made a public announcement that agreement had been reached in the negotiations. The only explanation Manfredo could come up with was that the morale of Zonians (US citizens born in the Zone, as it was then called, and working for the Commission) had seriously declined as they saw their world ending and they did not concentrate on their work.

According to Article V of the Neutrality Treaty "only the Republic of Panama shall operate the Canal and maintain military forces, defence sites and military installations within its national territory". But it is not clear whether this means that Panama has to establish military forces to defend the canal and if so who would pay for them. Canal users or Panamanian tax payers would not be prepared to absorb the cost. The United States has never recovered its military costs through the toll system – it is borne by US tax payers. Maintenance of and security of the military facilities costs over US$50 million a year. Furthermore, toll increases after 1999 are limited by the understanding added to the Neutrality Treaty by the US Senate during the ratification process (see below). Not surprisingly, there is a growing feeling that not all US troops will pull out and that some kind of defence agreement will be reached with the United States (see Chapter 2). In 1992 an Army War College study concluded that "Either renegotiation of the Panama Canal Treaties or negotiation of some other agreement may result in a limited US military presence at least during the first decade of the 21st century."

By the time the canal is transferred to Panama, virtually all jobs will be carried out by Panamanians. Between October 1979, when the Torrijos–Carter Treaty became effective, and 1995 the proportion of Panamanians in the permanent workforce increased to close to 90 per cent from 69 per cent. The remaining 10 per cent held key technical, high skilled and top level management positions and the goal is to increase Panamanian participation in these positions (see Exhibit 10.6). A Panamanian replaced a US citizen as the chief executive office (known as the administrator) in 1990. The Commission is supervised by a nine-member Board of Directors, five of whom are US citizens and four are Panamanians. However, a 100 per cent Panamanian labour force is not *per se* a transition goal as it could have a negative impact on the need to assure a skilled workforce. By the turn of the century, nearly all workers will be under Panama's Social Security Retirement Scheme and the majority of employees will not yet be eligible for retirement. It is estimated that around 1,600 employees (1,300 Panamanians and 300 US citizens) will be retirement eligible. Of more critical concern than whether a job is done by a Panamanian or a US citizen is how to mitigate the possibility that 20 per cent of employees will leave at the time of the handover, many of whom hold key positions. In the Office of Executive Planning, for example, 12 of 16 individuals in grades of NM-12 and above (which the Panama Canal Commission has identified as key personnel) are, or will be, retirement eligible before the year 2000. This situation is also true in the Engineering and Construction Bureau, where 80 per cent of the key personnel are, or will be, eligible for retirement before the year 2000. All of this emphasises the importance of Panama's need to work with the

Exhibit 10.6

Panamanians in key areas, 1979 and 1995

	Oct. 1979		*March 1995*	
	No.	*%*	*No.*	*%*
Professional & managerial	44	14	206	57
Skilled crafts	568	59	1,007	90
Floating equipment	39	20	202	76
Pilots	4	2	135	56

Source: Panama Canal Commission.

Panama Canal Commission to establish an Employee Retention and Succession programme that assures continuation of an adequately trained work force to operate the Canal efficiently after the handover.

Relations between labour and management are a potential minefield if not handled properly. One immediate problem is what to do about those contracts that come up for renewal before the handover but which go beyond the year 2000. The Constitutional Addition states that employees at the time of the canal's transfer will be guaranteed employment under the same terms and conditions.

Tolls

The canal is in excellent condition. It is run on a break-even basis. Operating, maintaining and improving the canal costs about US$550 million a year, including US$90 million in treaty-mandated payments to Panama. Toll rates are established at levels sufficient to cover costs of operating and maintaining the canal, including interest, depreciation, capital for plant replacement, expansion and improvements and payments to Panama. Every effort is made to maintain the rates at the lowest possible level to remain competitive with alternative routes. Despite the increase in the number of larger ships (see Exhibit 10.2), the average Canal Water Time for transiting ships has remained at less than 24 hours including time waiting to transit.

Once it assumes full control, and faced with the need to offset the loss of income from the closure of US military bases, Panama will be tempted to increase tolls. It currently earns US$90 million a year without having to invest a cent or take any risks: as one long-time employee of the Panama Canal Commission observed, this a very profitable return and will Panama "make" as much profit after the transfer although the canal has a non-profit status? Joe Reeder, Under Secretary of the Army and chairman of the Panama Canal Commission Board of Directors, warned in 1994 that any attempt to restructure the toll system before Panama establishes its ability to manage and maintain the canal would be a "recipe for major diversions to the existing and planned land bridge options."[2]

The last tolls increase was in 1992 (see Exhibit 10.7); the first one in the canal's history was not until 1974. The Panama Canal Commission does not envisage a toll rate increase until at least through FY 1996. The Commission changed the tonnage system on 1 October 1994 to bring it into line with the worldwide standard of tonnage measurement as promulgated in the 1969 International Convention on Tonnage Measurement of Ships. Known as the Panama Canal Universal Measurement System (PC/UMS), tolls are assessed on the basis of the PC/UMS net tonne. PC/UMS applies a formula to ships' total volume measurement to determine the PC/UMS net tonnage. The total volume measurement is the same as used in the ship's International Tonnage Certificate (1969). The appropriate toll rate, laden or ballast, is applied against the PC/UMS net tonnage figure to give the tolls for each ship. Ships assessed the laden rate are those carrying passengers or cargo. In order for a ship to receive the reduced rate in ballast without passengers or cargo, the volume of fuel on board must not exceed the volume certified for the ship's own use as shown in the PC/UMS Net Tonnage Certificate. The toll on other floating craft, including warships, other than army and navy transports, colliers, supply ships and hospital ships, is based on their tonnage of actual displacement.

Panama cannot change the tolls system until after the transfer. Options in the future include a continuation of the current system of operating the canal on a break-even basis, or alternatively maximising profits, maximising transits, or the establishment of a goal which synthesises profit and transit maximising objectives through the use of a selective toll structure. One of the reasons for building the canal was to keep freight charges low to promote US trade, and this goal serves as the basis of the toll policy.

As well as running the risk of diverting traffic into alternative routes, any changes in toll rates are constrained by the requirements stipulated in the Panama Canal Treaty and the Neutrality Treaty which protect US interests. Paragraph 1 (c) of Article III of the Canal Treaty states that before tolls can be increased:

Exhibit 10.7

Toll rates (in US dollars per Panama Canal PC/UMS net tonne and displacement tonne)

	Laden	*Ballast*	*Displacement*	*Average increase (%)*
Until 8 July 1974	0.90	0.72	0.50	–
8 July 1974	1.08	0.86	0.60	19.7
18 November 1976	1.29	1.03	0.72	19.5
1 October 1979	1.67	1.33	0.93	29.3
12 March 1983	1.83	1.46	1.02	9.8
1 October 1989	2.01	1.60	1.12	9.8
1 October 1992	2.21	1.76	1.23	9.9

Source: Panama Canal Commission.

the impact on the trade patterns of the two parties shall be given full consideration, including consideration on the following factors: (1) the costs of operating and maintaining the Canal; (2) the competitive position of the Canal in relation to other means of transportation; (3) the interests of both parties in maintaining their domestic fleets; (4) the impact of such an adjustment on the various geographic areas of each party; and (5) the interest of both parties in maximizing the effect of such an adjustment on the various geographical areas of each party and the interests of both parties on maximising their international commerce.

Furthermore, the Neutrality Treaty stipulates that:

for purposes of the security, efficiency and proper maintenance of the Canal the following rules shall apply: a) The Canal shall be operated efficiently. c) Tolls and other charges for transit and ancillary services shall be just, reasonable, equitable and consistent with the principles of international law.

There is no provision in the Treaty to measure the Canal's performance nor whether it is operated "efficiently". The efficiency determination is left to the United States. And the phrase "consistent with the principles of international law" is very vague.

If Panama takes any unilateral action based on its sovereign rights, the United States, according to the Treaty, can denounce a violation of the neutrality of the canal and this gives it the right to intervene in Panama. Such a course of action would be an extreme one but it does illustrate the complexity of the situation. The lack of an arbitration clause in the Neutrality Treaty leaves the door open for a confrontation. The conditions imposed on Panama by the Canal Treaty are more onerous than those in the Constantinople Convention governing the Suez Canal and the Versailles Treaty for the Kiel Canal in Germany.

Some analysts believe Panama may change its toll system from one based on the size of the ship to one based on the volume of cargo (as done by the Suez Canal). This would probably generate more revenue. Panama has three toll rate options other than continuing the current policy of full cost recovery pricing: marginal cost pricing, maximisation of economic development and increasing revenues. The problem for Panama is that the non-profit status of the canal will deprive the country of potential fiscal revenues, without the additional indirect benefits such as the ones enjoyed by the United States whose international trade greatly benefited from the canal (less so today). The canal also played an important role in the development of certain areas in the United States, such as the coast of California.

Under marginal cost pricing, toll rates would be set to recover the incremental costs associated with the services provided to ships. Marginal cost pricing is only valid up to the point where congestion occurs. Though the canal is not congested at the moment, such conditions could develop in the future. When there is congestion, the optimum strategy is to apply prices in such a way that the extra costs generated by the congestion (increased delays, higher operating costs, etc) are absorbed by those responsible for the congestion, whether by time for the transit or by the cost of the transit. The application of a marginal cost approach would result in substantially lower toll rates, and though more traffic would be attracted, it is likely that deficits would result.

A policy to maximise economic development would view the canal as part of Panama's infrastructure and its value would be assessed not in terms of the actual cost of the facilities but in terms of the economic and trade development objectives in the Canal Area. The primary motive is to maximise the developmental impacts to the region. Under this option toll rates would have to be set to encourage traffic to not only transit through the canal, but also stop in Panama, thereby stimulating economic development associated with the ships. Activities would include ship repair and refuelling, transhipment and loading and off-loading facilities. This would mean an available level of skills covering all aspects as well as interest for the proposed services and activities.

The third strategy is to set tolls to increase revenues to a defined point above current levels. Bearing in mind the monopoly position of the canal and assuming a relatively inelastic demand schedule, toll rates could be increased and though traffic would decline revenues would increase, at least in the short term. The drop in transits, however, would work counter to any long-term development strategy. Increases in revenues could also be enhanced by using a toll rate that differentiates the traffic in ways that are not currently applied. The toll structure does not differentiate between routes, cargo and type of ship. Differentiating between each of these attributes could increase revenues.

The full cost recovery pricing approach calls for setting toll rates sufficiently high enough to cover all costs. The system has worked well. It is easy and inexpensive to administer but does not promote economic equity on the basis of the cost of the service, value of the service to the user or the user's ability to pay. Nor does it promote efficiency by encouraging the use of optimum

Exhibit 10.8

Maritime sectors

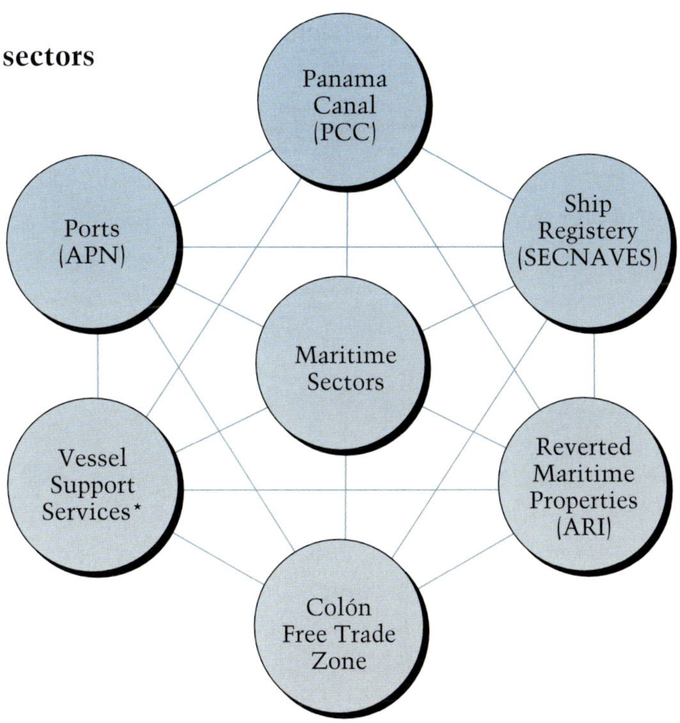

*Includes bunkering, chandlery, banking, insurance, etc.
Source: Presidential Commission for Canal Affairs.

sized ships or promote economic development. If economic criteria were included toll rates would be set at less than full cost recovery and the balance collected from the public (taxes or from the budget) who, though non-users, receive benefits. The Presidential Commission for Canal Affairs which drew up a report in January 1994[1] during the Endara government said changing this approach to incorporate economic development criteria makes "good sense".

Financial analyses were undertaken in 1993 in which net income levels were projected to FY 2010. The results indicated that based on a continuation of the present toll pricing system and rates (with no increases of any kind) tolls would have to be increased shortly after the transfer date (around FY 2003) in order to offset the shortfall between revenue and expenses due to inflation. There is not expected to be an increase during the transition period. The Commission said that a particularly promising option for a toll structure is one that maximises transits for particular types of ship but encourages cost reduction and profit maximization. "A selective toll policy coupled with a mandate to maximize profits embodies the advantages of both the transit objective and the profit objective by encouraging financial managers to more fully utilize Canal capacity and control costs while still promoting Canal usage by specific vessel types." Selective toll structures which apply a unique rate for each type of ship are almost universally used by port authorities and are frequently used by canal authorities (e.g. the Saint Lawrence Seaway).

A pricing policy that took economic development more into account would dovetail with Panama's ambition to strengthen and broaden its maritime sector (see Exhibit 10.8). The Commission believes that if "properly planned, coordinated and controlled, this emerging national maritime strategy will change the way the nation looks at the Canal and the mission of the future Canal Authority.[1] A key element in this are the reverted properties in the Canal Area managed by the Interoceanic Regional Authority (ARI). Such a strategy would mean developing services related to transits of the canal, such as: ship construction; repair maintenance; supplies and lubrication; ship management; ship related tourism; ship bunkering; container repair, etc. The Pérez Balladares government began to draw up an international maritime strategy in 1995.

Sea-level canal

Experts believe the canal can handle the volume of traffic until 2020, barring any unforeseen and significant growth in the number of ships, and that options will have to be reviewed around 2010 because of the long lead-times involved in any expansion project. Nicaragua, once considered as a rival site for a canal, is exploring a proposal to build a 400-kilometre railway linking the country's Pacific and Caribbean coasts. Backers include Germany's Siemens and investors from Hong Kong and China. Double-stacked container trains running from California to Texas already take traffic that might once have congested the canal. Average yearly growth in Panama Canal traffic is put at 1.5 to 2 per cent until 2010 when traffic is seen as flattening out. The traffic flow in the early 1980s (when there were backlogs of more than 100 ships having to await passage for between three and five days) was eased by the opening of the transisthmian oil pipeline which takes Alaskan North Slope oil that was previously shipped through the canal in tankers.

The tripartite commission, formed by Japan, Panama and the United States, to study alternatives concluded in 1993 that a sea-level canal was not needed. Japan disputes this and is still pressing for a sea-level canal. It took issue with the traffic projections made. The other options are to enlarge the canal with another set of locks with the capacity to take 150,000 dwt vessels, and to upgrade rail (a high-speed train) and road facilities.

Besides the United States, Japan would be the chief beneficiary of a sea-level canal, and probably China, whose rapid economic growth and growing resource needs as the country becomes richer are an important (and largely unquantified) factor to be taken into account. The average route length of four important Japanese imports – cereals, minerals, coal and oil – is much longer than that of Japan's world competitors. The freight tariffs of a sea-level canal might not be lower, but the passage time would certainly be much quicker and there would be no limit on the size of ships. As Charlotte Elton points out in her book,[3] a sea-level canal would not only reduce the cost of Japan's imports from the United States, but would also allow Japan to take advantage of new sources of raw materials in South American countries such as Brazil where Japan has large investments in raw material extraction projects. Japan is interested in increasing imports of cereals from Latin America and in reducing food dependency on the United States. Brazil is already Japan's third largest supplier of soya beans, while Argentina's importance as a source of corn and sorghum is growing. Japan is participating in the agricultural development of the Cerrado region in Brazil which – with 66 million hectares – is larger than the Asian archipelago.

Energy costs make the use of large ships up to 250,000 dwt increasingly attractive, but the canal's locks preclude the passage of ships larger than 70,000 dwt (the so-called Panamax size). These ships have to go round Cape Horn. The shipping industry estimated in 1981 that it cost US$2.4 million to transport cargo in four 62,500 dwt ships from Japan to New York through the canal. The same load, transported in one 250,000 dwt ship via Cape Horn cost US$2.1 million, despite the fact that the journey is an additional 5,600 miles. If the 250,000 dwt ship could go through Panama, the cost would have been reduced to US$1.7 million.

Building a sea-level canal is a centuries old dream. In 1542 Hernán Cortés told Charles V of Spain that joining the Atlantic with the South Sea (as the Pacific was then called) "would be worth more than the conquest of Mexico". Such a waterway would move trade far more quickly than the present locks-based canal, but the cost of building it would be astronomical (who would pay the bill?) and the environmental consequences could be enormous. The oscillating flow could result in a massive migration of species between oceans and their eventual extinction. Tidal gates, however, could be built to reduce this problem.

One advantage of a sea-level waterway is that the canal could continue to operate while it was under construction, which would not normally be the case if it were expanded. A route 10 miles west of the current waterway was chosen in a US government study carried out in 1970. The area is underdeveloped except for small farms and grazing land interspersed with jungle. About 50,000 people live in the area. However, a sea-level canal would nullify Panama's maritime strategy as ships would not have to stop.

The Gaillard Cut

The canal is some 50 miles long. A ship entering from the Atlantic sails at sea level from Cristobal to Gatun Locks, a distance of seven miles (see Exhibit 10.9); it is then lifted 85 feet to Gatun Lake in three lockages or "steps". From Gatun it sails, 85 feet above sea level, to Pedro Miguel, a distance of 31 miles. A single lockage at Pedro Miguel lowers the ship 31 feet to Miraflores Lake. A mile further south the ship enters Miraflores Locks and in two lockages is lowered 54 feet to the Pacific Ocean level. The last leg of the journey is four miles to the Balboa port area before entering the outer harbour.

Water to move ships up and down at each set of locks is fed by gravity from Gatun Lake, which is one of the largest artificial bodies of water in the world. Water enters the locks through a system of main culverts: 10 sets of lateral culverts extend under the lock chambers from the side walls and 10 sets from the centre wall. Each lateral culvert has a set of five holes, each measur-

Exhibit 10.9

Panama Canal profile

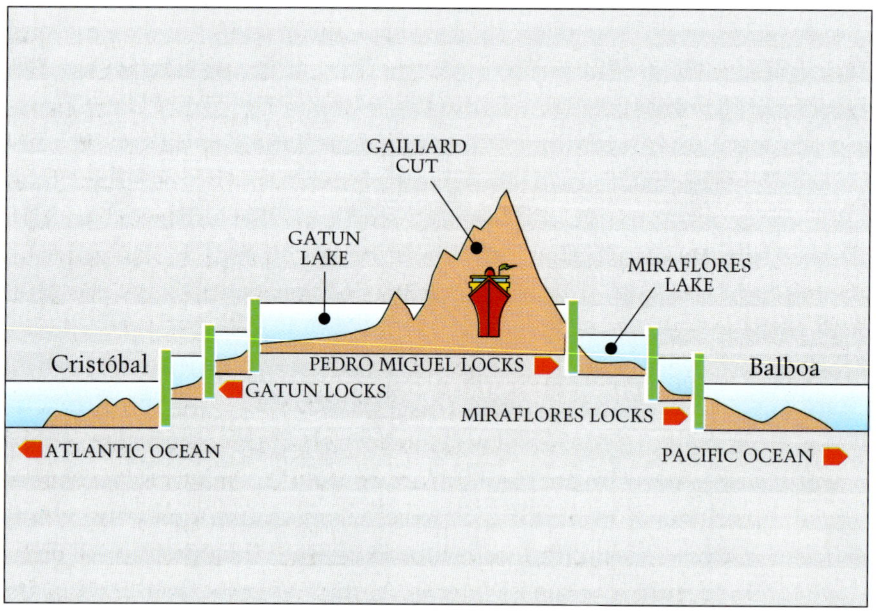

Source: Panama Canal Commission.

"The eighth wonder of the world" – completed in 1914, the canal is being improved and modernised constantly

ing 4.5 feet in diameter. As the water is released into the main culverts, it is diverted into the 20 lateral culverts and distributed through 100 holes in the floor of the chamber. Each ship passing through the canal uses about 52 million gallons of fresh water, fed by a gravity flow system through the locks and spilled into the ocean. No wonder the canal is gushingly referred to as "the eighth wonder of the world".

The Gaillard Cut, an eight-mile long stretch of the canal where Panamax ships and some others, because of their size, are restricted to one-way passage during daylight hours is being widened. This portion of the canal (appropriately called "the Snake") is the narrowest and it was carved through the rock and shale of the Continental Divide between the Atlantic and Pacific slopes for most of the distance. About one-third of the canal's business consists of Cut-restricted ships.

The area is the most susceptible to landslides. It was here that the largest slide occurred in 1915, the only slide that has closed the canal (the other time was when the United States invaded Panama on 20 December 1989). It took seven months to clear the waterway. Since then there have been several more slides, the worst of which occurred on 13 October 1987.

The width of the navigational channel, currently 500 feet, is being increased to a minimum of 630 feet in the straight sections and a maximum of 730 feet at the curves. The widened cut will allow greater flexibility in the scheduling of ship transits, improve the quality of transit service and reduce the risk of landslides. Completion will allow virtually unrestricted two-way passage of all ships.

Other improvements

The canal is an operation that demands constant improvements to ensure that traffic is handled efficiently at competitive rates. Other improvements include the purchase of new and more powerful towboats; ongoing replacement of locomotive turntables at all locks to facilitate ship handling during relay lockages; acquisition of new towing locomotives providing added transit capability and maintenance flexibility; high mast lighting at all locks to ensure safer transit of large ships during early daylight and dusk hours and completion of a new signal station at Cristobal to permit improved, unobstructed view of all vessel movements at the Atlantic entrance and harbour.

In addition to the modernisation and improvement programmes, annual major overhauls are performed on the 700-tonne lock gates and other lock equipment; towing locomotives are overhauled and reconditioned at a specially designed repair facility; the 50,000 feet of locomotive towtrack are regularly maintained and replaced; and continuous dredging keeps the canal at maximum navigable depth.

Improvements to operational procedures have also been accomplished to increase efficiency and safety. A transit reservation system allows customers to schedule a guaranteed day of canal transit and an upgrading of the computerised traffic management system provides for more controlled movement of ships.

The reverted areas

Not only the canal will be handed over to Panama at the end of 1999, but also the surrounding land, buildings and US military bases (see Exhibit 10.10). The Canal Treaty called for the return to Panama of 16 military sites, comprising 33,000 hectares and over 7,000 buildings. Between 1979 and 1994 6,500 hectares and 405 buildings were transferred, including the railway between Balboa and Colón, the ports of Cristobal and Balboa, dry dock facilities and part of Fort Gulick (now Fort Espinar) on the Atlantic side that housed the US Army School of the Americas. The government estimates the total value of the land and property is US$20 billion, just over three times Panama's GDP, though this figure is hotly disputed. Because of their strategic location, the reverted lands present substantial economic potential, especially those near to Panama City. Nicolás Ardito Barletta, declared the winner in the fraudulent 1984 presidential elections, who took over as ARI's administrator in 1995, optimistically speaks of generating 150,000 jobs and US$1.5 billion of exports.

Ultimately, the value of the areas depends on their proper up keep, which constitutes a considerable expense for Panama – as much as US$50 million per year. The sooner plans are developed and implemented, the greater the net economic beenfits will be.

Great care, however, will have to be taken to conserve the canal's watershed which must be protected from deforestation to prevent lakes from silting up and reducing the storage capacity of fresh water for lockages and drinking water for Panama City and Colón, the main cities.

The Interoceanic Regional Authority (ARI), created in 1993 under the Endara government, is in charge of developing and administering all reverted properties except the Panama Canal and its area of operations. ARI's legal framework was to be changed during 1995 to make it less autonomous and bring it more under the wing of the executive, and this generated fears that the organisation would become more vulnerable to political interference, though most of the directors appointed by the last government were close to the Christian Democrats, one of the parties supporting it. The Legislative Assembly approved measures President Pérez Balladares had demanded to obtain veto power over larger-scale ARI projects. There is also criticism that ARI is highly influenced by powerful businessmen trying to push through their own interests.

The Panama Canal Area has the potential to be developed for all kinds of activities, and a master plan was being drawn up in 1995 by a Panamanian-US consortium which will be submitted to the Legislative Assembly for approval in 1996. The area at Fort Amador, between Panama City and the banks of the canal, with spectacular views across the bay, reverts to Panama at the end of 1995 and has already been declared a tourist zone; the Foreign Ministry has moved out of its cramped building in the old part of Panama City into the more spacious former headquarters of the US Army; Telfers Island, at the Atlantic entrance to the canal near Colón is well positioned to become a container terminal (though it already faces competition from other projects); low-wage light manufacturing or assembly facilities could be established on some of the land;

Exhibit 10.10

Panama Canal Area

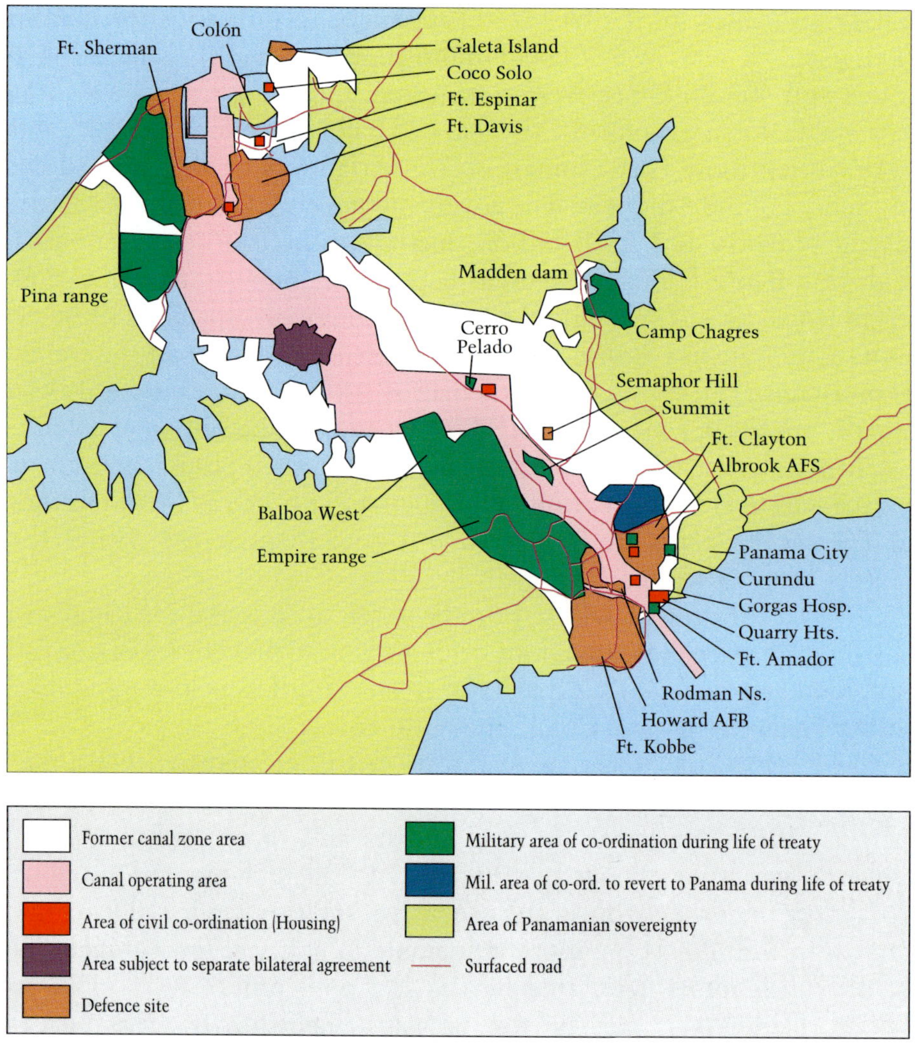

Source: US Southern Command.

housing is provided in many areas; and Fort Sherman, where there are 400 species of birds, has ecotourism potential. The government also proposes to create the *Ciudad de Saber* (the City of Knowledge) on land occupied by military sites. This would incorporate the University of the Americas, the International Health Services Centre, the Latin American Centre for Asian Studies and the Advanced Technology and Computer Institute, and would be administered by a non-profit private foundation. In 1995 Taiwanese businessmen were evaluating the prospects of setting up an industrial zone.

The government is not short of ideas; the problem is whether it will be able to attract Panamanian and foreign private sector investment which so far has been low. Another problem is the cost of cleaning up the military sites (the cost for sites in California which cover a smaller area than Panama is estimated at US$2.5 billion) and making them fit for other uses. Under the Panama Canal Treaty the US military will clean up toxic materials, industrial solvents and low-level radioactive waste and unexploded ordnance "in so far as may be practicable" (a vague term that is not defined).

Half of the 34,000 hectares are firing ranges that have been used for more than 60 years. They contain unexploded ordnance and cannot be cleared thoroughly because of the limitations of technology, and this will severely limit or even make impossible new uses of some areas.

The idea of using some of the reverted areas to make Panama a more

Exhibit 10.11

Transfer of US military property to Panama, 1996–99

Site	*Service*	*Location*
Diablo Heights Elementary School	Army	Pacific
Morgan Avenue Housing	Army	Pacific
Curundu Elementary School (on Fort Clayton)	Army	Pacific
East Corozal except commissary	Army	Pacific
Los Ríos Elementary School	Army	Pacific
Quarry Heights	Army	Pacific
Fort Clayton	Army	Pacific
Chiva Chiva Antenna Farm	Army	Pacific
Herrick Heights Housing	Army	Pacific
Ancon Hill Communications	Army	Pacific
Panama Canal College	Army	Pacific
Balboa Elementary School	Army	Pacific
Corozal Commissary	Army	Pacific
Gorgas Hospital	Army	Pacific
Fort Kobbe	Army	Pacific
Cocoli Housing	Army	Pacific
West Corozal	Army	Pacific
Cerro Gordo Communications	Army	Pacific
Building 1501, Balboa (Military Traffic Management Command)	Army	Pacific
Empire Range	Army	Pacific
Fort Sherman	Army	Pacific
Rodman Naval Station	Navy	Pacific
Farfan	Navy	Pacific
Arraijan Tank Farm	Navy	Pacific
Marine Barracks	Navy	Pacific
Galeta Island	Navy	Atlantic
Albrook Air Force Station	Air Force	Pacific
Howard Air Force Base	Air Force	Pacific
Semaphore Hill Caribbean Basin Radar Network	Air Force	Pacific
Balboa West Range	Air Force	Pasific
Curunda Junior-Senior High School	Army	Pacific

Note: Specific transfer dates have not been publicly announced; the above sequence does not imply any order by transfer dates.
Source: US Southern Command.

industrial country, including low-wage assembly plants known as *maquilas*, is tied to larger discussions of working conditions and wages, regional trade and economic policy generally. There are around 5,000 Panamanians working in the US military sites and they earn US$8–12 an hour, far more than the minimum Panamanian wage. Displaced base workers will be given priority for jobs created by projects in the reverted areas, but there will be considerable resistance to accepting lower wages. One possibility is that workers assume control of the light industrial equipment on bases to form their own businesses. There are shops for sheet metal, machine repair, indoor and outdoor electrical work, refrigerator and appliance repair, sign painting, carpentry and a print shop.

Workers will probably have no option but to accept lower wages.

Notes and references

1. This chapter draws on the *Transition Plan for the Transfer of the Panama Canal* (Presidential Commission for Canal Affairs, January 1994); *The Future of the Panama Canal*, a paper presented by Fernando Manfredo at the North-South Center, University of Miami,
4 June 1993; and the Annual Report for the 1994 fiscal year and other documents of the Panama Canal Commission.
2. Memorandum for the Secretary of the Board of Directors, Panama Canal Commission, 8 March 1994.
3. Charlotte Elton, *Rivales o Aliados? Japón y Estados Unidos en Panamá* (CEASPA, 1990).

Chapter Eleven

Foreign investment environment

Panama has long had an open doors policy for foreign investment, but there has been no major investment in the country for more than 10 years. The last foreign direct investment project of any significance was the joint venture between Northville Industries, the Chicago Bridge Company and Panama's Corporación Financiera Nacional for the building of the Transisthmian oil pipeline (see Chapter 3) which began to operate in October 1982; and that was only because Panama has an absolute competitive advantage in moving Alaskan oil.

The Pérez Balladares government is attaching great importance to attracting foreign investment: membership of the World Trade Organisation (formerly known as GATT), rescheduling of the commercial bank portion of the foreign debt, more flexible labour market regulations, cleaning up Panama's international image (tarnished by money laundering) and restoration of democracy have enhanced the investment environment, while privatisation is presenting opportunities. Foreign investment protection was strengthened in 1995 when Panama signed the Multilateral Investment Guarantee Agreement, under the wing of the World Bank. It had been one of the very few countries in Latin America not to adhere to MIGA. Panama's national credit-risk rating improved in the first quarter of 1995 to C (55 points) according to the Economist Intelligence Unit's ranking. The highest risk is E.

Panama has long provided several important incentives for foreign investors, but they have not been sufficient to attract investment. They include: the US dollar-based economy (the only such country in Latin America) offers low inflation and zero foreign exchange risk; total absence of exchange controls; equal treatment of foreign and local citizens; one of the most flexible company laws in the world; no restrictions on 100 per cent foreign-owned companies; no restrictions on mergers, acquisitions or joint ventures; and a high percentage of the labour force is bilingual. Nevertheless, the stock of foreign investment at the end of 1993 was only US$432 million (see Exhibit 11.1), down from US$533 million in 1985. The Foreign Ministry began to spearhead efforts to increase foreign investment through a commission headed by the president.

Most of the investment is in manufacturing (see Exhibit 11.2). The Panamanian Trade Development Institute (IPCE) provides investors with

Exhibit 11.1

Foreign direct investment, 1980–93 (US$m and as % of GDP)

	(A) Stock	*(C) GDP*	*(A)/(C) (%)*		*(A) Stock*	*(C) GDP*	*(A)/(C) (%)*
1980	386	3,592.6	10.7	1987	534	5,363.3	10.0
1981	395	3,921.4	10.1	1988	502	4,604.5	10.9
1982	429	4,324.6	9.9	1989	504	4,639.3	10.9
1983	471	4,428.0	10.6	1990	486	5,009.4	9.7
1984	490	4,609.9	10.6	1991	467	5,496.4	8.5
1985	533	4,948.3	10.8	1992	469	6,015,4	7.8
1986	491	5,190.9	9.5	1993	432	6,564.9	6.6

Exhibit 11.2

Foreign direct investment by sector, 1979 and 1993 (US$m)

	1979		*1993*	
	US$m	*%*	*US$m*	*%*
Total	342	100.0	432	100.0
Agriculture, forestry & fisheries	55	16.1	36	8.2
Manufacturing	175	51.1	188	43.5
Commerce	67	19.6	74	17.1
Transport, storage & communications	8	2.3	52	12.0
Finance	36	10.5	60	13.9
Services	1	0.4	10	2.3
Other	0	0.0	12	2.8

Source: Comptroller General's Office.

Exhibit 11.3

Foreign direct investment by country of origin, 1993 (US$m)

	US$m	*% of total*
United States	321	74
Costa Rica	24.3	5.6
United Kingdom	16.7	3.8
Japan	16.2	3.7
Venezuela	3.5	0.8
Other	50.4	11.6*
Total	432	100

*Percentages may not total 100 due to rounding up of figures.

Source: Comptroller General's Office.

information, expedites specific projects, leads investment-seeking missions abroad, and supports foreign investment missions in Panama.

The United States accounts for more than 80 per cent (see Exhibit 11.3). US companies present in the manufacturing and agricultural sectors include Bridgestone/Firestone International, Colgate Palmolive, Eastman Kodak, Kimberly-Clark International, Nabisco Brands, Phillip Morris, Revlon and United Brands.

One of the deterrents to investment has been the rigid labour code. One US bank, for example, was unable to fire some of its staff and so put them in an office with no work to do, in the hope that they would become bored and leave voluntarily. They did not. Some companies have looked at Panama over the last few years but decided not to invest because they regarded the regulations as not flexible enough; companies already in the country, however, have found they can sometimes get around the restrictions with the help of smart lawyers, of which there is no shortage. Indeed, some lawyers privately do not welcome the changes to the labour market regulations (see Chapter 2) because it would deprive them of business.

State companies also provide relatively high-cost public services, such as electricity, water and telecommunciations (international calls from Panama are very expensive, for example). The combination of relatively high costs for both utilities and labour makes Panama's unit costs higher than the average for the region. Privatisation of INTEL, the telecommunications company, and allowing IHRE, the power company, to grant concessions to private companies to generate electricity will help to lower costs in these areas.

Cumbersome legal procedures have also sometimes delayed resolution of contract and other business disputes. Setting up shell companies, however, is very easy, so much so that it is an open secret that they have been used for money-laundering purposes. The government planned to tighten laws in 1995 concerning lawyers' responsibility for such companies as part of a "get to know your customer" policy.

Corporate laws

Corporate laws[1] are very flexible and the time period for setting up a company is from one to two weeks. Lawyers' fees range from US$600 to US$1,500. Every company set up pursuant to the laws of Panama must have a resident agent within Panama, who must be a lawyer. The annual fee for this service is about US$200.

Advantages offered to Panamanian corporations include:

- Two or more persons, even though not domiciled in Panama, may organise a company. The articles of incorporation may be executed anywhere, even outside of Panama, and in any language.
- There are no requirements regarding the amount of paid-in capital.
- Ownership of a Panamanian company may reside in a single individual or corporation and no part of the capital needs to be held by a Panamanian.
- There are no nationality or residence requirements for shareholders. Neither the directors nor the officers are required to be shareholders.
- The Board of Directors must be composed of at least three directors, but one person may hold more than one position;
- Meetings of shareholders or directors may be held outside of Panama.
- Proxies may be used by shareholders and directors.

Export processing zones

Locations designated export processing zones (EPZs) under a 1992 law offer tax-free status and special immigration and labour code privileges, as well as licence and customs exemptions to manufacturers who locate there. The only active EPZ is at Isla Margarita near Colón.

Companies allowed to set up in EPZs must be engaged in manufacturing, assembly, high technology or specialised services such as computer data entry. Firms in EPZs are exempt from taxes, duties and other charges related to imports of machinery, equipment, raw materials, semi-processed goods and other materials such as packaging, fuel and lubricants used in the manufacturing process. Profits arising from exports are exempt from income tax and there is also no exports sales tax. The developer is exempt from taxes, duties and other charges related to the importation of machinery, equipment, accessories and other materials used in the construction of the facilities during the life of the contract (the maximum is 20 years). The developer is also exempt from property and income taxes, and taxes on capital or assets for the first 10 years of operation. From the 11th year until the end of the contract, the developer is exempt from income tax on net earnings reinvested in the development and expansion of the EPZ, provided that the amount exceeds 20 per cent of the net taxable income for the fiscal year the reinvestment is made.

Petroleum export zones

Some analysts believe Panama has the potential to become a major oil and downstream products redistribution centre. The Panama Canal creates a national bunkering market as well as a trans-shipment point, and Panama is the narrowest isthmus between the Atlantic and Pacific oceans to pipeline oil from South America to the Far East.

Under two 1992 decrees, which were the first serious attempt to promote the development of a petroleum service industry in Panama, companies are allowed to establish operations in a petroleum export zone (PEZ) to produce, refine and export products, and can also sell directly to ships transiting the Panama Canal and to foreign airlines. Companies in PEZs are exempt from municipal or federal taxes and are not subject to government regulations affecting the local market. The government has authorised the following for PEZ: Petroterminal de Panamá, Refinería Panamá, Autoridad Portuaria Nacional (the national ports authority) and the Tocumen international airport.

Expropriation and compensation

Panama has no current cases of expropriation of property for public or any other use. There is a constitutional prohibition against foreign land ownership within 10 kilometres of a national border or on an island. Neither Panamanian citizens nor foreigners may own beaches or the shores of rivers or lakes. Builders and investors generally rent the land for 20–30 years, via the Ministry of Finance. The tourism incentives law (see Chapter 4) expands this period for up to 40 years.

Dispute settlement

Disputes with foreign investors are rare. Panama has a court and judicial system, like many other Latin American countries, built around a civil code, rather than the Anglo-American system of reliance upon case law and judicial precedent. Business, corporate and banking laws are relatively modern and sophisticated and in general are enforced so as to create a favourable business climate, although there is no modern bankruptcy law.

There is a public property registry. The judiciary is independent, in law and practice, of the executive branch of government. Unique features of Panamanian law and practice in specific areas (including but not limited to banking, accounting requirements, formation and functioning of companies and taxation) make retention of local legal counsel advisable in many cases.

Intellectual property rights

Panama is a member of the World Intellectual Property Organisation, the Geneva Phonograms Convention, the Brussels Satellite Convention and the Universal Copyright Convention. In 1994 representatives of some US industrial sectors alleged Panama provides inadequate trademark and copyright protection. New laws to modernise copyright protection and to strengthen industrial property protection (patents, trademarks and trade secrets) were due to be approved in 1995. The law provides 20 years of patent protection in place of the previous five to 15 years for foreigners and five to 20 years for Panamanians. Patent protection is granted from the date of filing. Pharmaceutical patents are granted for only 15 years, but can be renewed for an additional 10 years if the patent owner licensed a national company (minimum of 30 per cent of Panamanian ownership) to exploit the patent.

Mining sector

The most promising sector for foreign investment, apart from the major opportunities presented by the former US military areas being reverted under the Panama Canal Treaty (see Chapter 10), is mining (see Chapter 2). A mining consortium including two Canadian companies (Adrian Resources and Tech Corporation) was at the advanced feasibility stage in 1995 for a US$500 million gold/copper project, and the rise in copper prices has sparked renewed interest in the Cerro Colorado copper deposit. Of the 45 projects under exploration, 35 are option or joint ventures, mainly with US and Canadian companies. New regulations introduced in 1988 substantially amended mining legislation and made Panama much more attractive through the following tax and investment incentives:

- Total guarantee that the foreign or local investor in exploration has the exclusive right to exraction.
- The extraction concession grants the exclusive right to execute all geological and seismic investigations of minerals, all extraction operations of minerals, transport of minerals extracted, and warehousing, marketing and export of extracted minerals.
- A new classification in minerals was established.
- Exploration operations are subject to a rental fee per hectare per year of

around US$1 during exploration and US$2 during extraction. Exploration rental fees can be set off against exploration expenses up to 75 per cent of the total rental fees payable within a fiscal year. Extraction operations are required to pay a fixed amount increasing every five years, plus a fixed royalty.

- A production royalty of 2 per cent for all minerals and of 4 per cent for precious minerals in placers, both calculated over the gross production.
- Loss carry forward for three years after the fiscal period in which they originated.
- Total exemption from import taxes and custom duties for all equipment, spare parts and materials used.
- A 20 per cent discount from income tax for those mining operations starting production by February 1998.

Note

1. This section and others draw on the US Embassy's 1995 Country Commercial Guide for Panama.

Chapter Twelve

The fiscal environment

Taxation

Corporation and foreign investment regulations

Business organisation
Six types of business organisation are recognised in Panama: sole proprietorships; general partnerships; limited partnerships; stock-issuing limited partnerships; corporations; and co-operatives. Foreign companies usually choose to establish a corporation (*sociedad anónima,* or SA).

Requirements of a corporation (SA) in Panama
Capital
There is no minimum and no legal reserve requirement. Capital may be assigned in cash or kind. The board of directors assign a value to equity contributions in kind. Non-cash investments must be registered in the documents of incorporation as shares, with no nominal value.

Founders, shareholders
A minimum of two persons of legal age are necessary to found a corporation; once founded, a corporation needs only one shareholder. There are no nationality or residency requirements.

Directors
A minimum of three are required. There is no restriction on nationality of the board of directors.

Management
There must be three management officers (president, secretary and treasurer), but one person may hold more than one of these positions. There are no nationality or residency requirements.

Labour
There are no requirements that labour be represented in management or on the board of directors.

Disclosure
Apart from documents supplied at the time of incorporation and annual income tax returns, no other financial reports are required (although certain reports must be made for statistical purposes). Accounting books, etc., must be kept in Panama, except for those relating to transactions outside the country.

Taxes and fees on incorporation
Registration fees are based on the amount of authorised capital or, if that is not reported, on the number of non-par shares, which are assigned a value for the purpose of determining the appropriate registration fee. Registration fees range from less than US$100 for companies with capital of less than US$100,000 to about US$2,000 for companies with capital of US$20 million or more. The total amount of legal fees, notary charges, stamps and translation costs for incorporating in Panama typically ranges from US$500 to US$1,000. In addition, all corporations pay a US$150 annual public-registry fee.

Types of shares
All types of shares are permitted.

Control
A simple majority of shareholders may effect business; meetings may take place anywhere.

Establishing a Panamanian corporation
Establishing a Panamanian Corporation (SA) is not at all difficult, and a wide range of options is permitted. Any two persons, without regard to nationality or domicile, may establish a corporate entity for any legal purpose. If the amount of capital is fixed, the number and par value of the shares, which may be either nominative or bearer, must be stated. A corporation formed with no par-value shares need not state any amount of capital but must state the number of shares authorised. The articles of incorporation may be written in Spanish or in any other language, and they may be executed in Panama or elsewhere. If the amount of capital is fixed, it may be stated in Panamanian currency or any other lawful currency. There are no restrictions as to the nationality or domicile of the shareholders, directors or officers, or as to where meetings of the directors or shareholders may be held.

Upon establishment, a notarised copy of the company's articles of incorporation must be filed with the government setting out: the name and domicile of each incorporator; the name of the corporation set out in such a way as to distinguish it from other types of business organisations; the principal objectives of the corporation; the amount of capital and the number of shares (and, if pertinent, the amount) that each subscriber agrees to take; the domicile of the company. The name and addresses of at least three directors, and of the president, secretary and treasurer of the corporation, must be provided. (Panamanian law permits the same person to hold more than one office, and a corporation's directors and officers need not be shareholders.) If the articles of incorporation are executed abroad, they must be legalised by a Panamanian consul.

In addition, to engage in local business, companies must secure a *patente comercial* (a commercial or industrial licence) from the Ministry of Commerce and Industry, which first ascertains whether the operation complies with constitutional and other legal provisions.

Officers and directors are not required to be in Panama at the time of organising, but a resident agent must be duly authorised to carry out all legal functions. He may be a company employee, director or manager, but an outside legal representative will suffice.

Branch operations

Operating in Panama through a locally incorporated subsidiary, as opposed to a branch, offers no distinct advantages. To establish a branch, a foreign company must record in the Mercantile Registry its articles of incorporation (and amendments), its latest balance sheet, an indication of the amount of capital to be utilised in Panama, and a certificate showing that it is authorised to do business in its country of origin.

These documents must all be authenticated by a Panamanian consul in the country of origin and notorised before they can be recorded in the Mercantile Registry. The foreign company must designate a representative in Panama with power of attorney in case of legal proceedings. There is usually no significant delay in these procedures, especially if a Panamanian attorney does the filing.

Foreign investment

There are few requirements for foreign investment in Panama beyond those described above for establishing a Panamanian corporation. If incentives are desired, investors must apply to the Ministry of Commerce and Industry. Work permits for foreigners are mandatory, and rules governing their employment are strictly enforced.

Panamanian corporate law is conducive to organising a company in the country to direct operations conducted elsewhere.

Securing approval for foreign investments

No basic foreign investment approval mechanism exists. Both domestic and foreign investors must comply with organisational formalities and, if they intend to do business in Panama, must obtain a licence from the Ministry of Commerce and Industry.

Limitations on foreign investors

The law does not permit foreign companies to engage in retail trade or certain professional activities. In addition, foreigners may not invest in radio stations, which must be 100 per cent locally owned, and Panamanians (or the state) must have a majority interest in public utilities. Otherwise, there are no restrictions on the amount of equity that foreign investors may hold in Panamanian industries and business.

As in many Latin American countries, foreigners are prohibited to own land near the country's border.

Taxes on corporate income and gains

Corporations, partnerships, branches of foreign corporations, limited liability companies and any other entity considered a juridicial person by law pay income tax on any profits or income generated in or derived from Panama according to the tax table for legal persons. Income which does not arise in or is not derived from Panama is not subject to taxation in Panama.

Corporate taxation

Taxable income up to $500,000 is taxed at a rate of 30 per cent. Corporations registered in the Panamanian Official Register of Industry pay income tax according to the following:

Net income	*Tax rate*
Up to $500,000	30%
Over $500,000	$150,000 plus 34% on everything over $500,000

If a corporation does not declare any dividends during the year, it must pay a deemed dividend tax, or minimum dividend tax, amounting to 10 per cent of 40 per cent of its taxable income less income tax.

Branches of foreign corporations must pay 10 per cent of their taxable income less income tax as deemed dividend tax.

Taxes for companies operating in the Colón Free Zone are the same as above but only apply to income derived from sales to companies located in Panama, outside the Free Zone. Free Zone companies are subject to 15 per cent income tax on their net taxable income generated from re-export operations. In addition, for the re-export operations, companies in the Colón Free Zone have to pay income tax in advance. This prepaid income tax is calculated according to the rates in Exhibit 12.1 based on the re-exporting operations.

The tax payment will be recognised as a credit for the real income tax to be paid at year end, and the following year. It could also be used as a credit for

Exhibit 12.1

Prepaid income tax rates, Colón Free Zone

Re-exportations	*Income tax*
Up to $2,000,000	$8,500
From $2,000,000 to $5,000,000	$30,000
From $5,000,000 to $10,000,000	$60,000
From $10,000 to $20,000	$100,000
From $20,000 to $40,000	$175,000
From $40,000 to $80,000	$275,000
From $80,000 to $120,000,000	$400,000
Over $120,000,000	$500,000

the subsequent prepaid tax. If, however, there is still a credit it will be lost after the following year.

Free Zone companies are not subject to deemed dividend tax on their taxable income derived from re-export operations.

Capital gains tax

Gains on the sale or transfer of real estate are considered capital gains. For the assessment of capital gains tax the seller may deduct the following items from the selling price:

- the original cost of the property;
- the cost of any improvements to the property;
- any expenses incurred in the sales; and
- 5 per cent or 10 per cent of the original cost of the property or any improvements thereto, for every year the property was held.

The resulting gain is divided by the number of full calendar years the property was held and the result added to other taxable income to determine the tax rate for the capital gain. Any losses on sales of real estate may be offset against other gains on sales of real estate during the same tax year. Excess losses on the sale of real estate may not be offset against any other gains, nor may they be carried over to the following year.

A tax payer may elect not to declare the gain resulting from the sale of the real estate, and pay income tax at a rate of 5 per cent on the value of the property that results from increasing the original cost of the property and any improvements to the property by 10 per cent for each year the property was held.

Administration

The calendar year is the standard fiscal year. However, under certain circumstances, a special fiscal year may be requested from the Director General of Internal Revenue. Businesses having taxable income are obliged to file annual income tax returns. This applies even if the net result for the period is a loss. Corporations having no Panamanian taxable income or loss are under no obligation to file income tax returns.

Tax returns are due 90 days after the close of the fiscal year. The regulations provide for an extension of time of up to three months to file an income tax return, provided the corporation pays the tax estimated to be due. If an extension is obtained, any payments due on filing the returns are subject to an interest rate of 2 per cent above the domestic banking rate. Tax returns are filed on forms provided by the Ministry of Finance and Treasury.

Along with the tax returns filed each year, taxpayers must file an estimated income tax return, which is a section of the yearly tax return. The estimated taxable income may not be lower than the preceding year's actual taxable income. The estimated tax is payable in three quarterly instalments. If the actual taxable income the following year is lower than the estimated income, any remaining credits are applied toward the following year's estimated income tax. Free Zone businesses are not required to pay estimated tax on their re-exportation activities.

Dividends

Dividends derived from taxable income are taxed at the source at a single rate of 10 per cent for nominative shares, and at the rate of 20 per cent if the shares are issued to bearer. The corporation paying the dividend must withhold the tax and pay it to the government within 10 working days after declaring or paying the dividend, whichever comes first. Capitalised dividends are not subject to dividend tax. During the five-year period after the capitalisation, a company may not re-acquire its own shares as treasury share or make loans to its shareholders or partners. In addition, within six months of the capitalisation, the shareholders of the company must repay any amounts owned to the company that are outstanding on the date of the capitalisation. Dividends paid by Free Zone companies on income derived from re-export sales are not subject to dividend tax.

Foreign tax relief

Since Panama only taxes income produced in Panama, regardless of where payment is received or the residence of the taxpayer, no credit or deduction is available for any foreign tax paid.

Withholdings

A 6 per cent withholding tax is imposed on interest, commissions and financial charges paid to foreign companies. Lease payments and royalties paid abroad by companies not in the Free Zone are subject to withholding tax at one-half of the corporate rate (see Exhibit 12.1). Payments for professional services rendered in Panama are subject to withholding tax at a rate of 15 per cent. The withholding must be made by the enterprise which receives the benefits of the loans, leases or professional services, etc. and remitted to the government 10 days after the withholding has been made or the account has been credited, whichever comes first.

Determination of trading income

General

Revenues must be recognised during the year they are earned. Construction companies may recognise long-term contract revenues either by the percentage-of-completion method or by the completed-contract method, unless the cash basis of accounting is being used. The instalment sales method of recognising revenues is not permitted by the Panamanian Fiscal Code.

Earnings derived from the following activities are not considered as originating in Panama:

- invoicing, from an office established in Panama, sales of merchandise or goods for amounts greater than cost, provided the merchandise never comes into Panamanian territory;
- directing, from an office established in Panama, transactions which are completed, consummated or take effect outside Panama; and
- distributing dividends or participations when such dividends or participations are derived from income not produced in Panama, including income derived from the activities mentioned above.

The following income is specifically exempt from taxation in Panama:

- income of natural or legal persons which is exempt by virtue of public treaties or contracts authorised or approved by law;
- revenues arising from international shipping commerce of national merchant ships legally registered in Panama, even when the shipping contract has been entered into in the country;
- interest earned on or gains on the sale of government securities;
- interest earned on savings or time deposit accounts kept in banking institution established in Panama;
- interest paid to official or semi-official institutions of international organisations or foreign governments;
- interest paid to foreign investors, as long as the capital of the loan is used exclusively for the construction of housing projects for low-income persons, as determined by the Ministry of Housing, or if the loan is guaranteed by a foreign government or institution;
- royalties received or earned by persons or companies abroad from businesses established in the Free Zone; and
- farming income when gross sales are less than $100,000.

All expenses incurred wholly and exclusively in the production of assessable income or the conservation of its source are allowed as deductions for income tax purposes, regardless of where the expense was incurred. Expenses of any one taxable year may not be deducted the following year, except those which, by their nature, cannot be determined precisely.

Interest is a deductible expense as long as it is used on loans or credits necessary for the production of taxable income. When non-taxable income on account of interest from savings accounts or certificates of deposit is earned, the only interest deductible is the excess of the interest expense over the non-taxable interest income. Royalties are deductible, except for those paid abroad by Free Zone companies.

Under certain conditions, 30 per cent of annual investments in farming operations may be taken as a deductible expense up to a maximum of 40 per cent of taxable income.

Inventories

Inventories may be valued by using either Fifo, Lifo, or the average cost method. Other methods may be allowed by the Director General of Internal Revenue. Once a system of valuation has been adopted, it may not be changed for five years.

Provisions

The only deductible reserves are those for depreciation, bad debts (1 per cent of credit sales up to 10 per cent of total receivables) and certain fringe benefits. Reserves for personal insurance and contingencies are not deductible.

Depreciation and amortisation allowances

Depreciation allowances are permitted on capital expenditure of assets used in production of taxable income. Depreciation may be computed by the straight-

Exhibit 12.2

Other significant taxes

Nature of Tax	*Rate (%)*
Value-added tax, on the sale or transfer of any chattel and on imported goods; some goods are specifically exempt	5
Commercial and industrial licences, paid annually on corporate net worth (up to a maximum tax of $20,000)	1
Municipal tax, based on the nature of the business activity and the amount of sales (up to a maximum of S$500 a month)	Various
Social security contributions and education tax, based on wages or salaries: paid by	
Employer	12.25
Employee	8.5
Luxury tax levied on cable and microwave television services, transportation in armoured cars and rental of security boxes	5

line, declining-balance or sum-of-the-years digits methods. Under special circumstances, the Internal Revenue Service allows accelerated methods of depreciation.

Relief for losses

Commercial enterprises incurring a loss in a fiscal year may deduct 20 per cent of the loss in each of the five subsequent fiscal years. Any portion of a loss not deducted because of this limitation may not be deducted in a later fiscal year. Loss carrybacks are not permitted.

Other significant taxes

The rates for value-added tax, municipal fee, social security contributions and other significant taxes are shown in Exhibit 12.2.

Tax treaties

Panama has not concluded tax treaties with any other jurisdiction.

Accounting practice

Legislative background

Banks and Insurance companies in Panama are under the supervision of regulatory commissions established by law. They must file audited financial statements annually with the appropriate regulatory commission, and these statements must be prepared in accordance with the commission's specific regulations as to form and content. Financial statements prepared in accordance with ordinary commercial reporting practices may also be prepared, however, for distribution to the general public.

Panamanian corporations that have publicly traded shares or debt instruments are subject to the regulations of the National Securities Commission, which requires that audited financial statements be submitted within 90 days after the close of the company's fiscal year. The Institute of Authorised Public Accountants of Panama has prescribed written standards of presentation that are generally followed by companies registered with the Commission.

All corporations doing business in Panama must file an annual income tax return. A CPA (Contador Público Autorizado) must sign files of companies over a specific amount of capital or sales. A CPA is the Panamanian equivalent of a chartered accountant or certified public accountant.

The Panamanian Commercial Code specifies the accounting books the companies must have and their characteristics. In practice, these requirements of the Commercial Code are met through summary entries that are based on more detailed records of transactions prepared in modern accounting systems which are not considered to be in contravention of the Code's requirements.

Accounting Principles and Practices

There are three professional accounting organisations in Panama: the Institute of Authorised Public Accountants of Panama (Colegio de Contadores Públicos Autorizados de Panamá), the Association of Women Accountants of Panama (Asociación de Mujeres Contadoras de Panamá) and the Association of Accountants and Authorised Public Accountants of Panama (Asociación de Contadores y Contadores Públicos Autorizados de Panamá).

These three organisations formed the Financial Accounting Standards Committee (Comisión de Normas de Contabilidad Financiera). Its members must be active in the public accounting profession. This Committee is responsible for the development of the accounting standards of Panama.

Conformity with US and international standards

Panamanian Accounting Standards follow US GAAP, as expressed in the Statements of Financial Accounting Standard Board (FASB).

Chapter Thirteen

Constitution and government

The government of the Republic of Panama is unitary, republican, democratic and representative, divided into three branches: executive, legislative and judiciary, with separate powers. The present constitution, adopted in 1972, was amended in 1978 and 1983.

The executive branch includes the President of the Republic and the Ministers of State. The President is head of the executive branch, elected by direct popular vote for a five-year term. The ministers are named by the President. The ministries which comprise the executive branch are: government and justice, presidency, foreign relations, planning and economic policy, commerce and industry, treasury, agricultural development, public works, education, health, labour and social welfare and housing.

The legislative branch is called the Legislative Assembly and its members are elected for periods of five years by direct popular vote, one for each 30,000 inhabitants within an electoral district. At present, there are 40 electoral districts and 71 elected members of the Legislative Assembly.

The judicial branch is composed of the Supreme Court and other tribunals and courts as established by law. The judges of the Supreme Court are appointed by the executive branch and ratified by the legislative branch, for periods of 10 years. Justice is administered by the following tribunals:

- Municipal Courts: these sit in the districts or municipalities and have general jurisdiction over certain matters and with certain limits according to the claims or penalties involved.
- Circuit Courts: these sit in the capital of each province and have general jurisdiction over: (i) matters exceeding jurisdiction of municipal courts, (ii) appeals from municipal courts and (iii) cases related to bankruptcies and successions.
- Family Courts: these sit in the capital of each province and have general jurisdiction over matters related to adoption and divorce proceedings.
- Minors Courts: these have jurisdiction over offences committed by minors up to 18 years of age.
- Superior District Courts: these have jurisdiction over appeals from Circuit Courts. The First District Court hears civil cases and the Second District Court criminal cases.
- Supreme Court: this has jurisdiction over: (i) constitutional matters, (ii) mat-

ters involving the interpretation of administrative acts and certain Labour Court decisions, (iii) civil cases and (iv) acts as trial court in certain criminal cases involving high officials.

- Labour Courts: Sectional Courts sit in various cities and have general jurisdiction over labour cases. A Superior Labour Court has jurisdiction over appeals from Sectional Labour Courts and Boards of Conciliation and Decision.
- Boards of Conciliation and Decision: created by Law No. 7 of 1975, they have jurisdiction throughout the Republic of Panama and competence over: (i) dismissals and (ii) suits claiming labour benefits under US$1,500.
- Maritime Courts: created by Law No. 8 of 30 March 1982, as modified and supplemented by Law No. 11 of 23 May 1986, they have jurisdiction over all causes arising from: (i) maritime commerce and maritime traffic within the territory of the Republic of Panama and (ii) claims arising elsewhere from maritime commerce and traffic when actions are filed against a vessel or its owner and the vessel is attached within the jurisdiction of the Republic of Panama.

The banking system

The international banking centre of the Republic of Panama, one of the largest and most important of Latin America, has developed as a result of the adoption of Cabinet Decree 238 of 1970, which provides a modern and flexible banking legislation. Other elements that have contributed to the development of the banking centre are the acceptance of the United States dollar as legal tender, freedom of currency movement, exemptions of income tax on interests generated by time deposits, communications, modern infrastructure, geographic location and a skilled labour force. As of December 1994, banking assets exceeded US$32.8 billion and there were 111 banks operating, broken down as follows: 61 general licence banks, 31 international licence banks, 17 representative offices and 2 government banks. The banking industry directly provides 8,900 jobs. Major banks from all over the world operate in Panama. Among the countries represented are Argentina, Bahamas, Bolivia, Brazil, Canada, Cayman Islands, Colombia, Costa Rica, China, Dominican Republic, Ecuador, France, Hong Kong, India, Korea, Israel, Japan, Spain, Switzerland, Taiwan, The Netherlands, United Kingdom, United States and Venezuela.

Both domestic and foreign corporations need to obtain a permit from the National Banking Commission before setting up a banking operation in Panama. This permit is a prerequisite to the registration of the corporation in the Mercantile Registry and also to the filing of an application for a banking licence. Within a period of 90 days from the granting of this permit, the corporation must be recorded in the Mercantile Registry and must also file the petition to obtain the banking licence.

At the time the temporary permit is requested, the Banking Commission requires the filing of the following:

- Power of Attorney granted to a local attorney authorising the said attorney to request the temporary permit.
- Petition requesting the temporary permit.
- Draft of articles of incorporation and by-laws of the company to be organised in Panama if the licence is to be requested in the name of a Panamanian company; if the licence is to be issued to a foreign corporation planning to pursue banking activities through a branch in Panama, a certified copy of the articles of incorporation and by-laws duly acknowledged by a Notary Public and the latter's signature validated by the Panamanian Consul.
- Certificate stating the names of the members of the board of directors, administrators and shareholders of the bank, including a "curriculum vitae" of each one.
- Certificate stating the activities to be carried out by the bank in Panama.
- Certificate issued by the banking authorities of the country of origin confirming the parent bank is duly authorised to engage in banking activities in the said country (if applicable).
- References for the applicant bank from well-known international banks (if pertinent).
- Certificate stating the percentage of participation of the shareholders in the capitalisation of the bank.
- Certified cheque for US$1,000 to cover the fee payable to the Banking Commission for investigation expenses.

Once the corporation is organised (or qualified to do business in Panama in the case of foreign corporations), it needs to request the relevant banking licence from the Banking Commission. With this petition the following documents must be filed:

- Certified copy of the notarial document whereby the corporation was organised (or whereby the qualifying documents of a foreign corporation were approved, duly noted to be recorded in the Mercantile Registry).
- Copy of the last balance sheet, closed not more than 90 days from the filing of the petition, which must be duly approved by a certified public accountant.
- If a general banking licence is requested, US$1,000,000 must be deposited with Banco Nacional de Panamá. This deposit (which does not earn interest) will be released when the banking licence is issued, but the bank must always maintain active investments, as defined by law, of US$1,000,000 in Panamá.
- If an international banking licence is requested, that is, a licence to exclusively direct offshore banking transactions from Panama, US$250,000 must be deposited with Banco Nacional de Panamá.

The legal requirements for banks operating under a general licence are:

- Paid-in capital or allocated capital for operations in Panama must be at least US$1,000,000. Such capital must be maintained or invested in Panama. As a matter of practice, the Banking Commission now requires a minimum paid-in capital or allocated capital for operation in Panama of US$3,000,000.
- A capital reserve fund must be maintained. Paid-in capital plus this reserve fund may not be less than 5 per cent of the productive assets of the bank. The

law defines productive assets "as loans and investments made in Panama".

- The bank must be the beneficiary of a "contingency credit" granted to it by a foreign bank approved by the Banking Commission. Such credit should be not less than 10 per cent of the productive assets, as determined on 31 December or 30 June of each year.
- The bank must always maintain cash, which shall be not less than 5 per cent nor more than 25 per cent of local deposits. Between this minimum and maximum, the percentage shall be fixed by the Banking Commission. Until otherwise determined by the Commission, it shall be 12 per cent.
- Liquid assets, as defined by Article 44 of the law, must represent a given percentage of the total bank deposits. This percentage shall not exceed 30 per cent.

Securities

Comisión Nacional de Valores

Cabinet Decree No. 247 of 16 July 1970 created the National Securities Commission (CNV). The CNV is the government entity in charge of supervising the securities' market in the Republic of Panama. The Commission comprises five principal members and their alternates. They are one representative of the Ministry of Commerce and Industry, the general manager of Banco Nacional de Panamá and three representatives from the private sector.

The principal duties of the CNV are to authorise or reject the sale of securities to the public, grant or revoke licences to stock brokers, authorise or reject mutual fund operations and supervise stock exchange operations. The CNV is charged with approving and supervising any public offering by either a national or foreign company. To make such an offering, these entities must prepare a prospectus. The prospectus must include all characteristics or traits of the securities in question, the distribution plan, risk factors, audited financial statements of the company and any additional information which the Commissioners may deem necessary.

Stock exchange and stock brokers

Decree No. 44 of 1988, amended by Decree No. 37 of 1992, authorised the operation of stock exchanges in Panama, which are regulated by the National Securities Commission. Stock exchanges must have an initial paid-in capital not less than US$1,000,000 and must have personnel experienced in security operations.

The companies desiring to operate brokerage houses in Panama must be represented by stock brokers licensed by the National Securities Commission. In order to obtain a licence as a stock broker, the applicant must be a Panamanian or foreign individual with not less than five years of residence in Panama and must pass an examination on the subject.

Listing of securities

To comply with the registry and listing of the stock exchange, issuance of security titles by local companies must comply with the provisions of Cabinet Decree No. 247 of 16 July 1970, its Regulations and Resolutions and with the provisions of the Regulations Governing Issuances of the Primary Market of the Stock Exchange of Panama.

Securities of foreign countries and corporate securities of international companies active in the international secondary market may be listed on the stock exchange. For such purpose the interested party must comply with the security registration procedures and requirements.

Fiscal advantages

Interest yielded by debentures is not subject to income tax, provided the securities have been authorised by the National Securities Commission and placed through a stock exchange.

No capital gains tax is levied on the sale of securities if the titles are registered with the National Securities Commission.

Foreign investments

Industrial incentives

Investors of industrial enterprises who do business in Panama may qualify to be exempt from the following: import duties on machinery, and taxes on income, exports, sales, capital assets and dividends.

Tourism

The country offers miles of white sandy beaches, tropical islands, vast rainforests, and lush highlands and mountains, which are ideal for the establishment of tourist resorts. In addition, there is a rich variety of animal life, flora and fishing, ideal for the promotion of ecotourism.

Law No.8 of 14 June 1994 promotes investment of foreign capital in tourism activities within the Republic of Panama.

Among the incentives offered by the law are:

- Total exemption from import duties on machinery, equipment, spare parts and construction materials used in projects undertaken in areas designed as "special tourist zones".
- Exemption from property taxes for the duration of the company's contract.
- Exemption from income taxes on profits, beginning on the date of the contract, for a period of 15 years.
- Authorisation to carry forward losses for a period covering three fiscal years from the year of the loss.
- Total exemption for the duration of the contract from all taxes, contributions, duties or other levies on the use of docks or airports built or rebuilt by the corporation that was granted the incentives.

Mining

The mineral potential of Panama has been known of since the 15th century. Mineral exploration started in colonial times with the Spaniards, followed by

German, French, British and North American interests into the present century.

The Mineral Resources Department, part of the Ministry of Commerce and Industries, has carried out geological studies and mineral inventory projects through international funding. The result of those studies has been the impressive development of mining projects in Panama, both in metallic and non-metallic minerals.

The mining laws were modified in February 1988, to bring the Mining Code in line with the international free market and stimulate foreign and local investment. The following features of the reformed Mining Code illustrate the special advantages for investors:

- Guarantees to the explorer that the state is obliged to grant him an extraction concession for the minerals found.
- Royalties payable to the government were reduced to 2 per cent of gross production for the mining of precious minerals.
- Income tax discounts.
- A depletion allowance deduction may be applied annually, based on the mineral reserves and the units extracted.
- Use of accelerated methods of depreciation of physical assets.
- Losses may be carried forward up to three subsequent fiscal periods.
- All equipment, spare parts and materials required for mining operations may be imported duty-free.
- All minerals produced in Panama may be freely exported and are exempt from any tax.
- Exploration concessions are granted for a period of four years, extendible for two additional periods of two years.
- Extraction concessions are granted for periods of 20 to 25 years, depending on the class of minerals, and can be extended for three periods of ten, five and five years.

Offshore legal instruments

Companies

The Republic of Panama serves as domicile for over 150,000 active companies, attracted by the legal stability offered through Law No. 32 of 26 February 1927, General Corporation Law of the Republic of Panama, which has remained relatively unchanged since its adoption. In 1994, over 16,000 new companies were incorporated in the Public Registry.

Those who wish to form a corporation must sign articles of incorporation setting forth:

- The name and domicile of each subscriber.
- The name of the proposed corporation, which shall not be the same as nor so similar as to cause confusion with the name of any other existing corporation. The name shall include a word, phrase or abbreviation to indicate that it is a corporation as distinguished from a natural person or partnership. The name of the corporation may be expressed in any language.
- The general purpose or purposes of the corporation.

- The amount of the capital stock and the number and par value of the shares, or whether the corporation is to issue shares without par value. The capital stock and par value of shares of any corporation may be expressed in terms of the legal currency of the Republic of Panama or in terms of gold units of the legal currency of any other country, or of both.
- If the shares are to be classified, the number of shares to be included in each class and the designations, preferences, privileges and voting powers or restrictions of qualifications of the shares of each class.
- The number of shares of stock which each subscriber to the articles of incorporation agrees to take.
- The domicile of the corporation and the name and domicile of its resident agent, which must be an attorney-at-law or a firm of lawyers admitted to practice in Panama.
- The number, names and addresses of its directors, which must not be less than three.
- Any other lawful provisions which the subscribers to the articles of incorporation may desire to include.

The usual procedure is to organise the corporation by having the organisational subscribers execute the articles of incorporation before a Notary Public in Panama. Thereafter, the articles of incorporation are submitted to the Mercantile Registry for registration. Each subscriber usually subscribes one share.

Other points of interest are:

- Neither the stockholders nor the directors have to be residents of Panama.
- There are no legal requirements regarding minimum capital. According to law, there is no need to state that the capital subscribed has been paid in.
- As long as the corporation is not doing business in Panama, it does not incur any tax liabilities.
- There are no particular requirements in respect to the subsequent operations of the company, except that the company must pay an annual franchise tax of US$150. Of course, subsequent amendments to the articles of incorporation and elections of officers and directors should be filed for registration with the Mercantile Registry of Panama.
- The time required for the corporation to be formed will be approximately two days from the date on which the articles of incorporation are filed in the Public Registry.
- The corporation is not deemed to have legal existence, in respect to third parties, until it is registered in the Mercantile Registry. Therefore, business should not be conducted under the corporate name prior to this date.
- The corporation may execute in favour of one or more individuals a broad power of attorney to operate the company.
- Panamanian law allows 100 per cent foreign ownership of a Panamanian corporation.
- If an office is established in Panama for the purpose of handling offshore operations, or if such operations are handled through a local management company, the profits derived from such operations are not subject to income tax. In this respect, Article 694 of the Fiscal Code provides:

Income derived from the following activities shall not be considered as produced within the territory of the Republic of Panama: a) invoicing, from an office established in Panama, the sale of merchandise or products for a sum higher than that at which said products or merchandise had been invoiced to the offices established in Panama provided that said merchandise or products are handled exclusively abroad; b) directing, from an office established in Panama, operations which are completed, consummated or take effect abroad; and c) corporate dividends or participations when said dividends or participations are derived from income not produced within the territory or the Republic of Panama, including the income derived from activities mentioned in subsections a) and b) of this proviso.

Corporate bodies

Stockholders: With the exception of corporations engaged in retail business in Panama, stockholders need not be nationals or residents of Panama. Meetings of stockholders may be held outside Panama, if so provided in the charter. Stockholders may be represented by proxy.

Board of directors: There must be at least three directors, but unless otherwise provided in the articles of incorporation, directors need not be stockholders, nor nationals or residents of Panama. Meetings of directors may be held outside Panama, and directors may be represented at meetings of the board by a proxy, who need not be a director.

The board of directors is elected by stockholders, but vacancies may be decided by the vote of a majority of the directors in office.

Officers: There must be a president, a secretary and a treasurer, who shall be chosen by the board of directors. Any person may hold two or more offices, if so provided by the articles of incorporation or by the by-laws.

Trusts

The Trust Law is embodied in Law No. 1 of 5 January 1984, regulated by Executive Decree No. 16 of 3 October 1984. A trust may be created upon property of any kind, present or future.

A trust deed must contain the following: complete and clear designation of settlor, trustee and beneficiary; sufficient designation of substitute trustees or beneficiaries, if any; description of the property or of the estate or portion thereof on which the trust is created; and the powers and duties of trustee. The trust deed may further contain clauses that are not contrary to morals, laws or public order.

For all legal purposes, the assets of a trust constitute a separate estate from the personal assets of the trustee and cannot be attached or embargoed, except for obligations incurred or damages caused by performance of the trust, or by third parties when property has been transferred or withheld fraudulently and in detriment of their rights.

Apart from a fixed annual tax of US$100, a trust is tax-exempt when it involves: (i) property situated abroad; (ii) money deposited by natural or juridical persons whose income is not from Panamanian sources or taxable in Panama; or (iii) shares of stock or securities of any kind, issued by corporations whose income is not from a Panamanian source, although such monies, shares of stock or securities are deposited in the Republic of Panama.

Executive Decree No. 16 of 3 October 1984, as modified by Executive Decree No. 53 of 30 December 1985, regulates engaging in trust business as regards requirements, granting of licence, guarantees, penalties and any other conditions to which trust companies, insurance companies, banks, attorneys and other natural or judicial persons engaged habitually in the trust business are subject to.

Regulatory power of the trust business resides in the National Banking Commission. In addition to professional qualifications and experience in the trust business, trust companies that engage in this business in or from Panama must maintain available to the Commission a guarantee of US$250,000, consisting of unencumbered assets kept at all times within the Republic of Panama.

Private Interest Foundations

The Legislative Assembly recently enacted into law the creation and regulation of Private Interest Foundations. Under this law, one or more individuals or corporations, by themselves or through a third party, may organise a Private Interest Foundation. For these purposes it is required that in the foundational minutes (articles of incorporation) a patrimony be expressly provided for, to be used exclusively to further the objectives or purposes of the foundation. The initial patrimony may be increased from time to time.

Private Interest Foundations are governed by the foundational minutes and its by-laws, as well as by the provisions of the law. Private Interest Foundations may not be profit-making. Notwithstanding, the foundations may carry out business activities in a non-habitual manner or exercise the rights arising from share certificates evidencing capital from business corporations that integrate the patrimony of the foundation provided that the result or economic income from such activities be dedicated exclusively to the purposes of the foundation.

A Private Interest Foundations may be organised to start operating at the time of incorporation or after the death of the founder by either of the following: (i) a private instrument, executed by the Founder, whose signature must be validated by a Notary Public at the place of its incorporation, or (ii) directly before a Notary Public at the place of its incorporation.

Shipping

For over 75 years, the Republic of Panama has offered facilities for the registration of vessels engaged in all types of maritime activities. Through Law No. 8 of 1925 a procedure for the registration of vessels was adopted which permits the registration of cargo and passenger vessels, as well as dredgers, barges, floating docks and other types of vessels. Currently, Panama is the world leader in terms of registered tonnage.

It is interesting to note that the law does not require that the owner of the vessel be a national of Panama, or an entity organised under the laws of Panama.

The application to register a vessel under the Panama flag may be filed with a Consul of Panama, who will supply all necessary application forms, or directly with the Shipping Bureau in Panama through a local attorney. This application can request the issuance of the Provisional Navigation Patent and Radio Licence, either in Panama or through an authorised Consulate.

Within six months following the issuance of the Provisional Navigation Patent, a copy of the title deed of the vessel in favour of its owner must be duly recorded in the Public Registry Office of the Republic of Panama. Following this, an application for a Permanent Navigation Patent (valid for two years in the case of pleasure or recreation yachts and for four years in the case of other vessels) should be filed in Panama. Before expiration of the Permanent Navigation Patent, the owner of the vessel must apply for a new Permanent Patent, which shall be issued for the applicable period, provided that all taxes have been paid and that the safety and technical certificates have been updated. The Permanent Patent of Navigation may be renewed indefinitely.

Trademarks

Trademarks may be represented by any word, phrase or symbol, or all of these combined, used to distinguish a specific product destined for industry or commerce. They shall be sufficiently different from one another, so that a given trademark can be clearly distinguished so that no confusion arises in the course of its use.

Any owner of a trademark, either foreign or Panamanian, may apply to the Ministry of Commerce and Industries for its registration to acquire the exclusive right to use it in the Republic of Panama. The application shall be published once in the *Industrial Property Bulletin*, and if after 90 days from the date of publication no claim to the contrary is filed, registration of the trademark shall be made. Registration is granted for a term of 10 years, indefinitely renewable for equal periods of time.

The requirements for trademark registration in Panama are:

- Power of Attorney.
- Sworn affidavit of the trademark.
- Six copies of the trademark.
- Basic registration or certificate of the trademark in the country of origin.

Colón Free Zone

Since its creation in 1948, the Colón Free Zone (CFZ), a segregated free trade area for wholesale operations located on the Atlantic coast near the entrance to the Panama Canal, has offered the world a unique centre for international commerce, becoming the leading free zone in the Western Hemisphere and the second largest in the world after Hong Kong.

Goods entering in the CFZ may be imported, stored, modified, repacked and re-exported without being subject to import duties or taxes. In addition, companies established within the zone are exempt from taxes on the export of capital and on the payment of dividends. There are no consular fees, nor any other charges levied on shipments destined to the Free Zone, nor on shipments from this area to consignees abroad. A Surveillance Service Fee is charged by the Customs authorities for the custody of re-exported goods. The fee charged is applied case by case.

As of January 1995, more than 1,500 companies were operating from this area, the re-export of products being the most important activity carried out. Record figures of nearly US$10 billion in trade movement were reached in 1993.

To operate from the Colón Free Zone, companies must obtain authorisation from the CFZ Administration, which grants the corresponding Operation Code. No business licence is required, nor does any company need to comply with any minimum investment requirements.

A company may operate in the zone in any one of the following ways:

- Leasing premises from the CFZ, provided that the company exports at least 60 per cent of the goods handled.
- Leasing land to build warehouse facilities for its own use or for the use of other companies.
- Leasing warehouse facilities owned by CFZ-established companies. This form of operation requires a special authorisation from the CFZ authorities, known as an Operation Permit, which requires the payment of US$1,200 per annum.
- Signing a contract with an established CFZ firm that will represent it.
- Using the public warehouse, where goods may be received and stored.

Immigration

Immigration is regulated by the constitution and Decree Law No. 16 of 30 June 1960, as amended. A permanent resident visa is issued to foreigners married to Panamanian citizens, investors and general managers of foreign companies established in Panama. A temporary visitor's visa is issued to foreign executives, for one-year renewable periods. A prerequisite to visa applications by foreign executives is the procurement of a work permit issued by the Ministry of Labour and Social Welfare. Under Article 17 of the Labour Code, only 10 per cent of employees may be foreign workers, or 15 per cent in the case of technicians or specialised employees.

Chapter Fourteen

Panama in the 1990s

The saying "small is beautiful" can be applied to countries as well as companies. With a population of only 2.6 million, a strategic location midway between Europe and Asia, a currency (the US dollar) free of exchange-risk, and other factors, Panama has some of the requirements to be a successful little economy. But this has not been the case so far.

While other small countries, most notably in East Asia, such as Singapore (to some extent the government's role model), managed to transform themselves from sluggish, high-cost, inward-looking economies into vibrant, rapid-growth, export-oriented societies within two decades, Panama was bogged down by a political crisis, culminating in the US invasion, and economic difficulties.

These countries also moved from high unemployment to virtual full employment and have been unusually successful, compared with developing countries in the rest of the world, at sharing the fruits of growth: they have lower and declining levels of inequality.

Democracy is now flourishing in Panama and the most important change of direction in the service-based economy in more than 45 years was underway in 1995, representing a complete break with the previous protectionist policies. Panama is a latecomer to the globalised world of free-market policies, and is charting unknown waters.

Although it may be invidious to make comparisons between Panama and, say, Singapore, none the less it is pertinent to ask why the country has not fulfilled its potential. Singapore's population of 2.7 million is not much bigger than Panama's, it too has a racially mixed society (in Singapore's case Chinese, Malays, Indians and Eurasians), a significant banking centre and the City state is also an important junction for world trade and an entrepôt.

Singapore was only four places ahead of Panama in the 1994 United Nations Human Development Index (Panama is ranked 47th out of 173 countries), but its real per capita GDP (purchasing power parity in 1991 US dollars) is three times higher than Panama's US$4,910. While Singapore's exports rose from US$918 million in 1965 to US$61.5 billion in 1992, Panama's (including services) only increased from US$240 million to US$2.2 billion.

Equally, there are many historical differences between the two countries. The legacy of British colonial rule in Singapore – for example, establishment of a professional and honest bureaucracy – is more positive than that of Spanish rule in Panama or, for that matter, being a virtual protectorate of the United States. A professional civil service increases a government's ability to design and implement policies. This is a key area and Panama must bring pay and perks more into line with the private sector in order to attract better-quality civil servants.

Another difference is that Singaporean society is much more regimented than Panama's and thus easier to mould and change direction: a government-decreed wage cut, a move taken by Prime Minister Lee Kuan Yew in the 1980s to improve international competitiveness, would not be calmly accepted in Panama.

One reason for Singapore's success is the much greater priority given to education, in general, and labour force skills, in particular, than Panama, a factor singled out by the World Bank in its attempt to discover the reasons for the East Asian "miracle".[1] South Korea, for example, spent US$450 per secondary education student in 1989, as against US$370 in 1992 by Panama in its state schools. The government's desire to invest more in education, a key area, will, however, be constrained by resuming the servicing of its commercial bank foreign debt. East Asian countries did not build up large foreign debts. Panama has no leeway for populist policies and will have to keep to orthodox ones.

Panama has clearly not realised its potential and can develop a stronger niche role in the maritime sector. In a country of its size and natural resources, there is absolutely no reason why the nation should have one of the most skewed income distributions in the world.

And because the country is so small the differences between rich and poor stand out all the more starkly. Like Singapore, Panama has a strong trading class, but it is much more voracious. The government's attempts to make firms in the Colón Free Zone pay a fairer share of taxes, after years of privileged status and massive tax evasion, and the protest of businessmen embodies this situation. It is regrettable that the government's proposals were not accepted, and it bowed to pressure.

Panama's lack of progress is also poor testimony to the protectionist economic policies of the past.

But this is not to say that success is automatically guaranteed by striking out on a new path; on the contrary, an export-oriented, market-based strategy is by definition a step into the dark. It is worth remembering that such a change in East Asian countries, unlike the free-market policies in Latin America, was accompanied by interventionist policies including some state capitalism, agrarian reform, mandatory savings mechanisms, directed credit and export promotion, as well as traditional government obligations such as providing adequate infrastructure.

The economic growth that has resumed in Panama since 1990 has been based mostly on unused existing capacity. Sustaining growth now requires investment in new capacity, and it is difficult to see how Panama can achieve this without changing the structure of its economy. This is certainly the government's belief.

Trade liberalisation and deregulation of the labour market in a US dollar-based economy are tantamount to devaluation and should make the economy more competitive. But these policies will not significantly increase Panama's exports of goods and non-factor services. The canal, the oil pipeline, the Colón Free Zone and the three traditional export crops (bananas, sugar and coffee) account for more than 70 per cent of the total, and they are mature sectors. There is scope for increased exports of goods but it is small and it will take years, as Juan Jované, a leading economist, points out in a critique of the government's economic policy unless the government quickly succeeds in attracting foreign investment to spearhead its export policy.[2]

Labour market reforms are bound to reduce wage costs indirectly or directly, and they will encourage greater investment. Panama's salaries (the average montly wage was around US$520 in 1995) are the highest in Central America, but they are hardly generous: an economic model based on competing in terms of low wages means competing with monthly salaries of not much more than US$100 in El Salvador, around US$80 in Guatemala and less than

Exhibit 14.1

Forecasts, 1995–2000

	1995	*1996*	*1997*	*1998*	*1999*	*2000*
Population (millions)	2.7	2.7	2.8	2.8	2.9	3.0
Per cent change	2.1%	2.1%	2.1%	2.1%	2.1%	2.1%
GDP per capita (US$)	2,698	2,826	2,948	3,098	3,241	3,411
Per cent change	2.2%	4.7%	4.3%	5.1%	4.6%	5.2%
Real GDP per capita (US$)	2,545	2,580	2,615	2,658	2,707	2,758
Per cent change	1.4%	1.4%	1.4%	1.6%	1.8%	1.9%
GDP (US$m)	7,200	7,700	8,200	8,800	9,400	10,100
Per cent change	4.3%	6.9%	6.5%	7.3%	6.8%	7.4%
Real GDP (US$m)	6,793	7,030	7,276	7,549	7,851	8,165
Per cent change	3.5%	3.5%	3.5%	3.8%	4.0%	4.0%
GDP (local currency, millions)	7,200	7,700	8,200	8,800	9,400	10,100
Per cent change	4.3%	6.9%	6.5%	7.3%	6.8%	7.4%
Consumer price change, year-end	2.5%	3.0%	3.0%	3.0%	3.0%	3.0%
Exports merchandise FOB (US$m)	6,020	6,440	6,890	7,370	7,890	8,440
Per cent change	6.9%	7.0%	7.0%	7.0%	7.1%	7.0%
Imports merchandise FOB (US$m)	7,290	7,900	8,560	9,260	10,040	10,920
Per cent change	8.3%	8.4%	8.4%	8.2%	8.4%	8.8%
Trade balance (US$m)	–1,270	–1,460	–1,670	–1,890	–2,150	–2,480
Current account balance (US$m)	–50	–90	–160	–250	–300	–440
International reserves without gold (US$m), year-end	710	720	710	710	760	670
International reserves with gold at market prices (US$m), year-end	710	720	710	710	760	670
Total external debt (US$m), year-end	7,985	8,485	9,035	9,685	10,435	11,185
Exchange rate (L.C./$), year-end	1.00	1.00	1.00	1.00	1.00	1.00

Date: March 1995.
Data are expressed in nominal terms unless otherwise indicated.
Real GDP is at constant 1990 prices and 1990 exchange rates. Exports and imports include the figures of the Colón Free Zone.
Source: Bank of America World Information Services.

US$65 in Honduras. Panamanians would not accept this. More important is the need to improve quality, design, service and marketing.

Assuming successful implementation of the reform programme and continued structural adjustment, real GDP could expand by an average of 3.7 per cent between 1995 and the year 2000, according to forecasts made by Bank of America (see Exhibit 14.1), which are optimistic. This would enable per capita GDP to reach US$3,400. Significant untapped opportunities exist for growth, particularly putting the reverted areas from the Canal Zone into productive use and developing the mining sector.

There is a danger, however, that expectations will be raised too high by the transfer of the canal and the surrounding area in the year 2000. Ownership is not a panacea for the country's problems, and it could bring as many headaches as benefits if not handled with great prudence.

Notes

1. *The East Asian miracle* (World Bank Policy Research Paper, Oxford University Press, 1993).
2. Juan Jované, *La probreza de la política económica* (CECADES, 1995), p. 31.

The co-publishers

THE PRIVATE ASSET MANAGEMENT GROUP

GROUP STRUCTURE

The Private Asset Management Group has solid ethical and professional principles and vast experience in different areas of business. We have dedicated our time and attention to build a solid and efficient organization. In doing so, we have established ourselves within the financial world community, as a group of companies that offers different types of services with the goal of satisfying the demands of a market that turns more complex and competitive by the day.

The group is formed by the following companies:

- The Private Asset Management
- AGB Consulting
- Global Management Services
- Private Discount Brokers
- Weil Asset Management
- Calle 50 Real Estate
- Inverarte

These companies act together or individually, according to the different needs of our clients.

OUR BACK UP

Our group is formed by highly qualified personnel with great experience in different business areas. We are always interested in finding the most convenient alternative for our clients, supported by dynamic and efficient personnel, that guarantees the correct execution of the decisions.

For the excecution of our operations in the financial markets, we work with the leading firms in clearing services. Such firms are Pershing, a division of Donaldson, Lufkin & Jenrette, as well as Refco. These companies back up at all times the security of our clients.

In the same manner, we offer an ample network of worldwide institutional relationships, which have access to precise and timely information, and locate the best opportunities for our clients.

OUR PHILOSOPHY

To promote the highest levels of services to each of our clients is our fundamental principle. The quality of the services we offer is based on an efficient, professional and personalized treatment, coupled with a flexible operation, through which we adapt to the requirements of each client, as well as to surrounding changes. Our constant search for opportunities and innovative solutions, which shall be sources of income for our clients, together with our vast expertise, profound knowledge of the markets and active participation in them, is our commitment.

SERVICES

Excellency is our goal, and The Private Asset Management Group is a faithful reflection of it. As head of the group, our main function is to make it easier for our clients to access international financial markets, and to advise them on different investment opportunities that Latin American markets offer.

Having the Panamanian Banking Center as headquarters, The Private Asset Management Group offers a wide variety of financial and investment products, offering these services to local and international investors in a personalized way, at the retail and institutional levels.

We have a staff of highly specialized professionals, keeping us up-to-date with the technology that allows us to analyse, excecute and follow all types of national and international securities markets transactions in an efficient, quick and dynamic way to achieve the best results to the benefit of our clients. Our services permit our clients to count on a permanent and actualized attention in an environment of constant evolution, adapting to the needs and requirements of the specific moment. We make constant analysis of market conditions and we have direct and instant access to information sources, so we can guarantee high-quality services with total confidentiality. We give our clients' investments a thorough follow-up through permanent and direct communication guaranteeing absolute dedication.

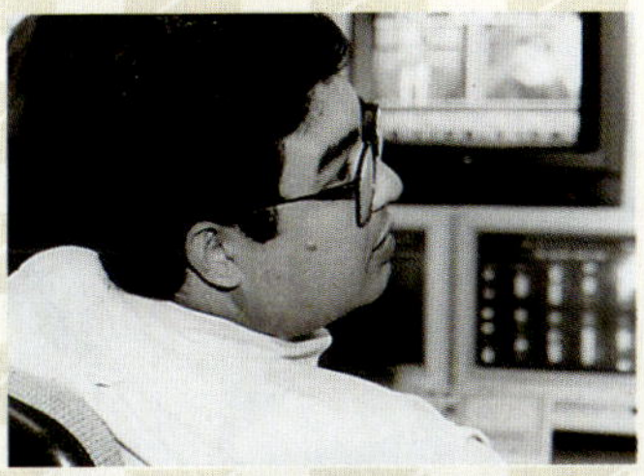

Among the many services offered to our clients are the following:

- **BROKERAGE :** The Private Asset Management Group offers access to the most important markets worldwide and, in a more precise way, to Latin American markets, as well as the widest variety of financial products with the help of professionals and the support of an organization designed to function successfully and efficiently.

- **ASSET MANAGEMENT:** The Private Asset Management Group offers personalized asset management services, which allow us to adapt to our clients' expectations in the RISK, YIELD and LIQUIDITY parameters in order to achieve their goals, as well as finding the best alternatives at every moment within market conditions.

- **PERSONAL AND INSTITUTIONAL FINANCIAL PLANNING:** To present alternatives to future requirements, offering different investment alternatives to assure our clients the financial planning that best fits their needs and requirements, in relation to retirement, education, investment and saving plans.

EXPERIENCE

During the last years, The Private Asset Management Group has actively developed operations in all international financial markets, especially in Latin American debt, trading securities in excess of 2 billion dollars for banking institutions and other Latin American corporations; domestic debt dealings in the secondary markets were in excess of 1 billion dollars, introducing for the first time re-purchase agreements and options in the Panamanian debt market. The Private Asset Management Group has acted as co-leader with other international financial entities in the underwriting of different debt instruments for important corporations in Argentina, Brazil, Peru and Panama, issuing over 200 million dollars in securities.

PROJECTION

With the goal of enhancing the many possibilities offered to our position in international markets, within the globalization tendency of the markets, The Private Asset Management Group has entered into a strategic alliance agreement with SOCIMER Finance Corp. with offices in Geneva, Switzerland. Through this association, we have accsess to their wide network of offices throughout all Latin America. SOCIMER established themselves in the last years as one of the leading investment banks in the region.

This alliance has the goal of complementing the assets and capacities of both firms, joining efforts and integrating activities in an independent way, building a more competitive and efficient structure to meet the challenges that international financial markets present.

With the same goal, we maintain a constant relationship with other first-rate international firms in Europe, Asia and the United States. For all these reasons, The Private Asset Management Group offers support and the necessary experience to satisfy our clients' most complex needs with a single objective: their benefit and satisfaction, as well as maintaining our values.

AGB Consulting is the consulting division of The Private Asset Management Group created to handle management needs produced by market globalization, which demands a fast reaction capacity and anticipation needs.

Since 1992 we have offered our clients both from the goverment and the private sector our experience, knowledge and specialized resources in different areas like business strategy, financial, administrative and business management. We focus for example on growth and development or corrective measurements like modernization and restructuring, maintaining a personalized profile adjusted to the characteristics and particularities of each company and its business sector, searching for solutions to satisfy a company's needs and consequently improve its administrative functions. To achieve these objectives AGB Consulting is staffed with a profesional team with vast experience, dynamic and up-to-date in every area in project management oriented towards client satisfaction with quick answers and service excellency.

Our purpose in the business world is to offer our clients an objective and documented vision and to back them up with our experience and knowledge in business development. We maintain a close relationship with our clients, knowing their objectives and priorities in order to combine their strenghts with the opportunities that arise in order to overcome their weaknesses and reach their goals. Our objective is to be close to our clients and fulfil a long-term relationship with constant and actual benefits for them.

ACTIVITIES

STRATEGIC CONSULTING

- Mergers and acquisitions.
- Strategic planning.
- Consulting on privatizations of goverment entities.
- Project feasibility studies.

FINANCIAL CONSULTING

- Financial engineering (Commercial paper issues, bonds, stocks, etc).
- Financial diagnosis.
- Money management for institutions.
- Financial planning.
- Financial information services.
- Corporate net worth assesment.

BUSINESS ORGANIZATION

- Analysis, diagnosis and design of a new organization within the company.
- Management and budgeting control.
- Re-engineer and optimization of business processes.

MANAGEMENT TECHNOLOGY

- Definition, selection and solution implementation in different business areas, as support to achieve changes and improvements in the business management.

Based on service quality and confidentiality principles, we offer our clients all types of services through our professional team and specialists, as complement to its business activity with the objective of achieving maximum profitability based on efficient management and the creation of new business opportunities.

PROJECTION

With the purpose of strengthening and enlarging our capacity of attention to the various needs of our clients in a world of constant evolution, particularly in the technology applied to business activities, we have formed in Panama a joint venture with a prestigious international firm in the auditing and consulting world: Deloitte & Touche Tomatsu. The development of administrative consulting and human resource areas through the merger of efforts and resources of both firms will allow us to be on top of the search for integral solutions for our clients.

THE PRIVATE ASSET MANAGEMENT GROUP

OTHER COMPANIES

PRIVATE DISCOUNT BROKERS

Private Discount Brokers was created as a discount broker offering low-priced execution services. Created to satisfy the needs of the sophisticated retail and the institutional investors that do not need financial advice and make their own decisions about local and international investments.

GLOBAL MANAGEMENT SERVICES

Global Management Services is the subsidiary of The Private Asset Management Group in the United States. Located in Miami, it offers the group's wide variety of services to clients in the Latin American area, as well as assistance and back-up to our clients in their business dealings in the United States.

Global Mangement Services consists of a team of professionals with vast knowledge in the fields of private banking and investment, and has the support of The Private Asset Management Group in relation to financial brokerage services, investment planning and consulting. In addition, it offers excecutive office rentals and services to cover the needs of our clients when staying in the USA, as well as providing administration services.

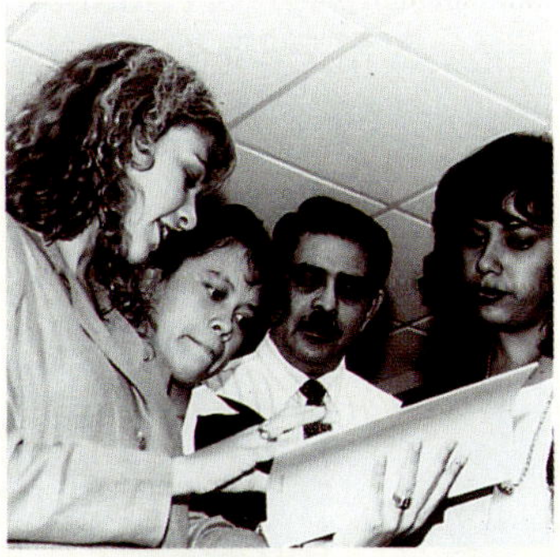

WEIL ASSET MANAGEMENT

Weil Asset Management was created as a company that offers financial design services, administration, and investment fund consulting. Having a vast experience in these fields, we have designed and manage different investment funds, being a pioneer in the constitution of investment funds in emerging Latin American markets.

CALLE 50 REAL ESTATE

This is a company engaged in real estate investments deriving its income from property rentals. Calle 50 Real Estate currently has, in a direct or indirect way, through the participation in other real estate companies' economical development, more than 4,000 square metres of prime commercial real estate in Panama City.

INVERARTE

The purpose of this company is to invest in the arts and to promote young talent in Latin American painting and sculpture. At present we have in our posession an important collection of art which is constantly being circulated through a buy-sell activity, as well as by renting pieces to local institutions.

PANAMA

Aseguradora Mundial

Aseguradora Mundail was established in April of 1968 by a group of investors motivated by their interest to offer an insurance alternative to the Panamanian market.

The company was designed to satisfy the needs of its client. Since then, it has been an innovative company, developing new products and utilising modern technology. Until 1993, it was the only company in Panama to offer all branches of insurance as well as full insurance services.

The 1994 figures show a constant growth in sales and market penetration as well as positive net results in its operations.

Premium Income of Aseguradora Mundial in the past five years has almost doubled, growing from US$22.5 million in 1990 to US$41.8 million in 1994, with constant yearly growth.

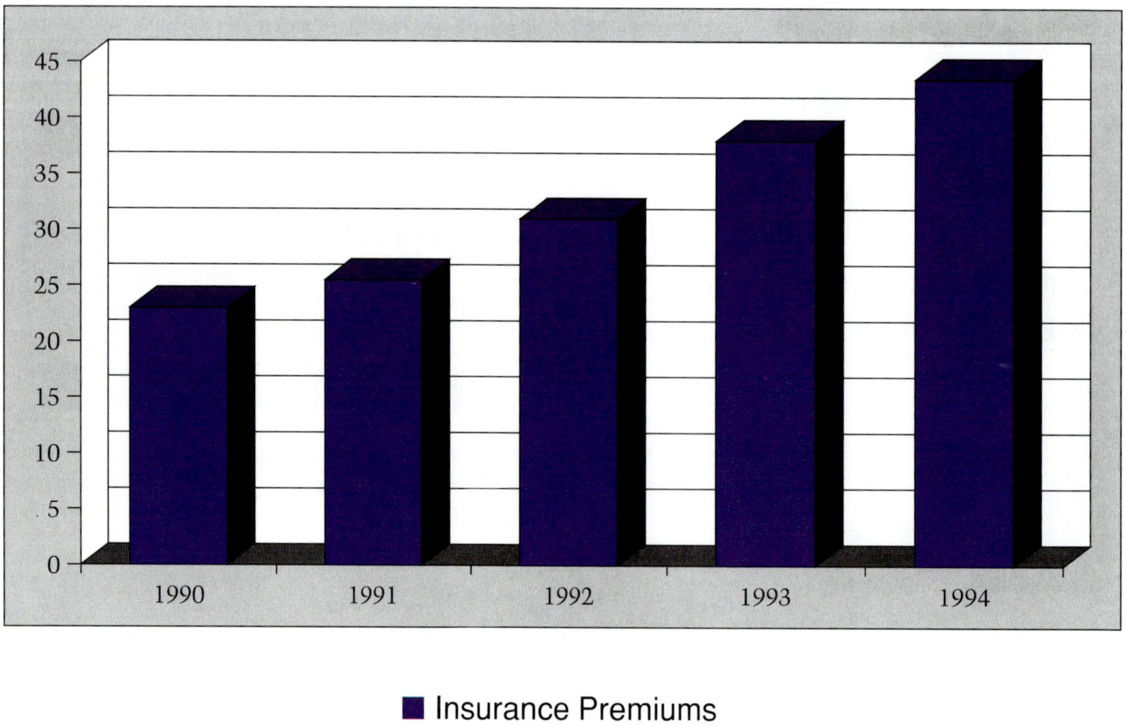

Premium income in 1994 was split among the most important lines, following a balanced company policy.

Premium income determines the size of an insurance portfolio. The quality of the portfolio is represented by the loss ratio between incurred losses and earned premiums. In the past five years, loss ratios have fluctuated between 41 per cent and 48 per cent; for 1994 it was 47 per cent.

Total resources, represented by the assets of the company, have increased from $36.3 million in 1990 to $56.1 million in 1994. The company adheres to a policy of high liquidity to meet its obligations, as demonstrated by the liquid assets, cash on deposit and investments.

The shareholders' equity of the company has been strengthened by favourable results in its operations and by a healthy dividend policy. The shareholders' equity has increased from US$5.1 million in 1990 to US$12.8 million in 1994.

A significant indicator of the operation has been the Return on Investments (ROI), i.e. the ratio between the net profits and the shareholders' equity. In the past five years it has exceeded 23 per cent, and for 1994 it reached 25.1 per cent.

For some time now, we have embarked on a programme of Total Quality Management towards a constant improvement of our operations. Because we are committed to our clients, priority has been given to human resources as well as the application of technology and the improvement of procedures in order to achieve an efficient and expeditious service.

We are sure that, with this central strategy, we will satisfy or even exceed the expectations of our clients, and this will allow us not just to maintain, but to improve our position in the insurance market of Panama as a modern and efficient company.

Prospects for 1995

We expect to continue the solid development of our portfolio, maintaining its quality, so that net profits produced by the operation are matched by its growth. We base our expectations on the growth of the Panamanian economy.

Satisfying the needs of our clients will continue to be our main objective and to that end we shall render the best service, giving special attention to the area of human resources, the improvement of our operations and the use of modern technology.

The Board of Directors

First bank that guarantees payment of

In 1995 Banco Disa became the first private Panamanian bank accepted by the Panama Canal Commission to guarantee the payment of Canal tolls on behalf of ship representatives. Thus, they constitute one of the first private sector moves towards Panama's management of the Canal by the year 2000.

PANAMA CANAL TOLLS.

BANCO DISA is the latest effort of the DISA GROUP. With the support of the United States Agency for International Development (USAID), Desarrollo Industrial, S.A. (DISA) was established by Panamanian entrepreneurs in response to the credit-market conditions in the Republic of Panama in 1963 when industrial development was an almost impossible task. • In order to provide an effective response to the situation of the times, DISA promoted its capitalization through the participation of all economic sectors of the Republic of Panama. Throughout the years, DISA developed into Panama's most important non-banking financial institution, decisively contributing to the creation of the nation's industrial infrastructure, channeling financial resources through the financing of the Industrial sector. • In 1986 the DISA GROUP, feeling they had achieved their goal in bringing about a new financial situation in Panama, created BANCO DISA, S.A., a private commercial bank. • BANCO DISA dedicates itself to offering its high-profile clients the best financial services, while at the same time helping those clients safekeep and increase their net worth by prudently and professionally managing their funds and looking after their financial needs. • Because BANCO DISA's objective is to stimulate economic growth while protecting and supporting its individual clients, the Bank emphasizes credit services directed toward financing the production of wealth rather than consumption. With this in mind, DISA has created strategic alliances so that they can offer the best services in the issuance of capital market instruments to corporations that, due to their structure, require more extensive financial resources to move beyond their present capacity.

INVESTMENT AND DEVELOPMENT BANKING

BROKERAGE HOUSE

CANAL TOLLS

DESTINED TO OFFER SERVICES TO A SELECT CLIENTELE, BANCO DISA HAS BECOME A MODEL OF PRUDENCE AND CONFIDENTIALITY, WHILE SCRUPULOUSLY SAFEKEEPING THEIR CLIENTS' INTERESTS.

In addition, because the internal development of Panama demands substantial credit-support, BANCO DISA puts considerable effort in obtaining international funds, not only from traditional organizations, but also through the issue of debt instruments that guarantee long term resources providing the national stability and rates of return required by foreign investors. • Furthermore, BANCO DISA has come to be known as "The Bank of Banks" because it supplies local banks with investment alternatives for their liquid assets, discounts on long term loans, and therefore, a mechanism that balances their assets and liabilities. • In 1990, after overcoming the most trying financial and banking crisis in the history of Panama, BANCO DISA founded Capital Traders of Panama, Inc.., a brokerage house dedicated to the issue and trade of national and international money and capital market instruments. • Capital Traders of Panama, Inc. guides clients through enduring financial operations that will increase their equity. BANCO DISA, then, will continue to earn its reputation as an innovator while retaining its traditional sense of responsibility to the individual client and the community at large.

BANCO DISA OFFERS ITS HIGH-PROFILE CLIENTS TRADITIONAL BANKING SERVICES AND ACCESS TO ALL THE RESOURCES AND EXPERIENCE NEEDED IN THE MODERN AND MUCH MORE COMPLEX FINANCIAL MARKET.

Banco del
ISTMO

Strength and Leadership

A sound capital base of US$ 50 million, an extensive nationwide branch system, a world-wide correspondent bank network, full financial services capabilities, product innovation, its entrepreneurial tradition, its civic activism, and its stated mission of "...being the preferred financial institution in the markets it serves..." are all strengths which have converged to provide Banco del ISTMO a unique and leading position in Panama's financial marketplace.

Panama's Bank

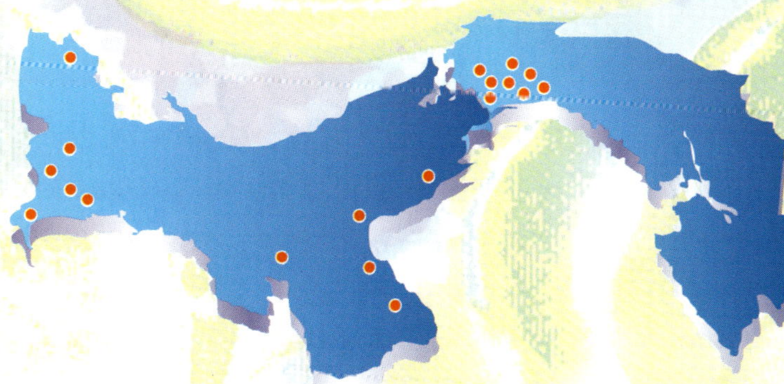

Banco del ISTMO's slogan, "El Banco de Panamá" (Panama's Bank), is a well-earned reality. The combination of its 20 branches, which provide the most extensive nationwide coverage of any private-sector bank, and the diversity of its credit and product portfolios, position Banco del ISTMO to reach and serve more Panamanians than any other commercial bank. This is one of the many reasons why world-class companies, such as Phillip Morris, Texaco, British American Tobacco, Glaxo, AT&T, Chiquita Brands International, and American Express have chosen Banco del ISTMO as a provider of financial services in Panama.

Commercial Banking

Banco del ISTMO serves the corporate, middle-market, and agricultural sectors through its wide range of commercial banking services. These include short and long term lending programs, import and export financing, trade collections, factoring, and cash management for businesses with a multi-province presence. Additionally, Banco del ISTMO is an active participant in U.S. Government programs, such as EXIM Bank financing for the importation of capital goods, and USDA's Commodity Credit Corporation facilities for the importation of grain.

Banco del
ISTMO

Consumer Banking

Banco del ISTMO uses its nationwide branch system to distribute its full menu of consumer banking products and services. These include personal loans, residential mortgages, VISA, Mastercard and a number of private label credit cards. This distribution channel is further complemented by Banco del ISTMO's affiliation with Panama's two ATM networks, which provides its customers access to 104 domestic ATMs and more than 213,000 Plus System ATMs internationally, through its debit card. This card also provides convenience and security through its direct-debit to the customer's account at 470 point-of-sale terminals located in commercial establishments throughout Panama, as well as the ability to pay public utilities from remote ATMs.

Investment Banking

Through its wholly-owned subsidiary, Banistmo Brokers, Banco del ISTMO and its customers have access to Panama's capital markets. A founding member of the Panama Securities Exchange, Banistmo Brokers has been the most active participant in the exchange in terms of number of trades for the past 2 consecutive years, providing its private banking and institutional customers with a diversity of investment opportunities. Banco del ISTMO also advises, structures, and places commercial paper and corporate bond issues for its corporate banking customers, in addition to providing its paying agent and trustee services. Since 1990, it has successfully structured and placed 24 issues.

International Banking

Customers have access to worldwide banking capabilities through Banco del ISTMO's correspondent bank network throughout Latin America, North America, Europe, and Asia. It's wholly-owned subsidiary, Banco Mercantil del ISTMO (formerly Banco Santander Panamá, S.A.), has a major presence in the Colon Free Zone, from where it offers a full range of international trade financing and services. This subsidiary is also a member of SWIFT, providing customers the most efficient electronic transfer means available.

Banco del ISTMO

Insurance

Compañía de Seguros Chagres, S.A. (Chagres Insurance Company), a wholly-owned subsidiary of Banco del ISTMO, offers a full product line: auto, homeowner, commercial property-casualty, life, pension, and others. Beginning this year, these products will be distributed through Banco del ISTMO's branch system, providing customers a complementary line of financial services.

Expertise and Commitment

Banco del ISTMO is a private-sector bank whose directors and management team bring a vast knowledge of Panama to bear on its strategies, product offerings, and advising capabilities. This expertise is forged by the many years of proven experience and success gained in the industrial, commercial, agricultural, and financial fields pre-dating the foundation of Banco del ISTMO. It is this knowledge and expertise which fills Banco del ISTMO with optimism and reinforces daily its full commitment to serving the people of the Isthmus of Panama. And, ever-conscious of its responsibilities as a good corporate citizen, this commitment is further exemplified through its program "Valores del ISTMO" (Isthmus Values), whereby Banco del ISTMO promotes civic and moral values to the community at large, as well as supports the preservation of historic sites, such as "Panamá La Vieja" (Old Panama), out of respect for the legacy of its name.

Colón Free Zone

Panama is a surprising country. The Colón Free Trade Zone is the latest surprise, with the Zone becoming fundamental to Panama's continued economic growth and prosperity.

The Colón Free Trade Zone was established in 1948 on a 35 hectare plot adjacent to the city of Colón with a couple of warehouses occupied by a handful of ambitious Panamanian merchants.

The last 48 years has seen the Colón Free Trade Zone grow rapidly, incorporating some 1,800 companies who are either fully operational or hold representation in the Zone, and which between them generate an annual turnover of US$10 billion.

Victoria Figge, General Manager

The Colón Free Trade Zone has allowed businesses to import goods in bulk from the Far East, Europe, and the US, and re-export them to a host of Latin American clients. Panama's strategic location allowed for fast transportation of goods into the Latin American marketplace ahead of European or Asian competitors. The variety of merchandise and brand names available is awesome, which is hardly surprising considering that any day's inventory can be in the region of US$1.5 billion. Companies can vary in size from large megastores which offer hundreds of famous luxury brands down to single agency businesses. A number of large multinational companies are also located in the zone.

Not all business conducted in the Free Trade Zone involves the physical transportation of goods into it. A registered Free Zone company is allowed to transport goods directly from source to client by simply completing the normal entry and exit paperwork, as if the goods had physically passed through the zone.

Any individual, or company, can set up operations in the Colón Free Zone by applying to the administration and supplying commercial and bank references, a Panamanian tax clearance (*paz y salvo*) and the articles of incorporation in the case of a company. No commercial licence is required and no minimum capital investment is stipulated.

Requirements to operate within the Colón Free Zone

According to Decree Law 18 passed in 1948, a national corporation may establish operations in the Colón Free Trade Zone. A foreign corporation may also operate in the Free Zone, as long as it is duly registered in the public registry of Panama. To commence operation in the Colón Free Zone corporations must comply with the following requirements:

General requirements

1 Application form duly completed and signed by the legal representative of the corporation.
2 Copy of the articles of incorporation and by-laws as well as amendments, if any.
3 Incumbency certificate certifying the corporation's existence, and date of incorporation, listing the members of the board of directors, dignitaries, and its legal representative.

4 Two "good standing" certificates issued by the Ministry of Finance, certifying that the corporation does not owe income tax to the government.
5 Two commercial and banking references. These references must include, among others, information about the type of commercial and banking relationship, length of relationship, relationship with legal representatives, offices, and directors of the corporation seeking to do business in the zone.
6 Copy of the passport, or identification documents of the legal representative.
7 Affidavit subscribed by the legal representative and its officers.
8 Any other information that the Colón Free Zone Administration may require from time to time.

Types of operation within the Colón Free Zone

There are four ways in which a company can set up operations in the Colón Free Zone:

Land lease contracts

According to article XXXVIII, section "d" of Decree Law 18 of 1948, the Colón Free Zone leases of land to local or foreign corporations to build warehouses and office space for their own use or for lease to third parties must be approved by the general manager.

The cost of the lease is established, from time to time, by the board of directors of the Free Zone, and it varies according to the area where the land is located. Current rates are as follows:

Developed areas: US$ 0.50 per square metre per month
Colón area: US$ 0.35 per square metre per month
France Field area: US$ 0.20 per square metre per month
Undeveloped areas: Costs of developments for these areas must be assumed by the corporation building the structure. These costs include building roads and installing water and electrical facilities for each private warehouse or office that is built. To promote the development of new areas, the administration of the Free Zone has in place a "lease-back programme". Through this programme any entity that constructs a warehouse or office in undeveloped areas must bear the cost of developing roads and electrical facilities, but is compensated by reducing the leasehold fees until the amount of the investment is repaid.

Land leases are negotiated for a minimum of 5 years to a maximum of 20 years, and may be renewed for a similar period.

Building lease contracts

Colón Free Zone buildings

Article XL, section "c" of Decree Law 18 of 1948, authorises the Colón Free Zone to lease its own building space to corporations that wish to set up operations in the area.

The cost of the lease is set by the board of directors of the Free Zone and will vary according to the location of the land:

Colón Area: US$2.40 per square metre per month
France Field Area: US$1.75 per square metre per month
Coco Solo Area: US$1.65 per square metre per month
Leases are granted for 1-20 years.

Private buildings

Article XL, section "d" of Decree Law 18 of 1948 also allows corporations to rent building space from private parties already established in the Colón Free Zone that are either leasing building space from the administration or have their own buildings.

In this case, the operation in the area is governed by an Operating Permit Contract entered into between the lessor, lessee, and the administration of the Colón Free Zone.

To obtain the operating permit, all the general requirements discussed above must be fulfilled. These include the presentation to the administration of an original copy of the lease contract between the private lessor and lessee.

Representations

Colón Free Zone Regulations, including Decree Law 18 of 1948, allow companies to be represented by another company already established in the Colón Free Zone. This method of operation is particularly advantageous for corporations that are commencing operations and do not wish to incur heavy operating expenses such as leasing or purchasing building space.

Both corporations must apply to the administration for the authorisation to enter into a representation contract. To obtain this authorisation, the company seeking a representation must comply with all the general requirements listed above, including:

Original copy of a letter requesting representation to another company already established in the Colón Free Zone.

Original copy of a letter from the company already established in the Free Zone, accepting to represent the petitioner.

Public warehousing

The Colón Free Zone provides public warehouse services to those corporations that want to do business in the Free Zone, but choose not to lease land or building space, or be represented by another corporation.

Corporations interested in using the Free Zone warehouse facilities must agree a warehouse contract with the administration. Said contract establishes the rights and obligations of the corporation. The fee for using the public warehouse is 0.5 per cent of the FOB value of the merchandise.

General rules and regulations

According to Decree Law 18 of 1948, companies operating within the Colón Free Zone are required to comply with the following rules:

- To employ a minimum of 5 local employees.
- To export a minimum of 60 per cent of their merchandise.
- To pay the rent within the first 20 days of the month. The administration will levy a 10 per cent annual surcharge on the rent for late payment to corporations leasing land or buildings directly from it. If the client is in arrears for more than two months his operating code will be suspended. While said suspension is in place the corporation is unable to operate in the Colón Free Zone.
- To report all imported and exported merchandise, in the appropriate forms, as the operations are made.
- To submit an income tax return and pay the corresponding taxes to the Ministry of the Treasury on a yearly basis.

Operating costs

Annual costs

Operating Code "Clave": US$200

Every corporation doing business in the Colón Free Zone must pay this fee, irrespective of the method of operation selected.

Operating Permit: US$1,200

This fee is only required from corporations operating through a private building lease contract.

Monthly costs

Leasehold fees which vary according to the type of lease.

To support a refuse collection service for corporations doing business in the Colón Free Zone, the administration has established a refuse collection fee. Depending on the space rented, the fee ranges from a minimum of US$25 to a maximum of US$100 per month.

One-off expenses

A deposit equivalent to three months' lease for those companies leasing land and/or buildings. In the latter case, including the equivalent of three months' lease when the building is leased from a third party.

Cost of registering the contract with the administration is approximatley US$23.00 plus official stamps based upon the total dollar value of the contract.

Should additional information be required, please contact the General Manager, the General Secretary, or the legal office of the administration on Fax (507) 45 2165, or mail them to P.O Box 1118, Colón Free Zone, Republic of Panama.

The Panama Stock Exchange

Carving a Niche

Five years ago, the Bolsa de Valores de Panama (BVP), started operations. On 26 June 1990 a mechanism was introduced to provide local investors and companies alike an alternative to allocate their savings and expand their operations. As years progressed and markets all over the world evolved, our role as a provider of capital to local corporations, and to others in the region, is gaining a predominant presence in Central America, as we try to be the Intraregional Stock Exchange of the Region.

In 1990, total volume traded at the Exchange amounted to US$3 million, while in 1994 we closed the year with a total volume of US$290 million, an increase of almost 100 fold.

More relevant than the larger volume increases are the composition and origin of the trading. The BVP has grown solely on the development of private business. Ninety-seven per cent of the volume traded are corporate securities where historically eighty per cent have been bonds and debentures with tenors ranging from three to five years. Commercial paper, an unknown security before the creation of the Exchange, accounts nearly 13 per cent of volume.

The Panamanian equity market volume has been less impacted by the creation of the Exchange. In the last three years volume accounted for just 3.5 per cent of total. In 1994, thanks to the privatisation programmes total volume rose to 24per cent of total. None the less, more telling than the volume has been the rise in trading values, due mainly to growing liquidity and increased exposure provided to the Exchange. Since 1993, the overall value of the most traded equities has risen some 150 per cent over its prior prices.

As business volumes continue to grow and government securities become more important than 3 per cent of total volume, the Exchange shall continue to enjoy strong fundamentals for development. Added to the microeconomic environment are the well-known advantages of Panama as a financial centre, a dollarised economy that allows the Exchange to thrive as the only dollar Exchange south of the United States.

As competition among emerging markets has increased in order to attract capital to fund economic expansions and restructuring, we can boast our zero currency risk to US dollar-based investors as our competitive advantage over the other markets. The investors are provided with the appropriate means to participate in the growth of undervalued companies, whose shares may sell below their industries' P/E norms and earnings prospects.

In 1994, the process to establish a central clearing, settlement and depository institution and mechanism finally took place thanks to a grant of US$2.9 million from the Interamerican Development Bank to the Association of Central American Stock Exchanges, also known as BOLCEN.

The implementation of the Harmonisation Project will enhance the structure and transparency of our market, since the aim of this programme is to develop, to the extent possible, a depositary system up to the standards outlined by the members of the Group of 30 nations. Ideally then, we will provide investors with the much needed centralised custody services, the ability to transfer payments and securities without physically exchanging the underlying titles and up-to-date mechanisms to prevent fraud or misallocation of securities.

Furthermore, the programme will provide a compatible depositary system among the Bolsa's in the region, so we can expect that Central American companies will look towards Panama in search of private capital to expand their operations, and then take advantage of our financial structure by issuing "Intraregional" securities.

As an example, TACA International Airlines, from El Salvador, through its finance arm, Taca International Finance Corp., just issued US$10,000,000 in debt securities as part of a total issuance for US$30,000,000 through the Bolsa de Valores de Panama. The company, through its lead underwriter, was able to allocate this tranche at a relative attractive cost which would have been more than twice if it would have place the offering in their local market. Panama provides issuers of debt with costs well below of that of other Central American countries, and we intend to exploit this niche.

Providing a framework for trading up to international standards on top of having the US dollar as our legal tender currency, the development of the Panamanian Depository Receipt (PDR) will be within our reach. The BVP will be then in the unique position to provide investors and corporations with an investment vehicle similar to that of the American Depository Receipt or the Global Depositary Receipt, further expanding their alternative to find new markets to raise new capital, diversify their portfolios and include us in their asset allocations models.

Taken together, the current and prospective developments; making aware local investors of the benefits of a corporate securities markets with the help of listed companies, the full implementation of programmes, such as the Harmonisation Project, providing effective information and the ease of registration for foreign securities, should further open the gate to the new emerging markets of the 1990s, with Panama once again being the bridge to the new age of borderless capital markets.

CAMBIOS, S.A.

Contact: Manuel D. Cabarcos
Juan M. Cabarcos
Telephone: (507) 264-6655
Fascimile: (507) 264-5204

Cambios S.A. is a founding member of the Panama Stock Exchange and is part of a Panamanian group which specialises in local and international financing and investing. We also provide securities and financial counselling to private and corporate investors preparing, structuring and selling bonds, debentures, shares and other financial obligation issues for the local market.

INVERSIONES BURSATILES DE PANAMA, S.A.

Contact: Ramón E. Fábrega G.
Samuel Espinosa
Julieta G. de Diego
Telephone: (507) 263-7150
Fascimile: (507) 263-7995

As a member of the Bolsa de Valores de Panama, we specialise in making a market to buy and sell securities, offering our customers investment plans aiming for the best returns. Included in our wide range of services is the structure and initial offering of corporate bonds and securities.

NEGOCIOS EN VALORES

Contact: Ellis Cano P.
Pedro Detresno
Telephone: (507) 264-4301/69-5135
Fascimile: (507) 264-7395/64-2878

We are an independent investment brokerage house with a founder seat on the Panamanian Stock Exchange. Through its highly professionally qualified, trained and experienced staff, NEGOVAL offers innovative and dynamic advice and services for sound investments, effective financial management and successful public or private placements.

TOWER SECURITIES INC.

Contact: Ricardo Sosa
Telephone: (507) 269-6900
Fascimile: (507) 269-2964

Tower Securities, Inc., established in 1990, operates a seat on the Panama Stock Exchange, currently the only operating stock exchange in the Republic of Panama. We specialise in the local financial market: sovereign debt, bonds, equity, privatisation projects and other investment opportunities. We conduct extensive research on financial, economic and business issues to provide our clients current information pertaining to the local market.

BANTAL BROKERS, S.A.

Contact: Javier Carrizo
Vicente A. Pascual
Mónica de Chapman
Telephone: (507) 263-7072
Fascimile: (507) 264-7106

Bantal Brokers S.A., a founding member of the Panama Stock Exchange, provides financial advice, dynamic brokerage services and portfolio management. Bantal Brokers, S.A. is part of the local financial group comprised by Banco Continental de Panama, S.A., Leasing Empresarial, S.A., and Norfolk and Hampton Bank. The group specialises in corporate banking and international finance.

CITIVALORES

Contact: Giselle de Tejeira
Telephone: (507) 263-5544
Fascimile: (507) 264-0659

CITIVALORES, S.A. brings Citicorp's proven experience in the emerging markets to the Panama Stock Exchange. Citivalores, S.A. provides debt brokerage and underwriting services and, through its affiliate network in Central America, is uniquely positioned to provide investors and issuers broad access to the region's capital markets.

BG Investment Co., Inc.

Contact: Juan Raúl Humbert
Francisco Sierra
Telephone: (507) 227-3200
Fascimile: (507) 225-2868

BG Investment Co., Inc. is a wholly owned subsidiary of Banco General, S.A., the largest privately owned bank of Panamanian capital, with total assets in excess of $950 million by year end 1994. Banco General S.A., is a subsidiary of Empresa General de Inversiones S.A., the public company with the largest market capitalisation on the

Panama Stock Exchange, exceeding $190 million as of 31 December 1994. BG Investment Co, Inc. is the entity of the Group that provides brokerage and investment banking services, and is the owner of a seat on the Panamanian Stock Exchange.

Franklin Guarantee Securities Corp.

Contact: Nicolás Ardito Barletta P.
Arturo Tapia
Telephone: (507) 269-5915/27-4577
Fascimile: (507) 264-1746/27-4100

Franklin Guarantee Securities Corp. is a Panamanian Investment Banking and Brokerage Firm specialising in corporate finance, mergers and acquisitions, underwritings and other brokerage activities through the Bolsa de Valores de Panama. Our experience is most noted for advising on and implementing for Panamanian corporations the benefits of going public with debt or equity issues, locally and internationally.

BICSA
BICSA VALORES (PANAMA), S.A.

Contact: José Francisco Ulate
Federico Echandi
Telephone: (507) 263-6822
Fascimile: (507) 263-6393

BICSA Valores de Panama is part of Banco Internacional de Costa Rica. As one of the foreign institutions that owns a seat on the exchange, we provide investors and institutions with an array of investments vehicles in order to take advantage of the opportunities presented in the region. With a seat also on the Guatemalan and Costa Rica exchanges, our predominance throughout the region provides investors the flexibility of diversification.

BINCAP
BROKERS, INC.

Contacts: Marielena Garcia Maritano
Guillermo Chapman III
Flor Ma. de Fonseca
Telephone: (507) 264-6833
Fascimile: (507) 263-4096

Bincap Brokers, Inc., founded in 1992, is a subsidiary of Banco Internacional de Panama - BIPAN. As a member of the Panama Stock Exchange we specialise in financial advising and trading of Panamanian securities, equity and privatisation projects with emphasis on the domestic corporate bond market.

IFS
ISTHMIAN FINANCIAL SERVICES INC.

Contact: Lloyd Smith
Michele de Benedetti
Telephone: (507) 263-9766/226-1769
Fascimile: (507) 264-7556/226-3967

Isthmian Financial Services Inc. was founded in 1993 by a team of experienced professionals. Since its inception, it has grown rapidly to be the third seat by volume in 1994. Although we specialise in Panamanian government securities, we are also involved in structuring, underwriting and selling corporate securities and in financial advising for private and corporate investors.